MARKS OF ACHIEVEMENT

FOUR CENTURIES OF AMERICAN PRESENTATION SILVER

Marks of Achievement

Four Centuries of American Presentation Silver

David B. Warren · Katherine S. Howe · Michael K. Brown
With an Introduction by Gerald W. R. Ward

The Museum of Fine Arts, Houston
In Association With
Harry N. Abrams, Inc., Publishers, New York

FUNDERS OF THE EXHIBITION

Foley's

Transco Energy Company

The Jesse H. and Mary Gibbs Jones
Exhibition Endowment Fund

Arthur Andersen & Co.

Mr. and Mrs. James H. Elder, Jr.

Mr. and Mrs. W. Temple Webber, Jr.

Gerald D. Hines Interests

Mr. and Mrs. William S. Kilroy

Englehard Corporation

William Hill Land & Cattle Company

This project was funded in part by funds from
The National Endowment for the Arts, a federal agency

J. C. Pangborn
Baltimore
George W. Ful
President
Cornelius Va
Chairman
Frank Thoms
Vice Presi
W. C. Van Horn
President
C. X. Lord,
Vice Presi
Edward H. W
Baldwin L
Edward Ellis
President
R. S. Hughes
President

STAGE COACH
1825

CONESTOGA WAGON

Lenders to the Exhibition

Albright-Knox Art Gallery,
Buffalo, New York

American Antiquarian Society,
Worcester, Massachusetts

The American Numismatic Society,
New York City

Anglo-American Art Museum,
Louisiana State University, Baton Rouge

Archives of the Archdiocese of Detroit

The Baltimore Museum of Art

J. Carter Brown, Trustee for Elissa L. R. Brown

Buffalo and Erie County Historical Society,
Buffalo, New York

Cathedral Church of St. James—St. Andrew's
Chapel, Chicago

Chicago Historical Society

Christ Church Devonshire,
Hamilton, Bermuda

Rector, Church Wardens, and Vestry Men,
Christ Church in Philadelphia

Christ Episcopal Church, St. Michael's Parish,
St. Michael's, Maryland

The Cliff Dwellers,
Chicago, Illinois

The Club of the United Bowmen of Philadelphia

Congregation Emanu-El of the City of New York

The Congregation Mikveh Israel in the City
of Philadelphia

Dallas Cowboys Football Club,
Irving, Texas

The Detroit Institute of Arts

Gerard L. Eastman, Jr.

Peter W. Eliot

The Fine Arts Museums of San Francisco

First and Second Church in Boston

First Baptist Church,
Philadelphia

The First Parish in Cambridge (Unitarian
Universalist), Cambridge, Massachusetts

Henry N. Flynt, Jr.

Franklin D. Roosevelt Library and Museum,
Hyde Park, New York

Rosalinde and Arthur Gilbert

Gorham Textron,
Providence, Rhode Island

Harvard University Art Museums,
Fogg Art Museum,
Cambridge, Massachusetts

Hennepin County Historical Society Museum,
Minneapolis

Henry Ford Museum and Greenfield Village,
Dearborn, Michigan

The Henry Francis du Pont Winterthur
Museum, Inc., Winterthur, Delaware

High Museum of Art,
Atlanta

Historical Society of Pennsylvania,
Philadelphia

Historic Deerfield, Inc.,
Deerfield, Massachusetts

Historic Mobile Preservation Society,
Mobile, Alabama

Mr. and Mrs. William S. Kilroy

The Lodge of Saint Andrew,
Boston, Massachusetts

The Maryland Historical Society,
Baltimore

Mead Art Museum, Amherst College, Amherst,
Massachusetts

Mr. and Mrs. John W. Mecom, Jr.

Memorial Art Gallery of the University of
Rochester, Rochester, New York

The Metropolitan Museum of Art,
New York City

The Minneapolis Institute of Arts

Munson-Williams-Proctor Institute Museum of
Art, Utica, New York

Museum of Early Southern Decorative Arts,
Winston-Salem, North Carolina

Museum of Fine Arts,
Boston, Massachusetts

The Museum of Fine Arts, Houston,
Houston, Texas

The Museum of Fine Arts, Houston,
Bayou Bend Collection, Houston, Texas

Museum of the City of New York

National Air and Space Museum, Smithsonian
Institution, Washington, D.C.

National Museum of American History,
Smithsonian Institution,
Washington, D.C.

National Museum of Natural History,
Smithsonian Institution,
Washington, D.C.

The Newark Museum, Newark,
New Jersey

The New-York Historical Society,
New York City

New York Racing Association, Inc.,
New York City

New York Yacht Club,
New York City

North Carolina Museum of Art,
Raleigh

Mr. and Mrs. Nicholas Sever O'Reilly

The Parish of Trinity Church in the City of
New York

Peabody Museum of Salem,
Salem, Massachusetts

Philadelphia Museum of Art

President Benjamin Harrison Memorial Home,
Indianapolis, Indiana

St. John's Church,
Salem, New Jersey

St. Michael's Episcopal Church,
Charleston, South Carolina

St. Patrick's Cathedral,
New York City

St. Paul's Episcopal Church,
Edenton, North Carolina

St. Peter's Church,
Lewes, Delaware

Mr. and Mrs. Samuel Schwartz

The Second Church,
Dorchester, Massachusetts

The State Museum of Pennsylvania,
Pennsylvania Historical and
Museum Commission, Harrisburg

State of Delaware,
Division of Historical and Cultural Affairs,
Dover

Charles V. Swain

Tennessee State Museum,
Nashville

Trinity Church,
Newport, Rhode Island

United States Navy and the City of Long Beach

United States Navy Marine Corps Museum,
Washington, D.C.

Vanderbilt University,
Nashville, Tennessee

Philip Van Rensselaer Van Wyck, III

Wadsworth Atheneum,
Hartford, Connecticut

David and Alice Greenwald Ward

Worcester Art Museum,
Worcester, Massachusetts

Yale University Art Gallery,
New Haven, Connecticut

PROJECT DIRECTOR: LETA BOSTELMAN

EDITOR: ELLYN CHILDS ALLISON

DESIGNER: CAROL ROBSON

Front cover: Vase, 1824, by Fletcher and Gardiner, presented to De Witt Clinton

Back cover: Two-handled covered cup, c. 1701, by John Coney, presented to Harvard College

(page 2). Salver, c. 1675–91/92. Timothy Dwight. *See pages 62–63*

(page 5). Vase (detail), 1893. Tiffany and Company. *See pages 148–49*

(page 7). Punch bowl (detail), 1889. Tiffany and Company. *See page 156–57*

Library of Congress Cataloging-in-Publication Data
Warren, David B., 1937–
    Marks of achievement.

    Catalog of an exhibition held at the Museum of Fine
Arts, Houston.
    Bibliography: p.
    Includes index.
    1. Silverwork—United States—History—Exhibitions.
2. Rewards (Prizes, etc.)—United States—Exhibitions.
I. Howe, Katherine S.   II. Brown, Michael K. (Michael
Kevin), 1952–   .   III. Museum of Fine Arts, Houston.
IV. Title.
NK7112.W37 1987 739.2'3773'07401641411 87–1251
ISBN 0–8109–1444–1
ISBN 0–89090–044–2 (Museum ed.)

Times Mirror Books

Printed and bound in Japan

Contents

FOREWORD

Marks of Achievement: Four Centuries of American Presentation Silver had its genesis when David B. Warren, the present Associate Director of The Museum of Fine Arts, Houston, was a student in the Winterthur Program in Early American Culture. He was impressed by both the high aesthetic value and the interesting historical associations of the American-made urn presented to Charles Thomson by the Continental Congress and of the silver presented to tutors by seventeenth-century students at Harvard College. In the mid-1970s Associate Curator Katherine S. Howe joined the museum staff. Her expertise in the later nineteenth century complemented Warren's knowledge of the eighteenth and earlier nineteenth centuries. Nearly ten years ago they decided to collaborate on an exhibition of American presentation silver. William C. Agee, then Director of the museum, encouraged them to develop a research and exhibition proposal. The arrival of Michael K. Brown in 1980 brought a specialist in earlier colonial decorative arts to the team. The project was expanded in scope to include the entire American past. All three curators have provided the essays and object descriptions for this book. In addition, an overview of the subject, written by Gerald W. R. Ward, noted silver scholar and author, provides the context for the specialists' analyses, putting them in perspective.

Warren, Howe, and Brown began a nationwide survey of presentation silver and eventually located more than two thousand examples. In selecting objects for the exhibition and this book, aesthetic merit rather than historic association was their touchstone. The works they gathered, therefore, represent the most beautiful American presentation pieces in silver and gold. I find it intriguing that, despite this purely aesthetic emphasis, the development of America from a seventeenth-century English-dominated, colonial culture along the Atlantic seaboard to a diverse nation, wealthy and self-confident, stretching from sea to sea by the end of the nineteenth century is mirrored in the variety of the occasions for presenting these superb objects. Presentation silver is one of our most enduring art forms, blending style and beauty with the simple human need to say thank you or congratulations. From colonial New England's ecclesiastical silver to the Super Bowl trophy, presentation silver bespeaks the whole history of America's interests and values.

I would personally like to thank those who have given financial support to this project. The exhibition would not have been possible without planning and implementation grants from The National Endowment for the Arts. Generous contributions from Foley's, a division of Federated Department Stores, Inc.; Transco Energy Company; The Jesse H. and Mary Gibbs Jones Exhibition Endowment Fund; Arthur Andersen & Co.; Mr. and Mrs. James H. Elder, Jr.; Mr. and Mrs. W. Temple Webber, Jr.; and Gerald D. Hines Interests enabled The Museum of Fine Arts, Houston, to present these precious objects in a stunning manner, conveying both their beauty and their historical importance. In addition, Mr. and Mrs. William S. Kilroy and the Engelhard Corporation have helped to make this exhibition and book a reality.

PETER C. MARZIO
DIRECTOR
THE MUSEUM OF FINE ARTS, HOUSTON

ACKNOWLEDGMENTS

An exhibition of this scope could not be planned, coordinated, and mounted without the assistance and encouragement of many people. In the earliest stages, William C. Agee, then Director of The Museum of Fine Arts, Houston, urged us to develop a proposal outlining our ideas for an exhibit of American presentation silver. Later, the benefit of Peter C. Marzio's belief and support was incalculable. His penetrating and thoughtful questions helped us refine and focus the project. We are grateful, too, to the silver scholar Gerald W. R. Ward, the present Assistant Editor at the Henry Francis du Pont Winterthur Museum. At an early stage he reviewed our data and encouraged us to proceed. Later, he joined us as a collaborator and contributed a thoughtful essay to this catalogue and book. William S. Kilroy, a Houston collector, believed in us and gave us the first dollars to begin our research and travel. Grants from The National Endowment for the Arts were pivotal to the exhibition's success, and we would like to express thanks to that important federal agency. We are also grateful to Foley's, the Transco Energy Company, The Jesse H. and Mary Gibbs Jones Exhibition Endowment Fund, Arthur Andersen & Co., Mr. and Mrs. James H. Elder, Jr., Mr. and Mrs. W. Temple Webber, Jr., Gerald D. Hines Interests, Mr. and Mrs. William S. Kilroy, and the Engelhard Corporation for their grants.

Without the support of our own museum staff, this exhibition would still be an idea and not a reality. Peter C. Marzio, Director, William G. Bradshaw, Associate Director for Administration and Finance, and Margaret C. Skidmore, Director of Development, have all contributed enormously to the project. In our own department,

Dorwayne Clements, Marilyn Allen, Laurie McGill, and Carla Carouthers have helped. Extra thanks go to those whose untiring attention to manifold details have smoothed the progress of this catalogue—Nina Nathan Schroeder, Mary Brimberry, and Ann Wood, who served as a special assistant. Thanks, too, to Karen Bremer, Linda Shearouse, and Gregg Most, who have aided us in a variety of ways. The publications staff, Celeste Adams and Carolyn Vaughan, worked with us to put the manuscript in order. Charles Carroll, Registrar, and Jack Eby, Designer, have afforded invaluable support in preparing the exhibition.

Excellent photography is vital to the success of a silver book, yet silver is exceedingly difficult to photograph. We are extremely grateful for the skill and enthusiasm of our two chief photographers, Lynn Diane DeMarco and Arthur Vitols.

We would also like to express appreciation to our colleagues in other museums. Morrison H. Heckscher and Frances G. Safford of The Metropolitan Museum of Art in New York City, and Donald L. Stover and Lee Miller of The Fine Arts Museums of San Francisco have been enthusiastic and supportive from the early days of the project. Others who deserve recognition include: Louise Todd Ambler, Oliver Ames, the late Kathryn C. Buhler, Rachel Camber, David Cassedy, John Cherol, Michael Conforti, Sharon Darling, John Davis, Bert Denker, J. Donald Didier, William C. Duffy, Allison Eckert, Nancy Edwards, Rosemary Estes, Jonathan Fairbanks, Martha Gandy Fales, Donald L. Fennimore, Oscar Fitzgerald, Donald R. Friary, Wendell Garrett, Beatrice Garvan, Bruce Gill, Jennifer F. Goldsborough, Anne Golovan,

Mrs. Richard W. Hale, Jr., Frank Horton, Patricia Kane, Mr. and Mrs. Joel Larus, Robert Macdonald, Robert MacKay, Christopher Monkhouse, Christine Oaklander, Francis J. Puig, Rodris Roth, Mr. and Mrs. Seymour Schwartz, Lewis I. Sharp, Alan Stahl, Margaret Stearns, Kevin Tierney, Philip Van Rensselaer Van Wyck, Deborah D. Waters, Gregory Weidman, and Eric M. Wunsch.

Among the many individuals who have lent their time and talents, we would like to mention: Charles Carpenter, Elenita Chickering, Stuart Feld, Edwin and David Firestone, Ann Green, L. W. Hanagan, Sohei Hohri, The Honorable Ernie Kell of the City of Long Beach, California, Bard Langstaff, John Leather, Nancy McClelland, Nicholas Sever O'Reilly, Eric Shrubsole, Robert Towse, Chase Untermeyer, Miguel A. Valencia, Ubaldo Vitali, and Capt. M. J. Weniger.

No exhibition can be developed without the help of dedicated volunteers. Ellen Avitts, Melissa Baldridge, Marsha Brown, Krystal Kirksey, Amanda Lange, Rena Minar, Nina Rutenburg, and Elizabeth Wastler have been selfless and hardworking, and we thank them.

We are grateful to the many museums, libraries, historical societies, historic houses, colleges, churches, synagogues, clubs, and other institutions whose staffs assisted us in our nation-wide search for silver. Similar thanks are due to a multitude of private collectors, individuals, and dealers who responded to our survey.

It would not be possible to mount a loan exhibition without the cooperation of collectors who are willing to part with their possessions for an extended period. To those individuals and institutions who have lent us silver we would like to express heartfelt thanks. The Museum of Fine Arts, Boston, and the Yale University Art Gallery have been especially generous in offering extensive loans.

In closing, we would like to express our gratitude to our families for their understanding, encouragement, and quiet support.

DAVID B. WARREN
KATHERINE S. HOWE
MICHAEL K. BROWN

AUTHORS' NOTE

The engraving on presentation silver is often quite as beautiful as it is meaningful. However, it does not always follow conventional rules of capitalization and punctuation. In the catalogue entries that follow their essays, the authors have altered the capitalization and punctuation of the inscriptions on some pieces in order to ensure their intelligibility.

MARKS OF ACHIEVEMENT

INTRODUCTION

GERALD W. R. WARD

At once the son of Peleus set out prizes for the foot-race: a mixing-bowl of silver, a work of art, which held only six measures, but for its loveliness it surpassed all others on earth by far, since skilled Sidonian craftsmen had wrought it well, and Phoenicians carried it over the misty face of the water and set it in the harbour, and gave it for a present to Thoas. Euneos, son of Jason, gave it to the hero Patroklos to buy Lykaon, Priam's son, out of slavery, and now Achilleus made it a prize in memory of his companion, for that man who should prove in the speed of his feet to run lightest.

W on by Odysseus, the silver mixing-bowl mentioned in this quotation from the *Iliad* is an early example in the long Western tradition of presenting silver and gold on special occasions.[1] Common in ancient Greek and Roman times, the use of silver for presentation objects continued throughout the Middle Ages and the Renaissance, primarily among royalty and the hereditary aristocracy. Gifts and presentations of silver were frequent in sixteenth- and seventeenth-century England and Holland, whence the custom was transported to this country by the immigrants, who perpetuated the tradition in the New World. Continued through the eighteenth century, especially in personal, small-group contexts, the custom blossomed during the nineteenth century. Beginning with a flurry of objects produced for heroes of the War of 1812, presentation silver became more widespread and, in effect, was institutionalized during the next hundred years. After World War I, the tradition declined somewhat, reflecting the generally diminished social role of precious metals in the twentieth century, but the use of silver and gold for presentation purposes has persisted and is implicit in modern society, as the twentieth-century examples selected for this exhibition so clearly attest.[2]

For the purposes of this book and exhibition, presentation silver has been defined as objects of silver or gold given by an individual (or group) to an individual (or group) to mark a specific occasion. (Silversmiths and silver manufacturers have always worked in both precious metals, but because most presentation objects fashioned in this country—with some important exceptions, such as the Adams Vase [fig. 178]—are of silver, the discussion in this book will focus primarily on silver, with the understanding that, in most instances, a reference to silver is meant to include both silver and gold.) This broad definition admits a wide spectrum of presentations, ranging from the rather impersonal kind undertaken by large groups to the intimate kind made by one person to another. Presentation pieces are usually inscribed with the names of the donor and the recipient, and often a sentence or two concerning the occasion and the date is

included as well. Presentation silver of all periods frequently bears an engraved image depicting an event, scene, or decorative device relevant to the presentation, and examples from the nineteenth and twentieth centuries are often ornamented with a three-dimensional cast-silver sculpture directly related to the event in question. Early examples of presentation silver tend to be functional objects, such as bowls, cups, beakers, or porringers, whereas later examples are often more purely symbolic creations, self-consciously designed works of art, or trophies meant purely for display. During the last century and a half, this trend toward literalness has produced such overt symbols as the Vince Lombardi Trophy (fig. 202)—a silver football complete with laces, mounted on a stylized silver kicking tee.

Presentation silver and gold presents us with a vast number of time capsules, each representing a unique exchange and many with a fascinating tale to tell. The circumstances surrounding each presentation provoke our curiosity and raise questions about specific people, places, and events that beg to be answered. Because of these personal associations, later generations have been inclined to save presentation silver from the melting pot, and thus the survival rate has been high, providing us with a substantial body of documented objects. The superb examples in this exhibition constitute only the pinnacle of a mountain of presentation silver. Each object stands for fifty, or a hundred, or even more examples in private hands and public collections.

In addition to their inherent historical interest, which stimulates our antiquarian impulses, high-style presentation pieces are often among the most ambitious works produced in a silversmith's shop or by a silver manufacturer. They represent out-of-the-ordinary, often special, commissions on which the patron was willing to spend more than the usual amount of money and on which the craftsman was encouraged to lavish his attention and time. Because these objects were made to commemorate a specific event, both patron and silversmith imagined future generations looking over their shoulders, and the one was willing to extend his pocketbook and the other

4. Belmont Memorial Challenge Cup, 1897. Tiffany and Company. *See page 159*

his skills to create works of art that could withstand the scrutiny of time. That presentation silver should be something out of the ordinary was stated explicitly by Admiral Samuel Francis Du Pont. In recognition of his service as a superintendent of the New York Crystal Palace exhibition of 1853, the directors voted to present him with a suitable gift. When he was offered a choice of silver that had been shown at the Crystal Palace, Du Pont demurred, explaining, "the idea of selecting anything ready made . . . is quite repugnant to me . . . and takes away all sentiment and much of the value of the tribute." Tiffany and Company was thereupon commissioned to make Du Pont's presentation service.[3] Presentation awards at this level of quality and importance are thoroughly represented here. Superb and stunning works of art, they are the equal in sophistication and workmanship of any examples of silver and gold made in this country. Many pieces—such as Richard Humphreys's urn of 1774, one of the first known examples of American neoclassical silver (fig. 62)—have become landmarks in the evolution of styles and design.

At the other end of the scale is the presentation silver that we might characterize as vernacular because it is the common, everyday expression of this type of object. This form of presentation piece—often a small beaker, cup, or trophy—flourished in the nineteenth and early twentieth centuries, especially during the period between 1850 and World War I. It persists in our own time, for example, in the form of the Revere bowl presented to volunteers and retirees at many institutions, including Colonial Williamsburg and the Winterthur Museum.[4] Usually supplied ready-made from stock, with an area held in reserve for a suitable inscription, vernacular presentation silver fills an important niche within our artifactual world. There is no evidence to suggest that these small beakers and bowls, no matter how trite they seem to a disinterested party, hold any less meaning for their recipients than a larger and more ambitious commissioned work. We must not forget that in many cases the act of presentation and the thoughts, sentiments, beliefs, and emotions that encircle that act matter more to the individuals involved than the physical qualities of the object itself.

Because of the intrinsic historical interest of all presentation silver, both vernacular and high-style, and the superb aesthetic quality of high-style examples, it is often easy to focus on individual objects and to lose sight of the larger patterns of behavior and meaning that these objects exemplify. This book and exhibition make a substantial contribution to our understanding of the nature and function of presentation silver by organizing the enormous body of surviving objects into five major categories—religion and education, industry and progress, pursuits of leisure and avocation, politics and the military, and rites of passage and friendship—and selecting important examples from each category and describing them in detail. Objects of silver and gold have been used as tangible "marks of achievement" along almost all of life's highways. Christening gifts, wedding and anniversary presents (fig. 225), and other "threshold" gifts represent strong elements of continuity during the past four centuries. Other forms of presentations, such as those associated with wars (fig. 134), industrial and agricultural progress (fig. 104), or sports and other leisure activities (fig. 189), memorialize a specific and unique event. The essays and descriptions that follow explore these threads of continuity and change in the history of American presentation silver.

While presentation silver was made and used throughout American history, the nineteenth century seems to have been the period of its greatest popularity and widest use. Charles Carpenter has called attention to an early exhibition that underlines the importance of presentation silver crafted during this era. Organized by Tiffany and Company and presented at the Main Exhibition Building of the 1876 Centennial Exhibition in Philadelphia, this show of some 125 objects was entitled, in part, "A Retrospective Exhibit of Silver Presentation and Commemorative Pieces, Presentation Swords, Yachting, Racing, Rowing, Shooting, and Rifle Cups, made by Tiffany & Co. During the Past 25 Years." It included such high-style masterpieces as the Bryant Vase (fig. 217) and in its scope reflected many of the preoccupations and avocations of the upper class, especially yachting, whose trophies are perhaps the quintessential artifacts of the second half of the century.[5] Trade catalogues issued by silver manufacturers in the nineteenth and early twentieth centuries often devote several pages to ready-made trophies, cups, testimonials, and premiums, offered in an eclectic range of styles and at prices gauged to appeal to a wide audience. Reed and Barton's 1884 catalogue, for example, contained numerous prize cups for bicycle races, regattas, and baseball, agricultural, shooting, polo, lawn-tennis, trotting, skating, and foot-racing competitions, and fireman's trumpets for presentation as well (fig. 118). The C. F. Monroe Company catalogue entitled *Prize Cups and Trophies in Sterling Silver and Other Metals* (Meriden, Connecticut, 1908–9) offered presentation silver in sterling priced between $5.50 and $2,000, thus blanketing the market from top to bottom. Some companies specialized in the more expensive presentation pieces: Bailey, Banks, and Biddle's catalogue of trophies (Philadelphia, c. 1908), contains no trophy costing less than $1,000, and several examples in the $2,000 range. Throughout the nineteenth century and during the first few decades of the twentieth, every event, no matter how large or how small, seems to have been deemed worthy of commemoration with an object made of silver.[6]

The reasons for the abundance of presentation silver in the nineteenth century are explored in detail by Katherine S. Howe in her essay. They include the opening of the great mines of the American West during the second half of the century. The consequent increase in the supply of the metal and the government's deregulation of the industry resulted in lower prices. Greater affluence and more leisure time meant that there was more money to spend on presentation silver and that there were more events—such as organized athletic contests—requiring a tangible prize or award. The War of 1812 and the Spanish-American War sparked acts of heroism that called for vernacular and high-style presentation silver (figs. 132, 203), as did notable achievements in agriculture and industry (figs. 100, 176). In particular, Howe has called attention to the phenomenon of conspicuous consumption prevalent among the upper class in the last quarter of the century, behavior that made the tangible expression of one's achievements particularly meaningful.

One other factor contributed to the steady call for presentation silver in the nineteenth century, especially in contexts of military, political, and technological achievements. In a recent work, the English historian Eric Hobsbawm has called attention to the "invention of tradition" in societies practicing specific types of behavior in order to establish a sense of continuity with the past and thereby pass along values and attitudes that are seen as desirable. These invented traditions, he speculates, are most likely to appear when societies are undergoing substantial and rapid changes, as was America during the nineteenth century. The use of presentation silver can readily be seen as a means of inventing tradition; the choice of historically acceptable forms reinforced values and attitudes in a new nation struggling to achieve a separate identity. For example, the presentation silver awarded to Stephen Decatur after the War of 1812 featured an abundance of neoclassical ornaments, including satyrs' heads, anthemia, and even a cast figure of Neptune (fig. 131). These classical elements, executed as part of the prevailing Empire taste for ancient forms, had an ideological function, serving to associate Decatur with an acceptable past—namely, the republics of ancient Greece and Rome and the virtues associated with them. The years that followed the War of 1812, as David B. Warren points out, represent a high point in both the production and the quality of presentation silver, but the invention of tradition continued throughout the self-conscious and highly pretentious nineteenth century.[7]

Although presentation objects have been and continue to be fashioned from a variety of materials, from the Biblical frankincense and myrrh to the bronze Heisman Trophy of today, gold and silver have long been at the top of the presentation hierarchy. Gold has long exerted a powerful influence upon the human imagination because of its rarity, durability, and unique luster. Silver is a wondrously flexible metal that can be worked with a wide variety of tools and techniques. It can be hammered,

cast, rolled, or spun into almost any imaginable shape, and therefore can be fashioned into the forms of almost any stylistic vagary. Moreover, it, too, is a durable material, befitting an object meant to last for the ages. It is easy to engrave, and thus is suitable for the lengthy inscriptions that presentation objects almost invariably bear. Its color, luster, and reflective ability, unusual in nature, also make it suitable for commemorating life's significant occasions. Objects of silver and gold are both portable and serviceable, making them additionally attractive for presentation pieces. Both metals have been endowed with intrinsic worth by Western society for thousands of years, and their monetary value literally enriches the act of presentation. While ivory, rhinocerous horn, cowrie shells, coral, amber, jet, jade, and precious stones have all been used as "symbols of excellence" in different cultures, silver and gold have been and remain the dominant materials for presentations in the Western tradition.[8]

Although the reasons for creating presentation silver are almost infinite in their variety, they can be assessed in light of several organizing frameworks, including the categories of temporal and situational analysis adopted here. We might also address what some of the latent functions of presentation silver have been since the seventeenth century. Although many kinds of presentation silver, and especially those objects made in the seventeenth and eighteenth centuries, can be used in the course of normal, everyday life, they were not designed solely, or even primarily, as practical, utilitarian objects. They served a variety of functions that represent contexts of social interaction, and were given, presented, and awarded for a complex mosaic of motives, both manifest and latent. We will briefly summarize some of these contexts and motives in the pages that follow, bearing in mind that any given object can, and frequently does, fulfill more than one—or perhaps even all—of these functions simultaneously. Like most objects, examples of presentation silver are polysemous, distinguished by a multiplicity of meanings.[9]

To commemorate: At its most basic level, presentation silver provides a three-dimensional, tangible record and reminder of an event or accomplishment that otherwise can only be perpetuated in the mind or on paper. Presentation silver thus serves as a form of substitute imagery in the way that Alan Gowans has defined the term in the pictorial arts: "substitute images of things or ideas whose memory it was desirable for some reason to preserve."[10] A presentation piece freezes a moment—almost like a snapshot—encapsulating the emotions stirred by an event in a process of reification. The objects, perhaps not regarded with much affect at the time of presentation, become even more powerful as they refresh the memory of events that recede into the past, often with what seems to be accelerating speed. "When you're playing," the late

5. "Yaght," 1884. Tiffany and Company. *See pages 153–54*

baseball star Hank Greenberg noted, "awards don't seem like much. Then you get older and all of it becomes more precious. It is nice to be remembered. When you're sixty, maybe that's all you've got."[11] Presentation silver thus can function as an icon of continuity, a term used by Eugene Rochberg-Halton and Mihaly Csikszentmihalyi to describe family photographs. These two sociologists found that "the most cherished objects" in the homes of eighty modern Chicago families were those that evoked memories, associations, and experiences of the owner and his or her family and friends. A silver trophy or award, like a photograph, has the ability "to provide a record of one's life, and of the lives of one's ancestors, and can be handed down to one's descendants."[12]

To satisfy altruistic impulses: In at least some cases, an example of presentation silver represents the unselfish regard for or devotion to others that characterizes the best impulses of the human spirit. Many personal types of presentation silver—those identified here with friendship, weddings, births, baptisms, anniversaries, and even deaths—reflect this willingness to give to others in honest appreciation and without thought of return. Although gift theory, as we shall see, posits that every exchange involves obligations between giver and recipient, we should not overlook the fact that presentation silver provides evidence of love, affection, and respect that reflects creditably upon mankind.

To motivate: Presentation silver can function as a lucrative prize to be striven for, one that carries significant monetary value as well as symbolic overtones. Because of the metal's intrinsic value, a gold or silver presentation piece can always be converted into cash should the need arise. Winners of horse races in the eighteenth century were often rewarded with a gold or silver tankard, two-handled cup, or teapot, but the value of the object in pounds sterling was almost always stated, and even emphasized, in announcements concerning the race. Thus, we find in the *South-Carolina Gazette* of 1 October 1750 a notice of a quarter-mile race to be held at the house of Mr. Isaac Peronneau in Goose-Creek, in which the winner would receive "a three pint silver Tankard and a silver Punch Bowl, value *Two Hundred* and *Fifty Pounds*." Racing for a handsome cup (rather than a bag of gold and silver coins) lent an air of gentility to the races, for most contestants had no need of cash, a conspicuous form of the display of wealth.

Small medals and prizes used to motivate children in their studies were common in England and America in the nineteenth century, and similar practices are known today.[13] "Silver incentive awards" are a favored management tool, designed "to reward top sales people, improve industrial safety, thank good customers, and recognize and applaud employee service and outstanding achievements." Such awards include "a wide variety of pens,

trays, tea services, boxes, frames, bowls, desk accessories, trophies and all types of fashionable silver designer jewelry," as well as silver medals and small silver ingots. As the pamphlet promoting these awards notes, management "won't have to convince your award winners that silver has a high perceived value or that it is desirable. They already know these things!"[14]

The modern practice of presenting both a silver object and a cash award blends tradition and expediency, symbolism and reality. In the eighteenth century, it was not uncommon for students at Harvard or Yale to present their teachers with objects made of silver. (As Michael K. Brown points out in his essay, Harvard tutor Henry Flynt received so much tutorial plate that some of his students, in an attempt to select a novel form, elected to present him with a silver chamber pot.) Today, the presentation of silver to faculty members is not especially common, but when it does occur, the donor is likely to be the administration rather than members of the student body. Such is the case with the Arthur G. B. Metcalf Cup and Prize for Excellence in Teaching, awarded annually by Boston University, "to establish a systematic procedure for the review of the quality of teaching and the identification and advancement of those members of the faculty who excel as teachers." The award, named for the current chairman of the university's board of trustees, consists of a large, silver, two-handled covered cup made in 1905, in Sheffield, England, basically English Georgian in style, and a $5,000 cash prize. Thus, the silver award lingers on—and often appears in photographs of the presentation ceremony—but its tacit purpose is in some cases to give a suitably genteel veneer to the presentation of a monetary award. In the case of the Arthur G. B. Metcalf Cup, the use of an eighteenth-century English form—rather than a style of the late twentieth century—may represent an unconscious attempt by a large, disparate, metropolitan university founded in the nineteenth century to invent for itself an older tradition.[15]

To compensate: Sometimes a gift of presentation silver was made when a gift of cold cash would have been gauche. In a famous English instance, the principle was stated quite clearly. In 1803 Lloyd's of London sought donations for a "Patriotic Fund," designed to reward those "who may be engaged in the Defense of the Country, and who may suffer in the Common Cause." Lloyd's understood that "many of those meriting awards might be offended by a gift of cash, [thus] it was proposed that a vase or sword would prove worthy substitutes."[16] This function may well have been at work in the case of the Tyng cup, one of the most famous examples of eighteenth-century American presentation silver. This large, graceful cup was given in 1744 by grateful merchants of Boston to Captain Edward Tyng for his part in the first American naval engagement in King George's War. Made by Jacob Hurd, the monumental cup weighs 96 ounces, 5 pennyweight. In 1744 silver was valued at 33 shillings per troy ounce in Boston, making the value of the metal alone in the Tyng cup worth about £159 in Massachusetts currency, or about £25 in pounds sterling. The cup was thus worth as much as the entire worldly estates of about 30 percent of Boston's population in the early 1740s. The Tyng cup was therefore a gift of substantial value, but one presented in a socially acceptable form. [17]

To influence: This is the dark side of presentation silver. According to gift theory, every present involves the obligation to give, the obligation to receive, and the obligation to reciprocate. [18] Therefore, we might speculate, a presentation gift implies an obligation upon the recipient to reciprocate either in kind or through an action; in effect, the presentation can function as a bribe. It is understandably difficult to marshal evidence that demonstrates this hidden agenda of presentation silver. The so-called Indian peace medals of the late eighteenth and early nineteenth centuries (figs. 58, 59) are, however, good examples of a type of presentation silver in which the desire to influence plays a large role. [19] These medals, and armbands, gorgets, and other forms of personal adornment were worn as badges of military alliance and were prized for the status and rank they conferred upon the recipients. We also might speculate that the San Francisco businessmen who in 1860 gave Senator Edward Dickinson Baker a fascinating set of presentation silver "as a token of their esteem and confidence" were probably attempting to secure Baker's support for a bridge across the Golden Gate and for the completion of the transcontinental railroad. The Baker urn and pitcher are replete with railroad imagery, and the message to Baker was undoubtedly clear and apparently effective. One wonders what was the motivation for the presentation of the so-called Phillips Gold Service. Consisting of 196 pieces of flatware and 175 pieces of hollowware, and made of fourteen-karat gold, this service was a gift to John M. Phillips from "certain sewer contractors in and about New York" in 1927. The next year, Phillips, known as the "sewer-pipe king" of the borough of Queens, New York, was "accused of defrauding Queens taxpayers of from $8,000,000 to $10,000,000 through monopoly of sewer pipe." Phillips died shortly before he went to trial, having only briefly enjoyed the presentation bestowed by those certain contractors, who apparently had every reason to be very grateful. [20]

To enhance the reputation of the donor: Presentation silver can represent an attempt at self-aggrandizement on the part of an organization. By making a presentation to an exalted or famous person, an individual or a group may hope to gain some reflected status-by-association. Was this part—even a small part—of the motivation of New York's Common Council in presenting gold freedom boxes to Governor George Clinton, George Washington, John Jay, the marquis de Lafayette, and Baron von Steuben (fig. 121)?

The modern essayist Andy Rooney has provided us with a personal statement of his views on this aspect of presentation gifts. When his college fraternity wished to honor him in later life, Rooney observed, "There is often a fine line between who's being honored, the individual getting it or the organization giving it. A lot of times the presence of the recipient does more honor to the giver than the getter." Rooney declined his fraternity's award and indicated that he much preferred the "small, tarnished cup with most of its thin plating of silver gone" that he won "for writing an article in my school magazine when I was fourteen, and I wouldn't swop it for any award in the world. When they gave it to me, they meant it." [21]

Some of the humbug surrounding testimonials was exposed in a satire entitled "The Mutual Piece-of-Plate Presentation Club," written by Laman Blanchard and published in the English periodical *The Illuminated Magazine* in September 1844. Noting that merit without its reward and certificate was "of no more consequence than an unfeathered peacock," Blanchard poked fun at the proliferation of testimonials awarded for "Humanity and Gentleness," or inscribed with "The Apostle of Temperance" or "An Honor to his Country" or other vague and generalized sentiments. [22]

To enhance the reputation of the maker: Many nineteenth-century presentation objects served to demonstrate the prowess and promote the sales of the manufacturer. The makers of these objects were aware that these awards and trophies would receive considerable attention and they expended extra effort and care on them, just as they did upon large showpieces made for expositions and fairs. The Philadelphia firm of Fletcher and Gardiner, for example, inscribed their name on the outside of the magnificent vase they made in 1812–13 for Captain Isaac Hull and used a depiction of the vase on their advertising trade card. Fletcher and Gardiner received many presentation commissions in the 1810s and 1820s, suggesting that this small bit of advertising was effective. In 1858 Tiffany and Company received much favorable attention when they were asked by the city of New York to make a gold box for presentation to Cyrus W. Field in recognition of the completion of the first Atlantic cable. The box was exhibited in Tiffany's show window prior to the presentation. Later in the century, firms competed for the right to make major presentation pieces. For example, in 1875 Black, Starr and Frost; Gorham; Starr and Marcus; Tiffany; and the Whiting Manufacturing Company vied for the right to produce the Bryant Vase (fig. 217), knowing full well that the publicity surrounding the receipt of such a commission (awarded to Tiffany) would enhance their reputation and stimulate sales of their regular line of goods. [23]

To perpetuate existing class and social relationships: As Karl Marx noted, gold and silver "are appropriated and controlled by elites precisely to secure or maintain dominance in the social hierarchy."[24] The vast amount of presentation silver associated with politics and military events, with captains of industry who saved sinking companies, and with business moguls who pioneered the telegraph and transatlantic cable, underscores this function. The ritual presentation of silver to these politicians, generals, and capitalists reinforced the perceived value of their work and provided tangible evidence of their status and power. A study by Eugenia W. Herbert of the role of copper in precolonial African societies showed that copper was an indication of status "in the sense of wealth, prestige, rank, and authority, but also status in regard to gender, age, and the stages of human life." The key to all of copper's uses in African society was its "connotation of power, understood not just in our narrowest sense of political power . . . but power defined within a view of the world that assumes the interpenetration of the political, religious, social, and esthetic spheres." She might well have been writing about the use of presentation silver and gold in America.[25]

The free-labor rituals of the mid-nineteenth century, as discussed by historian Brian Greenberg, provide another good case study of the function of presentation silver (and other objects) to solidify social relationships. "At the core of the free-labor ideology was the belief in the mutuality of interests between capital and labor," and employer-sponsored associations of employees, often in the form of volunteer corps, fostered and perpetuated this belief. In 1850 the Corning Corps went to a target-shooting competition, followed by a dinner paid for by the company, and the prizes "included such expensive items as a gold watch, a silver goblet, and a gold pen-and-pencil set, as well as the target itself." In 1855 company prizes given at a meeting of the Rathbone Guards included "a silver watch, six silver tea- and three silver tablespoons, and a clock," and in the same year, the awards given at an excursion of the guard corps of Boardman and Grey included "gold and silver watches, a gold chain, and a silver cake basket." The workers would feel obliged to reciprocate with similar gifts to their employers and foremen; Greenberg cites an instance in the mid-1850s when the employees of a boot and shoe manufacturer presented each of their employers with a silver cake knife "as a token of esteem and respect."[26]

Maintenance of social relationships may well have been a motivating factor in the practice of presenting silver to churches, a custom more common in the seventeenth and eighteenth centuries than in recent times. The motives of donors of church plate were undoubtedly mixed, but one of their reasons for giving pieces of suitably engraved, durable silver was to demonstrate their exalted role in the social hierarchy through their benevolence to grateful, yet suitably subservient, congregations. These donations would reflect well on the donor, and their continued presence in the church would help insure the status of the family name through subsequent generations.[27]

While presentation silver thus serves to reinforce the organization of society in political, commercial, and ecclesiastical contexts, it also functions in the same way on a personal level. Gifts of friendship and rites of passage act to strengthen the bonds of kinship, to emphasize the value of marriage and the family, and to reinforce other values that society regards with esteem.

It may well be that this function of presentation silver—that of solidifying and confirming relationships—is its paramount attribute. This is the view taken by the English scholar Grahame Clark, who argues that the "prime function" of precious materials of all kinds has always been social. "Even gifts made to individuals are as a rule intended to strengthen family links," he notes, "while in the public domain they are most overtly directed to promoting social ends. The notions of excellence they embody are used to fortify and legitimize the sacred and profane dimensions of authority while at the same time denoting official executants by means of appropriate insignia."[28] Paul Revere's Liberty Bowl, arguably the most famous example of American presentation silver, was commissioned by the Sons of Liberty and inscribed with the names of ninety-two patriots, with the purpose of defining and legitimizing the transfer of power and authority from the Old World to the New.[29]

Presentation silver and gold offer a significant opportunity to examine life from many perspectives. Each object illustrated and discussed here is a rich source of information on American values, assumptions, craftsmanship, technology, and a host of other topics. As this book indicates, each object is the nucleus of a historic event, the center of an act that involved the minds, hands, and hearts of many individuals; for the story of presentation silver is primarily the story of people—of their desires and ambitions, of their priorities and goals, and, ultimately, of their achievements.

THE COLONIAL PERIOD

MICHAEL K. BROWN

The presentation of silver and gold to mark a special occasion or as a tangible expression of a concept or feeling played a central role in the life of colonial America. Many such objects became the treasured possessions of the upper classes; others, symbolic of events and ideas, were created for Americans at every level of society. Gifts of these precious metals were imbued with meaning and fulfilled a multiplicity of purposes. Entries in the diary of Samuel Sewall, a Boston magistrate, suggest the ubiquity and variety of presentation silver from the late seventeenth century to the Revolution.[1]

When Sewall contributed a silver pike engraved with his name and the presentation to the Ancient and Honorable Artillery Company for its halberd, he may have intended more than simply meeting one of the company's needs.[2] Because of the pike's public use, his benefaction would become widely known, and perhaps he wished through his gift to attain an immortality of sorts. An enterprising, paternal motive probably induced him in 1707 to take a piece of silver to his son Joseph, a student at Harvard, who would present it to his tutor.[3] These same paternalistic instincts had surfaced before, when Sewall encouraged the relationship between his son Samuel and the young woman he was courting by sending her a piece of silver as an expression of his son's feelings.[4] Sewall gave silver and gold to satisfy his altruistic impulses, as the following tender passage from his diary indicates. On a visit to his daughter-in-law, Sewall went up to her "and gave her my Wive's Wedding Ring, saying I hoped she would wear it with the same Nobility as she did who was the first owner of it."[5]

The earliest references to American presentation silver are contemporaneous with the first European settlements along the Atlantic seaboard. Actually, the presentation of plate, a term by which silver vessels were then commonly known, had developed into a useful means of raising additional funds for the establishment of the American colonies. Just five years after the first permanent English settlement was established at Jamestown, the Virginia Company was granted a new charter giving it the prerogative to conduct a lottery. Appealing to people's generosity and fondness for gambling, the sweepstakes became immediately popular. In 1612 the First Great Virginian Lottery was drawn (fig. 7), and since the vestry of the Church of St. Mary, Colechurch, London, was the winner of "twoe spoones," it seems quite clear that there was little, if any, public opposition to it. "Thomas Sharplisse, a Taylor of London, had the chiefe prize, viz; foure thousand crownes in fayre plate, which was sent to his house in a very stately manner."[6]

American presentation silver in the colonial period is based almost exclusively on English models. French and Spanish colonies were established very early in Louisiana and the Mississippi Valley and in Florida and the Southwest, respectively. In addition, there was the short-lived Dutch colony of New Netherland, of which the English took control in 1664 and which they renamed New York. Some silver with histories of ownership in these colonies is known. Illustrated here is a Mexican-made chalice believed to have been presented to a Catholic church in New Mexico during the eighteenth century (fig. 8). But only the Dutch settlement seems to have exerted a significant cultural influence upon American-produced silver (see figs. 49, 68).

In British colonial America two completely different economies developed. In the northern colonies—from Delaware to New Hampshire—the population was relatively concentrated and could support a number of local silversmiths. With few major population centers, the southern colonies—Maryland, Virginia, the Carolinas, and Georgia—could not provide the economic base to support an extensive and specialized silversmithing trade. Instead, after exporting crops of tobacco, rice, and indigo to England, southern merchants imported a wide range of goods, including objects of silver. For example, the citizens of Boston, one of the principal colonial towns, presented fourteen churches with 245 silver vessels, of which 223 are of American origin. By comparison, throughout the entire colony of Virginia thirty-seven churches have on record only 120 examples of prerevolutionary silver. Of these, 92 bear the marks of London silversmiths and 24 others, although unmarked, are undoubtedly of English origin.[7]

As early as 1608 two London-trained silversmiths, Richard Belfield and William Johnson, settled at James-

6. Beaker, 1647–52. John Hull. *See page 32*

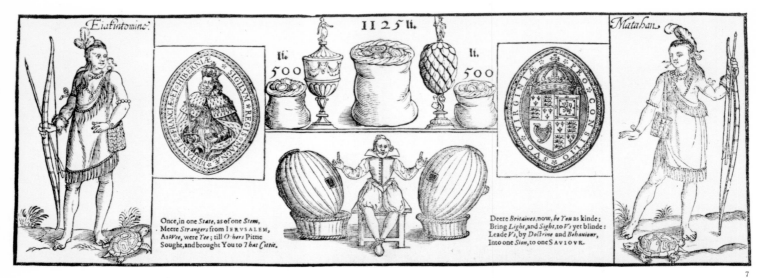

Once, in one *State*, as of one *Stem*,
Meere *Strangers* from IERVSALEM,
As *Wee*, were *Yee* ; till *Others* Pittie
Sought, and brought You to *That Cittie*.

Deere *Britaines* now, *be You* as kinde ;
Bring *Light*, and *Sight*, to *Vs* yet blinde :
Leade *Vs*, by *Doctrine* and *Behauiour*,
Into one *Sion*, to one SAVIOVR.

7. Illustration for *A Declaration for the certaine time of drawing the great standing Lottery*, London, 1615. Felix Kyngston. Woodcut illustration printed on paper. Society of Antiquaries of London

8. Chalice, c. 1750–1800. Mexico. Silver, h. 8⅝ in. (22 cm.). Courtesy Archdiocese of Santa Fe Collection in the Museum of International Folk Art, Museum of New Mexico, Sante Fe

town. Yet as Captain John Smith, president of the Virginia Colony, explained, these men would not found the silversmith's craft in America: "The lust of gold was apparent in sending out refiners and goldsmiths, who never had occasion to exercise their craft."[8] It was not until the middle of the seventeenth century that population centers sizable enough to provide the silversmith with sufficient patronage emerged, and only then did the craft become firmly established in America.

In 1643, when Jurian Blanck's daughter Elsje was baptized, the records of the Reformed Dutch church of New Amsterdam listed his profession as "Goutsmidt" (goldsmith), indicating that he was working as a silversmith by that date.[9] Some goldsmiths emigrated to America during the seventeenth century to escape the brutal policies instituted in France by Louis XIV in an effort to end Protestantism. Several of the Huguenot immigrants were responsible for introducing silversmithing to the colonies. Cesar Ghiselin settled at Philadelphia in 1681, while Nicholas De Longuemare and Solomon Legaré established the profession in Charleston during the following decade. In Boston, the partnership of John Hull and Robert Sanderson, which was formed in 1652 to operate the newly founded mint, was also responsible for firmly establishing the silversmith's craft in New England. A number of pieces of hollowware and a few spoons bearing the marks of these two makers survive and are recognized as the earliest known examples of the American silversmith's work (figs. 15, 17).

The largest identifiable body of colonial presentation silver is the group of vessels that were given or bequeathed to various religious and educational institutions and social and fraternal organizations. Although all of these pieces, like the rest of the colonial silver included in this book, were intended as utilitarian

9. Standing cup and pair of patens, 1618–19. Unknown maker, London. Marked "FG" (RG or IG) over a bird. Silver, h. of cup 8¼ in. (21 cm.). Inscribed on the base of the chalice "THE COMMVNION CVPP FOR Sᵗ MARYS CHVRCH IN SMITHS HVNDRED IN VIRGINIA" and on the rims of the patens "Whosoever shall eate this bread and drinke the cupp of the Lord unworthily shalbe gilty of the body & blood of yᵉ Lord Cor 1 XIᵗʰ" and on the second paten "If any man eate of this Bread he shall live for ever Jo VIᵗʰ". St. John's Church, Hampton, Virginia

objects, they also assumed a more elevated role as ceremonial or official plate.

Within this group, the silver presented to American churches and synagogues is the earliest and most plentiful. The first gift of ecclesiastical silver made to an American church actually took place in London, about 1618. There, "two persons, unknowne," as the Virginia Company's records state, gave "faire Plate, and other rich Ornaments" for a Communion table "for the Church of Mistresse Mary Robinson's founding"¹⁰ (fig. 9). The use of silver and gold ecclesiastical vessels is an ancient Roman Catholic tradition based upon the belief in transubstantiation, the miraculous conversion of the consecrated bread and wine into Christ's actual flesh and blood. This tradition continued to be observed by the Protestant sects that predominated in colonial America.

As in other British colonies, the Church of England was the officially established church, but in America a diversity of Protestant sects existed as well, including Congregationalists, Presbyterians, Methodists, Baptists, members of the Reformed Dutch church, Lutherans, Moravians, and Quakers. Maryland, along with the French and Spanish settlements, was largely settled by Catholics, while prominent Jewish congregations were established in New York; Newport, Rhode Island; Philadelphia; and Charleston.

The sacramental vessels employed reflected the beliefs and ritualistic requirements of each group. For example, the Protestants, to remove themselves from the taint of the Catholic church's popish rites, reduced the number of sacraments from seven to two—baptism and Holy Communion. The Catholic chalice, whose small cup held wine administered to the clergy alone, was replaced by a vessel of a form not identified with Catholic ritual, such as the late-Renaissance or Mannerist-style standing cup that Jeremy Houchin gave to Boston's First Church (fig. 16). This domestic vessel possessed a greater physical capacity, a practical advantage since, in

10. *Bishop William White*, 1814. Thomas Sully (1783–1872). Oil on canvas, 50 x 40 in. (127 x 101.6 cm.). Washington Cathedral, Washington, D.C.

the Protestant churches, some of the congregation usually participated in Holy Communion.

Church records identify some early religious silver that was acquired by subscription among the membership, but most of it was either presented or bequeathed by a donor. These individuals came from various levels of society. In 1694 King William and Queen Mary made gifts of silver to King's Chapel in Boston and the Chapel of the Fort in New York, which shortly thereafter became the property of the newly organized Trinity Church. The minutes of Christ Church in Quincy, Massachusetts, record that, at a meeting on Monday, Easter Week, 1 April 1771, the congregation "voted, that the thanks of this Congregation be given by the Minister, to Caesar, an aged Negro, servant to Major Ebenezer Miller, for his generous donation of a Silver Cup of the value of Twenty Dollars, for the Service of the Holy Communion."[11] Unfortunately, not all colonial record keeping was so precise, as evidenced by the inscription engraved on another cup: "This peice of plate is presented to ye first Church in Kittery by an Unknown Hand."[12]

Groups of people, or even churches, occasionally donated ecclesiastical silver. Two beakers, a pair belonging to the First Congregational Church in New

London, Connecticut, are engraved "The Gift of the Owners of the Ship Adventure of London 1699,"[13] and on the caudle cup presented by Mrs. Elizabeth Clement to the First Church in Dorchester, Massachusetts, in 1678 (fig. 17), a later inscription records its presentation in 1878 from the First Church to the Second Church of Dorchester. The silver presented in the Protestant churches includes many of the vessels that comprised the colonial silversmith's range of production. Often these pieces had originally been intended for domestic use and were subsequently bequeathed to a church by their owners; some, however, were commissioned expressly for ecclesiastical use. Although these pieces of silver were used as communion and baptismal vessels or as collection plates, they assumed a ceremonial status as well. An inventory taken in March 1729/30 of the plate belonging to the Second Church of Christ in Boston records no less than thirty-six vessels, including a baptismal basin, three bowls, four dishes, eleven cups, twelve tankards, and five flagons.[14] Certainly, not all of this silver was required for the administration of the sacraments, yet, assembled on the altar as ceremonial or official plate, it conveyed a clear sense of the church's prosperity and prestige within the community. In Thomas Sully's striking portrait of Bishop William White of Philadelphia, the eminent divine is depicted in his full complement of vestments, seated in an impressive mahogany armchair with a representation of his miter atop the carved crest rail and some of the church's communion silver displayed at his side (fig. 10).

Gifts of silver to secular institutions and organizations assumed an even more clearly ceremonial role since, unlike communion vessels, they were not actually requisite; in most instances, however, the givers' motivation was much the same. Certainly the magnificent grace cup that Samuel Sewall presented to Harvard College on behalf of the ailing Lieutenant Governor William Stoughton was intended by Stoughton to express the great prestige of his alma mater and to convey some measure of his devotion to it—as well as, doubtless, some sense of Stoughton's worth and generosity. The Stoughton cup (fig. 39) continues to be the focal point of Harvard's impressive collection of plate, most of which was amassed before the American Revolution.

Not all of Harvard's silver was presented in a spirit of disinterested beneficence. Seniority there was fixed not only between classes but, following an English practice, within each class as well. Simultaneously, the college established a system of rank among its undergraduates that appears to be unique. At the top of the system were the Fellow Commoners. Addressed and recorded as "Mr.," they were given the privilege of dining at the Fellows' table and, of course, were listed at the head of their respective classes. These privileges were not awarded in recognition of academic excellence but were granted in exchange for additional tuition and a silver vessel, worth

£3 or more, presented by the student to the college. Before 1650 only three Fellow Commoners were so designated:

> *By mr Thomas Langham ffellow Comonr, A*
> *peice to vallue of Three pound three shill . &*
> *ten pence. It is one Silver Beer Bowl .*
> *Mr Ven ffellow Commoner, One fruite dish*
> *& one silver Sugar spoon & one Silver tipt jug .*
> *Mr Richard Harris One great Salt & one*
> *small Trencher Salt .[15]*

One of these objects, the great salt presented by Richard Harris, remains at Harvard and is illustrated here (fig. 11). The plate was formally arranged at the high table where, like the churches' communion silver, it must have made an impressive display.

A second major group of presentation silver consists of the prizes and trophies that acclaim success in a variety of pastimes, such as lotteries or sporting competitions. Some of the lotteries held before the American Revolution were legally sanctioned and established for the benefit of the public. Others were conducted as private, entrepreneurial ventures. Of the public lotteries, no less than 158 were licensed. They were organized for a variety of purposes: to generate money for a city, county, or colony government; to pay for public improvements; to raise funds to benefit churches, schools, and industries; or for personal relief. Even more numerous, the private lotteries provided an alternative means to dispose of property. Newspaper announcements indicate that a wide. variety of prizes were offered, ranging from the inanimate ("new brick house, corner of Third and Arch streets," in Philadelphia) to the animate ("likely young Virginia Negro Woman, fit for House business and her Child").[16] Lotteries were also employed by the merchant and craftsman as a lucrative and more efficient alternative to merchandising. In 1737 Alexander Kerr, the Williamsburg silversmith, placed an advertisement in the *Virginia Gazette* announcing, "the Sale of sundry valuable Jewels, and Plate, amounting to Four Hundred Pistoles. By way of LOTTERY."[17] Another silversmith, Simeon Soumain, was probably a partner in John Stevins's lottery of "501£ of Silver & Gold Work, wrought by Simeon Soumain," the principal prize being "an Eight square [octagonal] Tea-Pot, six Tea Spoons, Skimmer and Tongs, Valued, at 18£ 3s.6d." The newspaper announcement specified that tickets could be obtained from either Stevins or a number of representatives stationed at several different locations, including "Simeon Soumain's in the City of N-York, which last place the good[s] are to be seen."[18] Regrettably, none of these objects or any other colonial lottery silver has been identified—a fact that may be explained by the absence of identifying inscriptions rather than by the loss of the objects. Silver trophies were frequently awarded to the winners of competitions. In 1702 Samuel Sewall judged

11. Great salt, c. 1637. Unknown maker. Marked on the inside of the bowl with partially effaced London hallmarks, indecipherable date-letter, and on each scroll or knop and on the bottom with a lion passant. Silver, h. 4³/₄ in. (12.1 cm.). Inscribed on the bottom "IGE [Jose and Elizabeth Glover]". Harvard University, Cambridge, Massachusetts. Bequest of Richard Harris to Harvard College, 1644

a marksmanship contest and afterward presented the winner, the silversmith John Noyes, with the silver cup that he had contributed.[19] In New York a similar event was held in 1766 for "Lovers of Shooting." The winner was presented a half-pint mug, and the runners-up received silver shoe and knee buckles and a stone ring.[20] Announcements of competitions and the trophies to be awarded were frequently published in newspapers, but only a few of these prizes—all of them for horse races—can be identified.

Organized racing was introduced in this country in the 1660s, at Hempstead Plain on Long Island by Richard Nicolls, the first English governor of New York, who was himself a horse fancier. In 1669 Governor Francis Lovelace, Nicolls's successor, wrote reassuringly that the races had been instituted, "not so much for ye divertisement of ye youth alone but for ye Encouragemt of ye bettering ye breed of horses."[21] The sport's popularity developed rapidly, and by the mid-eighteenth century several colonies had formed jockey clubs to encourage horse breeding. Here, too, different kinds of prizes were offered. Cash, usually raised through subscription, was frequently presented. In Philadelphia in 1767, with the governor's wife as the principal patron, a Ladies Contribution Purse was offered to the winner of the three-year-olds' race; the following year a number of Charleston craftsmen established a Mechanics Purse. The prize could be substantial; at an important competition held in

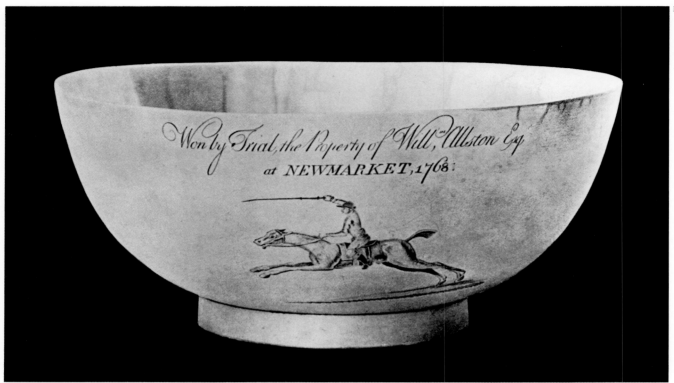

12. Punch bowl, 1768. Abram Portal (c. 1728–1809), London. Silver, diam. 9 in. (22.8 cm.). Inscribed "Won by Trial, the Property of Will.ᵐ Allston Esqʳ at NEWMARKET, 1768". Mr. and Mrs. John Alston Deas

1752, at Anderson's Race Ground, Gloucester, Virginia, Benjamin Jasker's horse Selima won 2,500 pistoles (a little more than £2,000). The English tradition of presenting the winner with a silver vessel is said to have been introduced in America by Governor Nicolls.[22] A porringer inscribed "1668 . wunn . att . hanpsted . plaines . march 25" was once believed to be one of these early trophies; however, since its maker, Peter Van Inburgh, was not actually working until about 1710, scholars now think that the porringer may have been remade from an earlier piece of silver.[23]

During the prerevolutionary period, the most prevalent form of racing trophy was the punch bowl. A fine London-made example was presented to William Allston of Charleston following his horse Tryal's win at the Newmarket Course in 1768 (fig. 12). Like other colonial presentation silver, these bowls were useful as well as symbolic and undoubtedly were put to service at the convivial gatherings that soon became an essential feature of the competitions.

Another category of presentation silver acknowledges the political and social contributions made by individuals for the benefit of mankind. Some of these commemorate acts of heroism—such as the punch bowl engraved with a naive and appealing picture of Andrew Gautier, a New York chairmaker, almost single-handedly bringing under control the fire that in February 1749/50 raged through the New Free School House and damaged Trinity Church (fig. 51). Most of this silver, however, was inspired by political and military events of the prerevolutionary period. Perhaps the earliest examples of this tradition are the ornaments presented to American Indians by the British, French, and Spanish governments. In a letter to William Carmichael and William Short of 30 June 1793, Thomas Jefferson described this practice as "an ancient custom from time immemorial."[24] A proposal made by Governor Robert Hunter in 1710 at Albany, while meeting with the chiefs of the Iroquois Nations, more fully identifies the ornaments as emblems of friendship and allegiance:

> Your Brethen who have been in England and have seen ye great Queen and Her Court, have no doubt informed you how vain & groundless the French boasting has been all along, how our Great Queens armys have year after year, routed all his forces, taken his Townes, and is at this time near his principle town and seat of Government, her Majty has sent them as a pledge of her protection, and as a memoriall to them of their fidelity, a medall for each Nation with her Royall effigie on one side, & the last gain'd battle on ye other, which as such she desires may be kept in your respective Castles for ever, she has also sent her Picture on silver twenty to each nation to be given to ye Cheif Warriors, to be worn about their necks as a token, that they shall allwaies be in readinesse to fight under her Banner against the common enemy.[25]

During the colonial period American silversmiths as well as their European counterparts fashioned thousands of these ornaments. The range of forms was extensive, including rings, wrist bands, arm plates, brooches, hair plates, and gorgets (fig. 58). Just a fraction of these objects are now known, undoubtedly because they were worn on the person and buried with the dead. The most splendid example known is a London-made frontlet that was intended to be worn across the forehead (fig. 13). This superb ornament is surely among the earliest and most sophisticated manifestations of the Baroque style in America. Presented in the name of Charles II, "King of England, Scotland, France, Ireland, and Virginia," to the Queen of the Pamunkey Indians in Virginia, it boldly conveys the consequence of these presentation pieces.

The importance of the Indian alliances became still more critical during the middle of the eighteenth century, when England and France were at war. Both King George's War (1744–48) and later the French and Indian War (1754–63) were fought to safeguard English territories and to protect commerce in North America. While the American newspapers were reporting the colonists' victories over the French privateers that were disrupting colonial trade, they also were frequently announcing that insurers and merchants were taking up subscriptions for a piece of silver to be presented to some triumphant captain (figs. 48, 57). Silver presentation vessels were also commissioned to honor colonial heroes who commanded victorious attacks against the French enemy. Most notable of these triumphs was the stunning American victory at the French fortress of Louisbourg, on Cape Breton Island. The remarkable campaign was organized under the direction of William Pepperrell, a merchant who had never before commanded troops in battle. For forty-nine days his New Englanders laid siege until the French finally capitulated. The expedition's success was heralded throughout the colonies, and indeed throughout the British Empire. Pepperrell received quantities of silver commemorating the momentous victory and, incidentally, became the first colonial to be created a baronet (fig. 14).[26]

Another significant body of presentation silver recognized the political figures of the day and honored distinguished individuals. In the American colonies this practice is most closely associated with New York. In 1702 Viscount Edward Hyde Cornbury, a cousin of Queen Anne, arrived as the colony's new royal governor, and the Common Council voted to award him the freedom of the city, symbolized by its seal contained in a gold box. This was not the first such presentation: in 1693 a gold cup made by Cornelius van der Burch was bestowed by the Council on Governor Benjamin Fletcher. Undoubtedly the custom reflected English and Irish traditions.[27] By 1775 the Council records had noted the gift of no less than twenty gold and three silver-gilt boxes. Some of them honored distinguished personages, such as

13. Frontlet, c. 1677. English. Silver, h. 6⅛ in. (15.6 cm.). Inscribed "HONI SOIT QUI MAL Y PENSE [Evil to him who evil thinks]" and "CHARLES THE SECOND KING OF ENGLAND SCOTLAND FRANCE IRELAND AND VIRGINIA". Above the central cartouche is a horizontal oval reserve engraved with a lion passant over a crown; below is a crescent-shaped reserve inscribed "THE QUEENE OF PAMUNKEY". The Association for the Preservation of Virginia Antiquities

Lord Augustus Fitzroy, a son of the duke of Grafton, who visited New York in 1732, and Andrew Hamilton, the Philadelphia attorney, for "his learned and Generous defence of the Rights of Mankind and the Liberty of the Press in the Case of John Peter Zenger,"[28] but the majority of these boxes were presented to newly appointed royal governors. Such generous presentations were intended to welcome and honor these dignitaries yet at the same time to ensure that government relations would be affable.

Silver was also an appropriate means of marking progressive accomplishments or of honoring an individual's professional station. Samuel Sewall writes of the visit of a grandson, for whom he "wrap'd up a Silver Cup with one ear, weighing about 3 ounces and 12 Grains, to give his Mother, which I had promis'd her. A Minister's Wife, I told her, ought not to be without such a one."[29] In 1642 Kiliaen van Rensselaer sent from Amsterdam to William Kieft, who as Director of New Netherland was repre-

14. Two-handled covered cup, 1749. John Wrigman (active c. 1740–1772), London. Four hallmarks on the base of the cup and on the cover of the lip: "JW", "O", lion passant, and crowned leopard's head. Silver, h. 15 in. (38.1 cm.). Inscribed "S.ʳ W.ᵐ Pepperell to his Son Andren." and "64–19" (ounces and penny-weight). Pepperrell Silver Collection, Portland Museum of Art, Portland, Maine

senting van Rensselaer's New World interests, several gifts including a pair of gold- and silver-plated spurs and a gold- and silver-plated rapier. Kieft wrote van Rensselaer:

The saddle, rapier, boots, spurs and baldric have been delivered to me and although I would rather these things had not been sent—first, because I am still pretty well provided with everything, secondly, because I expect to be called home next summer and, thirdly, because it is against my oath to accept presents—nevertheless, to show that it is my desire to render your honor and your honor's colonists as much service as I can and as is consistent with my bounden duty, I have neither been able nor willing to refuse the aforesaid articles and have accepted them on behalf of the honorable Company, as whose effects they have been entered on the books. I further thank your honor heartily and shall always try to repay this debt with gratitude.[30]

Most of this category of presentation silver is comprised of the pieces presented to college tutors, who were primarily responsible for the students' instruction. In the American colonies this tradition was established by the end of the seventeenth century. In 1695 William Brattle received from his Harvard students a great basin (fig. 38) as well as a porringer. Tutorial silver is most closely identified with Harvard College, although a few examples presented to Yale presidents and tutors are known (fig. 44). No particular form appears to have been favored over another. For example, in 1724 Nicholas Sever received from the graduating class at Harvard a small salver, a pair of candlesticks, and a pair of chafing dishes; four years later the class of 1728 gave him a large salver, a cann, and a teapot (fig. 42).[31] Another Harvard tutor, Henry Flynt, is said to have received a silver chamber pot from a class of students.[32]

The tradition of giving tutorial silver is most closely identified with the colonial period, the latest recorded examples being a tankard and pair of canns presented to Joseph Willard by his Harvard students in 1770.[33] Most certainly these gifts were presented as symbols of respect, yet one cannot help wondering whether, after reading of Sewall's taking his son a piece of silver for his tutor, if there might have been an element of opportunism as well.

Religious institutions, the principal recipients of presentation silver, occasionally themselves made gifts to acknowledge an individual's contributions. In 1758 the Parnassim and Elders of the Congregation Shearith Israel in New York voted "that a piece of Plate not exceeding Twenty Pound value be presented to Mr. Abm Abrahams for his zealous services to the Synagogue."[34] A few years later the Protestant Reformed Dutch church in New York presented Daniel Crommelin, an Amsterdam merchant, with a silver tankard in appreciation of his service in assisting the congregation in its search for a bilingual minister (fig. 35).

Gifts of silver to family members and friends are the most personal and common of all presentations. For the most part, these gifts are tangible expressions of love between spouses or other family members or of affection between friends. Sometimes they commemorate a holiday or specific event, as did the gold rings that Samuel Sewall presented to the governor of the colony in honor of the New Year, but the majority mark special occasions in family life, particularly those relating to birth, marriage, and death.[35]

In January 1725/26 Sewall entered in his diary the birth of a great-grandson to his granddaughter Mary and her husband William Pepperrell: "Gave my Grand Daughter Pepperrell a Silver Spoon in Remembrance of her Son Andrew, born Jany 4. 1725/6. A.P. 1725/6."[36] In addition to spoons, a number of other types of silver were presented as gifts for children. Bethiah Shrimpton owned several miniature silver vessels, and she wrote in her will that after her death, "her Sister Hunts Children Should have her silver Baby things."[37] In 1758 Mary Storer commissioned her brother, Samuel Edwards, the Boston silversmith, to fabricate a small pair of canns, engrave them with the Storer arms, and inscribe them for her granddaughters, Mary Smith and Mary Storer, Jr.[38] Spoons and canns could be used by their recipients, but some vessels, such as the saucepan that Edwards made in 1752 to be presented to Ebenezer Storer III, who died before his first birthday, had no apparent utilitarian purpose for the recipient.[39]

Some silver forms and specific decorative devices are archaic today, and therefore we may not understand their symbolic significance. The sugar box is an English form produced during the second half of the seventeenth century and briefly at the beginning of the eighteenth century (fig. 66). While the rich ornamentation of these boxes has long been admired, only recently have we been able to interpret the decoration as an expression of love, symbolic of marriage and fertility.

An extensive range of silver forms was produced as courtship gifts, for dowries, or to celebrate marriages. In 1768 Dr. William Paine ordered from the silversmith Paul Revere an extensive service for Lois Orne, his bride. When completed, the service consisted of a coffeepot, a teapot, a tankard, a pair of canns, a pair of sauce boats, a pair of porringers, a cream pot, a pair of tea tongs, eighteen teaspoons, four salt spoons, and a dozen large spoons.[40]

In addition to its functional aspects, the silver marking life's rites of passage and symbolizing friendship also took on a ceremonial role. Perhaps the most meaningful of all these forms is the wedding ring. In his diary for 1686, Samuel Sewall described the wedding of Elizabeth Babcock to Henry Vose, the first marriage performed by an Anglican clergyman in New England. Despite the historic nature of the occasion, the bridegroom seems to have lacked a ring, and so one was borrowed.[41] Relatively few of these early rings have been identified. One presented by Paul Revere to his wife, Rachel, is inscribed "Live Contented."[42]

Rings were also presented to the clergy and the principal mourners at funerals as mementos (fig. 78). Sewall's diary includes frequent references to the mourning rings he received. Dr. Samuel Buxton, a minister in Salem, Massachusetts, bequeathed his heirs "a quart tankard of mourning rings."[43] Expressive of personal loss, these precious tokens, together with the gloves and scarves that were also presented and the food and drink consumed, made mourning a costly practice.

Presentations in the form of bequests were a tangible expression of affection. In his will the Reverend Thomas Cheever bequeathed to his grandson John Burt, the silversmith's eldest son, "my silver Cann as a token of my love."[44] The bequest of silver vessels also underlined family permanence and continuity from one generation to the next.

One of the latest examples of colonial presentation silver is the great tea urn (fig. 62) presented by the first Continental Congress to Secretary Charles Thomson in 1774. Handsomely conceived and adeptly fabricated in the new neoclassical style, the urn was as much in the forefront of design as in the vanguard of politics. In that it honors a distinguished American for his service to his country, the Thomson tea urn is very much in the tradition of colonial presentation silver; at the same time, in its impressive size and richness it looks forward to the American presentation silver of the nineteenth century.

15

16

15. Beaker, 1647–52 *(cat. no. 1)*

John Hull (1624–1683), Boston. Marked on the bottom "IH" beneath four pellets. Silver, h. 3⅞ in. (9.8 cm.)

Inscribed "B$\overset{T}{*}$C [The Boston Church]"

Silver Collection, First and Second Church in Boston

16. Standing cup, 1639–40

T.G., London. Marked "T.G." beneath three pellets. Silver, h. 9⅜ in. (23.8 cm.)

Inscribed "The Gift of a Freind I*H" and "B$\overset{T}{}$C [The Boston Church]" Silver Collection, First and Second Church in Boston

This fine little beaker, bearing just the mark of John Hull, and therefore predating the partnership he formed with Robert Sanderson in 1652, is the earliest known piece of American silver. Hull was born in Market Hareborough, in Leicestershire, and emigrated to Massachusetts in 1635. Accompanying his family was Hull's older half-brother Richard Storer, who had previously completed five years of an apprenticeship under the London silversmith James Fearne. Although there were some other goldsmiths in the colony at this time, none is known to have established a workshop. So with the advantage of having a goldsmith in the family, Hull writes, "by God's good hand, I fell to learning (by the help of my brother), and to practising the trade of a goldsmith, and, through God's help, obtained that ability in it, as I was able to get my living by it."[45] Hull must have completed his apprenticeship by 1646, when Storer returned to England. The following year Hull, having by that date certainly established his goldsmithing shop, married Judith Quincy.

This beaker must have been made very early in Hull's career. The First Church records do not contain any entries that identify it; however, it has been suggested that the beaker may have been the bequest made to the church by the Reverend John Cotton in 1652: "Item for a shedule I give to the Church of Boston a silver tunn to be used amongst the other Comunion Plate."[46]

John Cotton was graduated from Trinity College, Cambridge, and in 1612, when he was only twenty-seven, he was chosen vicar of the parish church of St. Botolph's at Boston, Lincolnshire. Within a few years he began to question Church of England practices and slowly abandoned them for the simpler Puritan form of worship. In spite of his changing beliefs, he remained a respected member of the community and was treated with full consideration. Finally in 1633 Cotton, a friend of John Winthrop's, resigned his position and emigrated to Boston, Massachusetts. That same year he was selected teacher of the First Church, a position that he continued to occupy until his death. Eventually Hull became a member of the First Church, and, as his diary reveals, he did so as a result of Cotton's influence.

1647. It pleased God not to let me run on always in my sinful way, the end of which is hell: but, as he brought me to this good land, so he planted me under choice means — viz., in Boston, under the ministry of Mr. John Cotton — and, in the end, did make his ministry effectual (by the breathings of his own good Spirit) to beget me to God, and

RELIGION AND EDUCATION

*in some measure to increase and build me up in holy
fellowship with him. Through his abundant grace, he gave
me room in the hearts of his people, so that I was accepted
to fellowship with his church, about the 15th of October,
1648.*[47]

Four years later, Hull's diary elucidates his profound feelings
when, following a brief illness, Cotton died:

*23d December, 1652. The reverend teacher of the church of
Christ at Boston, viz., Mr. John Cotton, departed this life,
after he had kept his house, by reason of weakness, about
five weeks; a man so exceedingly useful and eminent, that
the loss seems unparalleled with respect to the living, and
no less gain to the dead.*[48]

Hull appears to have based the beaker's design on a London-made
standing cup bearing the date-letter for 1639–40 (fig.
16). This cup's bowl, like the beaker's, is embellished with a simple chased
decoration that was first used as an allover surface ornament in
England during the 1630s. The First Church's beaker, although
simple in appearance, is clearly a vessel that aspired to be current
with London fashion. The London cup was a gift to the First
Church from Jeremy Houchin. Houchin had emigrated to Massachusetts and became a member of the First Church in 1644. A
man of considerable means, he held public office and represented
the church as a delegate to the Synod of 1662, which approved the
Half-Way Covenant.[49]

The First Church beaker is of great historic importance,
whether or not it is the tunn that John Cotton bequeathed in 1652.
Its deceptively simple, utilitarian form seems compatible with the
Puritans' goal of removing virtually every aspect of Catholicism
from their practice, yet at the same time as a handsome reminder
of the prosperity and culture that were also important to the
Puritans.

17

17. Caudle cup, 1664–67 *(cat. no. 2)*

John Hull (1624–1683) and Robert Sanderson (1608–1693),
  Boston. Marked "IH" beneath four pellets and in a shield-
  shaped reserve and "RS" beneath a rayed circle. Silver, h. 3 in.
  (7.6 cm.)

Inscribed "A$^\text{C}$E [Augustine and Elizabeth Clement]"; "The gift of
  M$^\text{rs}$ Elizabeth Clement to the Church in Dorcester, 1678"; and
  later inscribed "Presented by the First Church Dorcester to the
  Second Church Jan$^\text{r}$ 1$^\text{st}$ 1878"

The Second Church, Dorchester, Massachusetts

This Mannerist or late-Renaissance-style cup, with its chased floral and matted decoration, was fashioned by John Hull and Robert
Sanderson for Augustine (c. 1600–1674) and Elizabeth Clement
of Dorchester, Massachusetts.[50] It is one of the two earliest extant
examples of the form in American silver.[51] The form represented
by the Clement caudle cup is the American progenitor of the two-
handled cup or "trophy," which is now used exclusively for presentation silver. Seventeenth-century descriptions of this vessel
often refer to it as a caudle cup, yet there can be little doubt that
caudle, which consisted of wine or ale mixed with eggs, bread,
sugar, and spice, was not the only beverage served in such cups.

Augustine Clement was a decorative and heraldic painter who
emigrated to Massachusetts in 1635. Legal documents indicate
that he continued to work as a painter after coming to America, at
a level of sophistication that remains unclear. Clement died in
1674 and, according to the records of the First Church of Dorchester, his widow donated the cup four years later. Like so much colonial church silver, it thus passed from domestic to ecclesiastical
use. Exactly two hundred years later, the Clement cup, along with
some other silver belonging to the First Church, was presented to
the Second Church, Dorchester.

18, 19. Tankard, c. 1704 *(cat. no. 3)*

John Noyes (1674–1749), Boston. Marked "IN" in an oval, on the
  lid near the thumbpiece and on the body to the left of where the
  handle is attached to the lip. Silver, h. 8¼ in. (21 cm.)

Inscribed "This belongs to the Church in Brattle-street 1704"

Peter W. Eliot

In 1699 a group of citizens established a liberal church in Boston.
John Noyes was among the founders of the Brattle Street Church,
which eventually drew Edward Winslow, John Edwards, and
other prominent silversmiths to its membership as it assumed a
prominent position in the town. Within the first year, the church
seems to have become well established and well supported. Its
records imply that it possessed some communion silver, since
"scouring yee plate" was listed as one of the responsibilities that
Job Ingraham was hired to undertake,[52] and since, at the same
time, the church minutes state that Thomas Brattle, elder brother
of the Reverend William Brattle (see page 48), would "speak to
Mr. Noyse to make a silver tankard," which the committee would
present to Deacon Barnard in acknowledgment of their gratitude
for his supportive assistance during the construction[53] of the
recently completed meeting house.

Although the inscription does not specify a donor, it seems
likely that the tankard illustrated here was a gift or bequest, since
there is no record that the church purchased any communion plate
during this early period. The church's minutes for 21 July 1704
state that "after the uncomfortable Church Meetings past we had
none for several years";[54] thus, during the period that the tankard
was acquired no records were kept so that now it is impossible to
document its acquisition. By 1839 record keeping had become
much more complete; end-of-year minutes clearly describe how
the tankard passed out of the possession of the church:

*Dec. 29, 1839. A meeting of the Church was held this day
at the House of Deacon Moses Grant, Cambridge Street,
at which the Committee appointed more than a year ago on
the unused plate of the Church made a report; presenting
a schedule of the different pieces, the number of ounces
in each, & the value of the same per ounce according to
the estimate of the most prominent jeweler in the city; &
recommending that it be sold according to that estimate*

Taken from the
ruins, after the fire
of November 9th 1872.

of appraisal. Objection was made that it was hardly respectable, certainly not pleasant for Brattle Street Church to offer its supernumerary pieces of plate most of them gifts for the communion service for sale in any public way. While it was very proper to sell it & make the income available to the poor of the Church, it should be done in a private & not public manner. It was then proposed that as there was a very full meeting of the male members of the church the plate should be sold then & there by auction; the Brethren to bid for choice & then select what piece or pieces he chose at the appraisal. This was done; & in a few moments the pieces were all sold. As the bidding grew slack at the very last, & only one piece remained unsold; it was moved that the piece be presented to the Pastor. The brother acting as auctioneer, "do you mean to the Pastor or to Rev Mr Lothrop?" the mover said, "I mean to our present pastor as his personal property"; & the motion prevailed. The proceeds of the whole sale amounted to nearly twelve hundred dollars.[55]

This great tankard has only recently come to scholarly attention. It clearly ranks among the most notable work by John Noyes, with its generous proportions and handsomely engraved plumage surrounding the engraved inscription. A closely related tankard by William Cowell, dated 1705 and engraved with a similar

inscription, was the remaining unsold piece presented to the Reverend Samuel Kirkland Lothrop in 1839.[56]

The tankard is a silver form frequently found in collections of New England church plate. A passage in Samuel Sewall's diary suggests that the adoption of the form as a communion vessel may have represented an extreme Protestant effort to distance their church from Catholic traditions: "Lord's Day, Decr 6th Lord's Supper . . . Deacon Checkly Deliver'd the Cup first to Madam Winthrop, and then gave me a Tankard. 'Twas humiliation to me and I think put me to the Blush, to have this injustice done me by a Justice. May all be sanctified!"[57]

20. left: Flagon, 1707–8

John East (active 1697–1734), London. Marked "E.A." in a shaped reserve with a trefoil below. Silver, h. 11½ in. (29.2 cm.)

Inscribed "Annae Reginae in usum Ecclesiae Anglicanae Apud Philadelphiam AD 1708 [(gift) of Queen Anne for the use of the Anglican Church in Philadelphia AD 1708]"

Christ Church in Philadelphia

20. right: Flagon, c. 1715 (cat. no. 4)

Philip Syng, Sr. (1676–1739), Philadelphia and Annapolis. Marked "PS" in a square three times. Silver, h. 11½ in. (29.2 cm.)

Inscribed "The Gift of Coll Robert Quary to Christ Church in Philadelphia this 29th 8br 1712"

Christ Church in Philadelphia

In making his land grant to the Quaker William Penn, Charles II of England included in the charter the provision that if as few as twenty people desired the establishment of an Anglican church in Philadelphia, then such a church could be organized. A few years later, a group of petitioners who did not share the "wicked and damnable principles and doctrines" held by the Quakers, described themselves as "uneasy and inquisitive after the truth and sound doctrines of the Church of England,"[58] Thus, in 1695 Christ Church came to be founded.

The fledgling church received substantial support from England, including missionaries and even ecclesiastical furniture and fixtures. The congregation, undoubtedly cognizant of their crucial position in the Quaker colony, made additional requests. In 1705 Evan Evans, Christ Church's minister, wrote to the London administration: "We are very well furnished with books against Quakerism but . . . the furniture for the Communion Table is not yet provided, & we have no plate for the Communion but a smal[l] one bestowed by one of our pious founders."[59] Evans's remark did not slip by unheeded, and three years later the church was presented with a paten, a chalice, and one flagon illustrated here—all the gift of Queen Anne, who was following a tradition established during the reign of William and Mary. (Anne also made gifts of silver to churches and chapels in Wickford, Rhode Island; in Albany, Hempstead, Rye, Westchester, and New York, New York; Burlington and Perth Amboy, New Jersey; and Chester and Oxford, Pennsylvania.) Silver flagons were often used at home in England but in America exclusively as the communion vessels from which the eucharistic wine was poured into the communion cup.

Colonel Robert Quary (d. 1713) held a number of public offices in the colonies, his last as a surveyor-general of the customs. He was an ardent and prominent Anglican and specified in his will the generous bequest of sixty pounds to Christ Church, "to bee layd out in silver Plate for the use of the Comunion Table."[60] With Quary's bequest the vestry and church wardens obtained two late-seventeenth-century London-made dishes and also commissioned Philip Syng to produce a baptismal basin and the flagon shown at right, which is a copy of the John East flagon presented to the church by Queen Anne in 1708 (left).[61]

Philip Syng, who only shortly before had emigrated to America, must have been apprenticed in Ireland. In November 1714 Christ Church records mention the death of his wife, indicating that by that date he had settled in Philadelphia and was attending services at Christ Church. This flagon must have been Syng's first major commission after arriving in Philadelphia. The care he took in copying this flagon is indicative of his capabilities.

21. Standing cup and plate, c. 1728 (cat. no. 5)

Attributed to Alexander Kerr (active c. 1728–d. 1738), Williamsburg, Virginia. Marked "AK" in a square. Silver, h. of cup 7¾ in. (20.3 cm.)

Inscribed "The gift of Colonell Edward Mosely for ye use of ye Church in Edenton in year 1725"

St. Paul's Episcopal Church, Edenton, North Carolina

It is ironic that this standing cup and plate, the most important known colonial examples of Virginia-made silver, were crafted for St. Paul's Episcopal Church in Edenton, North Carolina. There they have continued in use to the present.[62] It is generally believed that most of the silver produced in the South during the colonial period consisted of flatware and other simple forms. Larger and more complex hollowware pieces were more easily obtainable from England, which had close economic ties to the southern colonies. Most silver vessels in southern churches are either marked by or attributed to London silversmiths. In 1759 the Charleston silversmith John Paul Grimke ordered from London a "Challice" and two alms plates, on which he simply engraved a presentation inscription.[63]

Originally the standing cup and plate in the collection of St. Paul's were to have been paid for with the gift of ten pounds presented by Francis Nicholson, the royal governor of Virginia in 1703/4. The completion of the commission was delayed, however, and it was not until 1727/28 that the church actually received the silver. The story is complex, but by combining an analysis of the church records with a bit of logic, the entire affair can be reconstructed.[64]

After Nicholson contributed the funds for his gift, they were placed in the care of Henderson Walker, who soon died. Edward Mosely, who then married Walker's widow, was placed in charge of the estate, and became responsible for the Nicholson gift as well. The vestry's minutes record that in 1709/10 the church wardens asked Mosely to return the funds, but apparently he did not do so, and three years later Mosely was threatened with a lawsuit. On 15 July 1714, Mosely wrote to Francis Nicholson explaining that the money had been lodged in Mr. Pere [Jeremiah] Dummer's hands of Boston towards procuring Church plate," and suggesting that it "lyes to wait Yr Excellency's further orders."[65] The money may have been returned to Mosely, since by this date Dummer was in very poor health.[66] Throughout all of these transactions there can be no question as to Mosely's integrity. He was a member of the vestry for nearly twenty-five years and served three terms as

warden. Finally, on 20 February 1727/28, the vestry minutes record that Colonel Edward Mosely "made a Present to the Parish of a Silver Chalice and Plate with his Own Name Engraved thereon." At this early date there was no silversmith working in the colony, so Mosely must have commissioned the Williamsburg silversmith Alexander Kerr to produce the communion plate. Why the silver is engraved "1725" presents an enigma that has yet to be clarified.

22. Beaker, c. 1732–33 *(cat. no. 6)*

Cesar Ghiselin (c. 1663–1733), Philadelphia. Marked "CG" between stars. Silver, h. 4¹/₄ in. (10.5 cm.)

Inscribed "The gift of Magaret Tresse Spinston [Spinster] to Christ Church in Philadelphia"

Christ Church in Philadelphia

Cesar Ghiselin was born in Rouen, but eventually left France, undoubtedly because of increasing persecution of the Protestants by Louis XIV. In 1681 Ghiselin arrived in Pennsylvania, and he became the first to follow his craft in Philadelphia. By 1693 he had married Catherine Reverdy of Annapolis, and as a result of

the marriage he also became the earliest silversmith to work in that town. It appears that during the remainder of his career, Ghiselin periodically operated a shop in each town.[67]

When living in Philadelphia, the Ghiselins attended Christ Church, and Cesar's youngest child was baptized there in 1717. The goldsmith's most important known commission came late in his career, when he executed the beaker shown here and a plate for Christ Church. They were the gift of Margaret Tresse, a daughter of Thomas Tresse, one of the church's vestrymen. In December 1732, she died at the age of nineteen, only four months before Ghiselin's own death.[68]

23. Flagon, c. 1734 *(cat. no. 7)*

Benjamin Brenton (1710–1766), Newport, Rhode Island. Marked "BB". Silver, h. 12½ in. (31.8 cm.)

Inscribed "An Oblation from Nathaniel Kay a publican for the use of the blessed Sacrament in The Church of England in Rhode Island 1733"; "Lux perpetua Credentibus Sola [The sole eternal light for believers]"; and underneath "39 oz. 8 dwt."

Trinity Church, Newport, Rhode Island

24. Baptismal basin, c. 1734 *(cat. no. 8)*

Daniel Russell (c. 1698–1771), Newport, Rhode Island. Marked "DR" in a square with rounded upper corners surmounted by a circle. Silver w. 14¾ in. (37.5 cm.)

Inscribed "Legatum Nathanaelis Kay Armigeri, in usum Ecclesiae Anglicanae, in novoportu, in Insula De Rhode Island Anno Salutis 1734 [Bequest of Nathaniel Kay Esquire, for the use of the Anglican Church, in Newport, in the Island of Rhode Island, in the year of (our) Salvation 1734]" and underneath "52 oz. 12 dwts."

Trinity Church, Newport, Rhode Island

23

24

25   26

Nathaniel Kay's munificence to four Rhode Island churches is handsomely suggested, but certainly not fully represented, by the flagon and basin made for Trinity Church. When Kay died, in 1734, he bequeathed four hundred pounds to be divided among four Anglican churches in Rhode Island, "to be Disposed of by the Minister and Church Wardens of the four Respective Churches for the time being, to furnish each of them with a peice of plate for the holy Communion." Kay's full bequest, represented by no fewer than five flagons, a chalice, a beaker, a paten, and a basin, is unequaled in size by any other colonial church gifts.[69]

Kay served as the collector of royal customs at Newport and he is buried there, in the Trinity Church graveyard. He was a devout Anglican and in 1713 was among the Newport signers of a petition to Queen Anne requesting the appointment of a bishop to preside over the Church of England in the colonies. Certainly his notable bequests throughout the colony must reflect his zeal in promoting Anglicanism. A member of Trinity Church, Kay also bequeathed to each of the Anglican churches in Bristol, Narragansett (now Wickford), and Providence one hundred pounds. The commissions to execute all of this silver were carried out for the most part by Newport silversmiths, although some were completed by Providence and Boston makers as well.

This flagon and baptismal basin were commissioned from the Newport silversmiths Benjamin Brenton and Daniel Russell, who were also members of Trinity Church.[70] While Brenton's flagon is typical of its period, Russell has fashioned an unusual basin, in a unique interpretation of the form.

25, 26. Pair of salvers, 1737 (cat. no. 9)

Joseph Richardson (1711–1784), Philadelphia. Marked "IR" in an oval stamp. Silver, diam. 5½ in. (14 cm.)

Inscribed "The Gift of Samuel Sherlock Esq. to Devon tribe"

Christ Church, Devonshire, Hamilton, Bermuda

American silversmiths were occasionally commissioned to produce silver for a clientele living beyond the boundaries of the Thirteen Colonies. Close ties existed between Bermuda and the principal urban centers of Britain's northern American colonies. As a result, an economic and cultural system similar to that which existed between Britain and the southern American colonies developed between the American colonies and Bermuda.

Samuel Sherlock (1652–1736) was a prominent Bermudian. He was appointed a councilor first in 1694 and he served as chief justice from 1709 until 1722.[71] He was elected vestryman in 1724, and in his will he bequeathed "unto the Church in Devon Tribe aforesaid ten pounds money, to be Disposed and Laid out for that use as my Executor and Executrix thinks fitt." The following year Sherlock's bequest was completed, not by a Bermuda or London silversmith, but by another English colonial, Joseph Richardson.[72] In his account book, Richardson recorded the presentation inscription to be engraved on each piece. These fine late-Baroque-style salvers are now recognized as the earliest extant examples of the form from Richardson's Philadelphia shop. In 1987, two hundred and fifty years after their making, these salvers returned to America for the exhibition on which this book is based.

27, 28. Alms basin, c. 1747 (cat. no. 10)

George Ridout (active c. 1745–c. 1751), New York. Marked "GR" in a square. Silver, diam. 12¾ in. (32.4 cm.)

Inscribed in the well "For The Sacred Service of GOD OUR SAVIOUR; According To The Usage and Rites of the Church of England: The Reverend Henry Barclay Rector of Holy Trinity Church in New York PRESENTER In the NAME Of the DONOR FEST. ANNUNC. B. VIRG. MDCCXLVII". The cipher "RE". Around the rim "AN offering of a free heart will I give thee, and praise thy name O LORD: because it's so comfortable. Amen. Alleluia! Amen. LIV. Psalm VI. Verse". On the bottom the Elliston arms, crest, and motto.

The Parish of Trinity Church in the City of New York

George Ridout was listed as a plate-worker on Lombard Street, London, in 1743, but by 1745 he had left England, emigrated to America, and become a freeman in New York. There he established a shop where, in addition to silversmith's work and jewelry, he sold lavender water, hartshorn, and the "most fam'd and long experience Powder for Preserving the Teeth and Gumms."[73] Ridout's arrival in New York coincided with the death of Charles

27

28

with an inscription that is as reticent in identifying the donor as it is clear in stating the intended function of the piece. Elliston's name is not boldly engraved; instead a cipher of his initials is engraved in the well and the Elliston arms, crest, and motto are engraved—unusually and modestly—on the bottom (fig. 28).

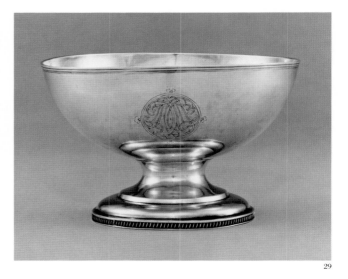

29

29. Bowl, c. 1751–1767 *(cat. no. 13)*

John Leacock (1729–1802), Philadelphia. Marked "I. Leacock" in a rectangle and "I·L" in two squares of different sizes. Silver, diam. 6⅞ in. (17.5 cm.)

Inscribed "Presented to St John's Church, Salem, by Jane Hall" and with the cipher "DH".

St. John's Church, Salem, New Jersey

This basin, like so many examples of American church silver, was presumably made for domestic rather than ecclesiastical use, for there exists a sugar dish in the Philadelphia Museum of Art bearing the same engraved cipher.[75]

By 1751 John Leacock must have completed his apprenticeship and been given his freedom, for that year he advertised his shop at the Sign of the Cup on Water Street. Two years later, following the death of his father, Leacock moved his business to Front Street, at the sign of The Golden Cup, a change of address that suggests the success of his goldsmithing shop, or perhaps a generous inheritance. Newspaper advertisements identify him as a silversmith, but like Joseph Richardson, William Ball, and other contemporary silversmiths, he appears also to have been employed as a merchant and importer of London-produced silver and jewelry. He continued to work as a silversmith until 1766 or 1767, when he left Philadelphia, purchased a small plantation in Lower Merion Township, and turned his attention to horticulture.[76]

In all likelihood, this piece was originally a slop bowl, into which cold tea was poured before a cup was refilled. The engraved cipher "DH," derived from Samuel Sympson's designs, must represent the initials of a member of the Hall family, for the bowl was eventually given to St. John's Church by Mrs. Jane Hall.[77]

30. Two-handled covered cup, 1762 *(cat. no. 14)*

William Ball (1729–1810), Philadelphia. Marked "WB" in a rectangle on the cover and on either side of the handles. Silver, h. 12¼ in. (31.1 cm.)

Le Roux, who had been the town's leading silversmith. Undoubtedly Ridout's European training and recent London employment must have enhanced his reputation in New York.

About 1747 Ridout was commissioned by Robert Elliston to produce an alms basin for Trinity Church. Shortly thereafter, the vestry passed a resolution acknowledging the gift: "The Rector Acquainted this Board that Mr. Eliston had Made a present to this Corporation of a very handsome Silver Bason to Receive the Offerings at the Communion. Which this Board Gratefully Accept, and unanimously return him their hearty thanks for the same."[74]

By this date the church had already amassed an impressive collection of communion plate, including the gifts of Their Majesties William and Mary and Queen Anne; and later it would receive silver presented by King George III.

Robert Elliston was the comptroller of the port of New York. At various times between 1713 and 1756 he was a member of Trinity Church's vestry. Unlike Thomas Hancock's gifts to the Brattle Street Church in Boston (figs. 33, 34), Elliston's dish is engraved

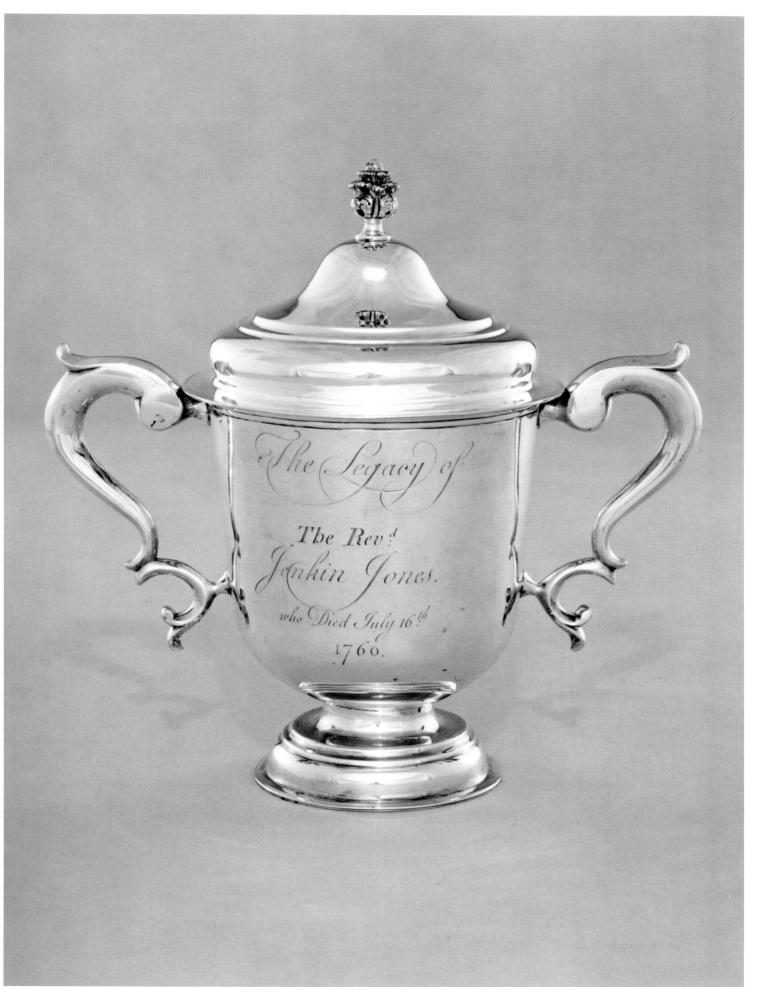

Inscribed "The Legacy of The Rev.ᵈ Jenkin Jones, who Died July 16.ᵗʰ 1760."

Lent by the Trustees of the First Baptist Church, Philadelphia

The Reverend Jenkin Jones (c. 1686–1760), the donor of this cup, served as the pastor of the First Baptist Church, Philadelphia, from 1746 until his death, in 1760. During his tenure, the church enjoyed an active period of growth. The trustees acquired property for a church building, and when a new parsonage was under construction, Jones contributed some of his own funds toward its completion. At his death, he willed the church £25 with the instructions that the interest should "be given, yearly, and every year, forever, to the Minister or Ministers, that suceseed me in the ministry, in ye said meeting house."[78]

It seems doubtful that Jones's bequest would have accrued much interest annually. For that reason, or perhaps because the trustees were not as sympathetic as Jones to a minister's needs, in 1762 they moved that the legacy should be applied toward the purchase of a communion cup.

Agreed that Rev. M. Edwards and Isaac Jones Esqr. do buy a two-handle silver cup or chalice for the wine in the Lord's-supper with the above said legacy; and in case the chalice should cost more than 25£ that the old silver cup (now belonging to the meeting) should be sold to help paying for the new. And that the Rev. Jenkin Jones' name be engraved on the front of the new chalice.[79]

The previous year William Ball had advertised his intention of leaving for England, but he must have suddenly returned to Philadelphia, or perhaps he never left, for he was given the church's commission.[80] His cup is reminiscent of Boston and New York examples (see fig. 57), but it is unique in the corpus of Philadelphia silver. It ranks as Ball's most important work and certainly is a very grand communion vessel. The estimate to the trustees was low, and when completed the cup cost the church not only all of Jones's legacy but also the old cup and an additional £12.17s.3d.[81]

31. Beaker, c. 1751 *(cat. no. 11)*

Jonathan Otis (1723–1791), Newport, Rhode Island, and Middletown, Connecticut. Marked "Otis" in a rounded rectangle on the side and "J. Otis" in a rounded rectangle on the bottom. Silver, h. 5¹³/₁₆ in. (14.8 cm.)

Inscribed "The Gift of Deacon EDWARD GLOVER Dec.ᵈ to the First Church of Christ In Rehoboth, 1751"

Yale University Art Gallery, New Haven, Connecticut, Mabel Brady Garvan Collection

This fine beaker, like the one presented to the First Church of Boston one hundred years earlier (fig. 15), reflects Protestant efforts to eliminate Catholic customs and trappings from their own services. At the same time, it casts light on the way styles in silver design filtered from major urban centers to the provinces.

In 1747 Edward Glover, a deacon of the First Church of Christ in Rehoboth (now East Providence, Rhode Island), died, having bequeathed to the church "a Silver Cup of the same dementions and value with one of those thereunto already belonging to be purchased by my said executrix." Meanwhile, during the few months after Glover drew up his will and before his death, the First Church also received bequests from Mrs. Mary Walker and Samuel Newman, each specifying that a cup be fashioned.[82] Both

31

the Walker and the Newman commissions were executed by the Boston silversmiths Jacob Hurd and Daniel Boyer, whose shops were up-to-date in the latest fashions and more experienced in producing large pieces of silver than shops in smaller centers.

But Glover's executrix turned to Jonathan Otis, whose shop was located in Newport, and Otis patterned the Glover beaker after the one Jacob Hurd had made to fulfill the Walker bequest. Not only did he carefully copy its form, dimensions, and decorative details, he even used two different marks, like Hurd, and struck them on the same places Hurd had chosen. Although the Hurd beaker bears the date of the donor's death, Otis's beaker is inscribed 1751, the probable date of the beaker's execution and presentation.[83]

32. Dish, c. 1755 *(cat. no. 12)*

Alexander Petrie (active c. 1742–d. 1768), Charleston, South Carolina. Marked "AP" on the bottom. Silver, diam. 8³/₄ in. (22.2 cm.)

Inscribed "The Gift of HENRY MIDELTON Esq. to Sᵗ Georges Church in Dorchester 1755" and later, "Presented to St. Michaels Church by Henry A. Middleton Esqʳ. Charleston S.C. April 1871"

St. Michael's Episcopal Church, Charleston, South Carolina

Henry Middleton (1717–1784) was born and raised at The Oaks, his father's plantation near Charleston, and later was educated in England. In 1741 he wed Mary Williams and through that union

acquired the plantation now known as Middleton Place. Eventually he owned nearly 50,000 acres and as many as 800 slaves. He was a generous benefactor of the church as well as an active supporter of colonial agricultural, commercial, and educational interests. In South Carolina he was a leader in the opposition to British policy, and in 1774 was selected to represent the colony at the Continental Congress. In October of that year he was elected president of the Congress but resigned in February 1776, when the radicals gained control of the body. Middleton did not favor independence, yet in spite of his political position he continued to be highly regarded by the public.

Alexander Petrie, whom Middleton commissioned to fashion this dish, was the finest silversmith then in Charleston.[84] Both his surname and the close relation of the basin to French silver suggest Petrie's origins. Perhaps he was a Huguenot. Like so many of the silversmiths working in the middle and southern colonies at that time, he imported work by London craftsmen as well as manufactured silver in his own workshop. When part of his estate was put up for auction in 1768 it included not only "articles of household furniture and plate; some work finished, suitable for the Indian trade; a few gold and silver watches"; but also "A Parcel of very valuable Negroes; among whom are two compleat house-Carpenters, a silver-smith, a barber, a taylor, a good waterman, and two likely young fellows."[85]

The Middleton dish is among the most original and beautiful American interpretations of the late-Baroque style. Though it is deep enough for a baptismal basin, it may have been employed as a communion dish or alms basin. It is probably patterned after the shallow French basins called "jattes."[86] The Middleton dish is one of four known silver objects from St. George's Church, the others being a standing cup, a paten cover, and a dish bearing the London date-letter for 1729–30. The cup and paten cover now belong to St. Paul's Church in Summerville, South Carolina, the dish to St. Michael's Episcopal Church.[87]

33

33. Communion dish, c. 1764 *(cat. no. 15)*

John Coburn (1724–1803), Boston. Marked "J. COBURN" on the bottom and upside down on the rim. Silver, diam. 13¹⁄₈ in. (36 cm.)

Inscribed "The Gift of the Hon;ble THOMAS HANCOCK ESQ^R: to the CHURCH in Brattle Street Boston 1764." Engraved with the Hancock arms and crest.

National Museum of American History, Smithsonian Institution, Washington, D.C.

34. Communion dish, c. 1764 *(cat. no. 16)*

Samuel Minott (1732–1803). Marked "Minott" in a rectangle, twice on the bottom. Silver, diam. 13 in. (33 cm.)

Inscribed "The Gift of the Hon;ble THOMAS HANCOCK ESQ^R: to the CHURCH in Brattle Street Boston 1764." Engraved with the Hancock arms and crest.

Worcester Art Museum, Worcester, Massachusetts

About Noon, the hon. Thomas Hancock, a Member of his Majesty's Council, was seized with an Appoplexy just as he was entering the Council Chamber. He was immediately carried home, and expired about 3 o'Clock, in the 62 year

34

of his age—He was Son of the late Revd. John Hancock of Lexington, came into Boston, as an apprentice to Mr. Henchman Stationer, which Business he followed for a number of years, but having a Genius for a more extensive Commerce, turned his Views that Way, and by the Smiles of heaven upon his Application and dispatch, he acquired a plentiful Fortune, and for many years has been considered as one of the principal Merchants in New England.[88]

Although it is less wordy than this contemporary encomium, the boldly engraved inscriptions on these communion dishes also clearly designate Hancock (1703–1764) as one of the principal figures in the New England of his day. His will included a number of generous public benefactions, including bequests for communion silver to the Brattle Street Church, where he worshiped, and to the church in Lexington, where both his father and his brother had served as minister.[89]

The communion silver produced to fulfill Hancock's bequests offers an interesting, and at times perplexing, insight into the silversmith's craft. Nathaniel Hurd (fig. 77) was selected to produce two silver cups, or beakers, for the Lexington church. Hurd must have seemed the logical craftsman to undertake the commission, having within the year cut a seal for Hancock on behalf of Governor Wilmott of Nova Scotia.[90] The bequest to the Brattle Street Church has a more complex history. Hancock specified two flagons in his will, but they were never executed. Perhaps the trustees decided that since the church already owned a magnificent set of four flagons as well as two tankards it did not actually require two additional flagons.[91] It appears that the decision was made to commission instead a set of six communion plates, a liturgical form that was not represented in the church's silver. The commission was divided equally between Samuel Minott and John Coburn.[92] Like Nathaniel Hurd, Minott had previously worked for Hancock, executing a teapot that the merchant is said to have presented to his brother Ebenezer;[93] moreover, Minott was also a member of the Brattle Street Church. The choice of Coburn is not as understandable. Perhaps he collaborated with Minott. Hurd (who was equally well known as an engraver), rather than Coburn or Minott, may have completed the inscriptions and coats of arms. The engraving varies slightly among the six dishes yet appears to be the work of the same hand. Hurd, who had already been chosen to work on part of the Hancock commission, would have been the logical person to engrave all the inscriptions.[94]

35

35. Tankard, c. 1764 *(cat. no. 17)*

John Brevoort (1715–1775), New York. Marked "IBV" in an oval to the left of the handle. Silver, h. 7½ in. (19 cm.)

Inscribed with the insignia of the Collegiate Reformed Protestant Dutch Church, New York: SIG.ECCL.PROT.BELG. REFORM.NEO—EBORACENSIS [seal of the Dutch Reformed Protestant Church of New York]" in a circle and

"VERITATE BIBLIA PLETATE" in the center. Later inscribed "The Gift of The Consistory of The Dutch Church of The City of New-York"

Historic Deerfield, Inc.

Most colonial silver associated with religious organizations consists of objects presented or bequeathed for sacramental use. But in a few instances, individuals received silver vessels from a religious organization by way of thanks for help or service. Such an example is this fine tankard with magnificently engraved Rococo ornament, one of three presented by the Consistory of the Collegiate Reformed Protestant Dutch Church of the City of New-York to David Crommelin, James Brinshall, and David Longuiville of Amsterdam. At a December 1762 meeting, the consistory discussed whether the church should hire a bilingual minister since Dutch was then being spoken less frequently in New York. A letter was sent to Brinshall and Longuiville in Amsterdam enlisting their assistance in the search. As a result of their efforts and Daniel Crommelin's financial assistance, the Reverend Mr. Archibald Laidlie, the minister of the Reformed English Church of Jesus Christ at Vlissingen in Zeeland, was hired for the position.[95] The consistory voted that "£25 New York currency should be given in acknowledgement of their pains in furthering the call on Do. Laidlie, and that this sum should be laid out on a piece of silver, such as would best please the parties, with the arms of our Corporation on the same"; and that "the cost of the three pieces of silver which were made [word omitted] tankards to be sent as a present to Amsterdam, be paid out of the pews sold; and that the Committee send the same by the first oportunity." The commission was given to Brevoort, who had been a member of the church since 1739.

36. Rimmonim, 1772 *(cat. no. 18)*

Myer Myers (1723–1795), New York. Marked "Myers" in script at the base of the stem. Silver and silver-gilt, h. 14 in. (35.5 cm.)

The Congregation Mikveh Israel in the City of Philadelphia

Philadelphia's first synagogue was opened in 1771, and the following year Myer Myers, who was Jewish, completed this and a second pair of rimmonim, or Torah finials, for the congregation. The rimmonim, a sacred ceremonial object, slips over the staves upon which the Torah scroll is rolled. Myers also fashioned two pairs for the Touro Synagogue in Newport, Rhode Island, and a pair for his own synagogue, Congregation Shearith Israel in New York; however, the rimmonim Myers made for the Congregation Mikveh Israel are his only well-documented set.

In January 1772, Myers enclosed a letter to the merchant Michael Gratz with the completed rimmonim: "The Bearor Mr. Aarons is kind enough to take the Rimonim with him, which hope he will diliver [to] you, and that they may meet your, and the Contributers Approbation."[96] Apparently Myers also assisted the Philadelphia synagogue in securing Torah scrolls and possibly a yad, or pointer. A letter from Barnard Gratz, who seems to have been in charge of the project, to his friend Michael Samson in London, elaborates on Myers participation:

In regard the sefer torah have only to say and to lett you know that we have the one you mentioned to me, that did belong to Mr. Jonas Philips from New York, from Mr. Myers, as Mr. Philips order'd, for which you will be kind anough to pay Mr. Philips for it. I suppose he will not charge too much for it, as he asked me but seven guenes, I

think, for it. But shuld he ask something more now, you must pay him. Mr. Myers of New York, I heard, told somebody he thinks it will be nine guenes, but hope Mr. Philips will lett it goe for the price he asked me for it, as above. However, I leave this to you to agree with him.

You need not send the silver yad I mentioned to you before, as we had one made a present for the shool *from New York.*[97]

The significance of the rimmonim, which means "pomegranates," is not clearly understood today. The Torah staves are symbolic of the Tree of Life, which in Judaism represents a joyous approach to life. The rimmonim celebrate the sacredness of the solemn part of the service when the Torah is either removed from or placed back in the Torah Ark. While meeting all the ritualistic requirements, Myers also successfully combined naturalistic and asymmetrical elements of the fashionable Rococo style.[98]

37

37. Covered standing cup, c. 1773 *(cat. no. 19)*

John David (1736–1793), Philadelphia. Marked "I. DAVID". Silver, h. 10 in. (25.4 cm.)

Inscribed "The Gift of the Hon:[ble] Iohn Penn Esq[r] to S[T] Peter's Church at Lewis Town June 10 1773"

St. Peter's Church, Lewes, Delaware

John David's unusual covered standing cup conveys a sense of strength and stature that one might say was only befitting a gift of John Penn (1729–1795), grandson of William Penn and lieutenant governor of Pennsylvania and of the three lower counties of Delaware. Actually, the cup—and a flagon and paten as well—were purchased for St. Peter's at Lewes with Henrietta Sims's estate, since Miss Sims left no heirs and designated no beneficiaries. Penn merely assumed the responsibility of assigning a legatee, and his choice was St. Peter's Church.[99]

In 1771 Penn departed for England. By August 1773, when he returned, the Sims estate had been settled and the communion service presented, complete with Penn's name engraved as donor. It seems most likely that one Daniel Nunez of Lewes oversaw the handling of the entire matter. There were a number of silversmiths working in Delaware at the time, but probably Nunez felt that none had sufficient expertise to carry out such an important order. Therefore, he gave the commission to John David of Philadelphia. It seems logical to assume that Nunez also specified the inscription, since Penn was out of the country and did not return until after the silver had been engraved.

38

38. Basin, c. 1695 *(cat. no. 20)*

Jeremiah Dummer (1645–1718), Boston. Marked "ID" over a fleur-de-lis in a heart-shaped reserve. Silver, diam. at the rim 14⅞ in. (37.8 cm.)

Inscribed on the rim "Ex dono Pupillorum [the gift of pupils] 1695" and "A Baptismal Bassin consecrated, bequeth[d] & presented to the Church of Christ in Cambridge, his Dearly beloved Flock, by the Rev[d.] Mr. W[m] Brattle Past[r] of the S[d] Church; who was translated from this Charge to his Crown, Febr 15; 1716/17". Engraved with the Brattle arms

The First Parish in Cambridge, Cambridge, Massachusetts

The ewer and basin must have been the largest and most impressive colonial silver forms. Such pieces were made in England by the fifteenth century and, like the great salt, they were frequently

RELIGION AND EDUCATION

displayed at high table. But ewer and basin also had a use: they were carried in at the end of a meal, when the diners would wish to wash their hands. As early as 1638, Elizabeth Glover "brought over in to this Country a very faire and large silver bason and eure."[100] Although we do not know that any ewers were produced by American silversmiths, both Jeremiah Dummer and John Coney fabricated domestic basins. Dummer's Brattle basin is the earliest of these, and, together with a porringer also by Dummer, it represents the earliest American tutorial plate.[101] William Brattle (1662–1716/17) was graduated from Harvard College in 1680, and a few years later became a tutor. During a smallpox epidemic, he remained to look after the students who were ill, instead of leaving town for safety. He, too, came down with the disease but recovered, and as a result won the students' affection, becoming known as Father of the College. In 1703 he was elected a member of the College Corporation and in 1707 he became a Fellow. Brattle accepted the pulpit of the First Parish in Cambridge in 1696 and was ordained later that year. He took a more liberal approach than his predecessors and early on demonstrated his independence regarding established church practices. He was popular and noted as urbane, scholarly, and philanthropic. In 1716/17 he bequeathed to his church the basin presented to him by his Harvard students more than twenty years earlier.[102]

39. Two-handled covered cup, c. 1701 *(cat. no. 21)*

John Coney (1655/56–1722), Boston. Marked "IC" above a fleur-de-lis, in a heart-shaped reserve. Silver, h. 10 in. (25.4 cm.)

Inscribed "The Gift of the Hon. William Stoughton, who died at Dorchester, July 7th, 1701". Engraved with the Stoughton arms and crest

Courtesy of the President and Fellows of Harvard College, Cambridge, Massachusetts; Gift of the Honorable William Stoughton, 1701

40. *Portrait of William Stoughton*, c. 1700. Unknown artist. Oil on canvas, 50¾ x 42¼ in. (128.8 x 107.3 cm.). President and Fellows of Harvard College, Cambridge, Massachusetts, Gift of John Cooper, 1810

John Coney's artistic sensibilities are very much in evidence in the Stoughton cup. Just as the sugar box he made for the Norton family (fig. 66) demonstrates his experience in manipulating the metal and thorough understanding of Mannerist design, here his technical skill and aesthetic sense were combined to create one of the masterpieces of early-Baroque-style American silver. The vigorous energy of the Baroque is expressed in the rhythmic move-

40

41

ment of the gadrooned and fluted ornament around the base of the body. Moving up from this decoration is the massive but plain central section, ornamented only by the plumage-encircled Stoughton arms and crest and the exuberant cast caryatid handles. The domed cover, like the cup's splayed foot, continues to evoke movement with its alternating reeded and plain bands that culminate in the great lobed knop.[103]

Stoughton (1631–1701), was graduated from Harvard College in the class of 1650. Afterward he went to England, where he received an M.A. degree from Oxford. In the years that followed his return to Massachusetts, he preached at the Dorchester Church, although he repeatedly declined to become pastor there. Instead, he assumed a number of government positions as a representative from, as well as within, the colonial administration. In May 1692 he was appointed lieutenant governor under Sir William Phipps, and after the latter's departure in 1694, Stoughton, still lieutenant governor, became the active head of government, remaining so, almost without a break, until his death.

Stoughton was totally dedicated to Harvard and was the college's most generous patron during the seventeenth century. Among his benefactions were funds for the construction of Stoughton Hall, which is depicted in the background of his portrait (fig. 40) and this magnificent cup. Its presentation in 1701 is recorded by Samuel Sewall, who represented the ailing Stoughton at the 1701 commencement activities:

Monday, June 30. Lt Govr said would go to the Commencement once more in his life-time; so would adjourn the Court to Friday, and did so. But was very much pain'd going home. Mr. Nelsen, Secretary, and I visit him on Thursday to disswade him from going, lest some ill consequence should happen. He consented, and order'd us to present his Bowl. After Dinner and singing, I took it, had it fill'd up, and drunk to the president, saying that by reason of the absence of him who was the Firmament and Ornament of

the Province, and that Society I presented that Grace-cup pro more Academiarum in Anglia.[104]

A week later, Harvard's great benefactor was dead. In addition to his gifts to the college, he also made generous bequests to the First Church of Dorchester and the first Congregational Parish in Milton for the acquisition of communion silver. Stoughton had selected John Coney to produce the grace cup for Harvard, but in carrying out the bequest, his executors commissioned Jeremiah Dummer to fashion the ecclesiastical silver.[105]

41. Pair of candlesticks, c. 1716 *(cat. no. 22)*

John Coney (1655/56–1722), Boston. Marked "IC" in an oval on top of the base. Silver, h. 7½ in. (19 cm.)

Inscribed "Ex dono Pupillorum [the gift of pupils] 1716"

Henry N. Flynt Jr., on permanent loan to Historic Deerfield, Inc.

Henry Flynt was born in 1675 in Dorchester, Massachusetts, where his father was minister. Henry, like his father, attended Harvard and was a member of the class of 1693. He remained at the college for two more years to work on his M.A. degree, and then left to preach. In 1699 he was offered an appointment as a tutor, which he promptly accepted. Traditionally, Harvard selected its tutors from a succession of recent graduates, who were expected to remain for a few years and then to leave for a parish. Yet Flynt did not relish the ministry and remained a tutor for fifty-five years. In Harvard's Charter of 1700 he was named a Fellow of the Corporation and remained one until his death, in 1760.

Although during his tenure there were periods when Flynt's relations with the administration were strained, he seems to have remained a great favorite with the students. This pair of early-Baroque-style candlesticks, with their lively, reflective faceting, were a token of the respect and affection felt for him by the class of 1716, of which Flynt was in charge.[106] In addition to these candlesticks, Flynt is known to have received in 1718 a two-handled covered cup, also by Coney, and in 1738 a teapot by Jacob Hurd.[107] He is also said to have received a silver chamber pot from one class![108]

42

42. Teapot, c. 1728 *(cat. no. 23)*

Attributed to John Burt (1692/93–1745/46), Boston. Silver, wood, h. 4³/4 in. (12.1 cm.)

Inscribed "Ex dono Pupillorum [the gift of pupils] 1728"

Mr. and Mrs. Nicholas Sever O'Reilly

Nicholas Sever's diminutive teapot is part of a large group of silver that was presented to him by his Harvard students. No fewer than eight pieces of tutorial plate, all marked by or attributed to John Burt, can be identified from an inventory that Sever compiled in 1728,[109] the year he resigned his teaching responsibilities, married Sarah Warren Little, and settled in Kingston, Massachusetts. There he established himself as a merchant and served in various capacities as a town official.

Sever (1680–1764) graduated in 1701. He was ordained in 1711 and accepted the pulpit in Dover, New Hampshire. In 1716 he returned to Harvard, where he was given a tutorship. There Sever became a rather controversial figure, yet he must have held the affection and respect of his students. The classes of 1724 and 1728 were placed under his guidance and he received from the former a pair of candlesticks, a pair of chafing dishes, and a small salver. The class of 1728 presented him with a pair of canns, a large salver, and this teapot.[110] Although it is unmarked, the teapot can confidently be attributed to John Burt since he is known to have produced all of Sever's other tutorial silver. Furthermore, this cast spout, while based on English designs, is only found on two other American teapots, both marked by Burt.[111]

The 1728 inventory also includes a two-quart tankard, a quart tankard, two porringers, a pair of salts, six spoons, two sets of six teaspoons, a pair of tongs, and a strainer. Some of this silver is known today; however, the absence of identifying inscriptions makes it difficult to determine how it came into Sever's possession. The teapot has descended in Sever's family to the present owner.

43. Two-handled covered cup, c. 1731 *(cat. no. 24)*

John Burt (1692/93–1745/46), Boston. Marked "John Burt" in an oval. Silver, h. 11¹/2 in. (29.2 cm.)

Inscribed "From the Bequest of Colonel Samuel Browne of Salem, 1731" and engraved with the Browne arms and crest

43

Courtesy of the President and Fellows of Harvard College, Cambridge, Massachusetts; Bequest of Colonel Samuel Browne, 1731

This impressive example was produced for Harvard College as a bequest from Samuel Browne in 1731. It embodies the late-Baroque style as eloquently as the Stoughton cup represents the Baroque of thirty years before (fig. 39). Samuel Browne, member of the third generation of a successful mercantile family in Salem, was also a prominent public servant. When he died, in 1731, he willed his church "seventy pounds, to purchase a silver flagon &c. for the Lords Table as my Exrs shall decide."[112] His benefactions to Harvard were even more generous, consisting of approximately two hundred acres of land, along with building and stock, the income from which was to be allocated for scholarships. In addition, he bequeathed "sixty pounds to be Improved for purchasing a handsome piece of Plate for ye College, with my Coat of Arms on it."[113] The covered cup that resulted from Browne's benefaction is a great ceremonial vessel, like the Stoughton cup. Like Stoughton, Browne commemorated his numerous accomplishments and benefactions by having his coat of arms engraved on his prestigious gift.[114]

44. Teapot, c. 1745 *(cat. no. 25)*

Jacob Hurd (1702/3–1758), Boston. Marked in a rectangle "HURD" and stamped twice. Silver, wood, h. 6 in. (15.2 cm.)

Inscribed "Ex dono Pupillorum [the gift of pupils] 1745" and engraved with what are believed to be the Clap arms

Yale University Art Gallery, New Haven, Connecticut, Gift of Robert Goelet

The tradition of presenting tutorial silver is most closely associated with Harvard; however, upon a few occasions silver was presented to members of the faculty of Yale College.[115] Thomas Clap (1703–1767) graduated from Harvard College in 1722, and after studying theology received his master's degree in 1725. That

same year he was ordained and accepted the pulpit at Windham, Connecticut. In 1739 he was offered the rectorship of the Collegiate School, the future Yale College. Under Clap's leadership the school began to place more emphasis on the ministry, but also developed a fine secular curriculum. In 1745 a new charter was secured, Connecticut Hall was constructed, and the school's name officially became Yale College. During a period of student strife in 1766, Clap resigned his office.

This handsome teapot was presented to Clap in 1745, the year the college received its new charter. Though the same year the Yale tutor Thomas Darling was presented with an elaborately chased punch bowl wrought by Cornelius Kierstede of New Haven, the Clap teapot was fabricated by Jacob Hurd of Boston.[116] Clap's engraved coat of arms do not appear in John Guillim's *Display of Heraldry*, but then neither does his surname, so they may have been devised for this commission.

45, 46. Medal, 1767 *(cat. no. 26)*

Unknown maker, New York. Engraved by Elisha Gallaudet (active c. 1756–c. 1767), New York. Silver, diam. 2½ in. (6.3 cm.)

Inscribed "PRAEMIUM LITERARIUM BENJAMINO MOORE COLLEGII REGALIS NOVI EBORACI IN AMERICA [Literary Prize to Benjamin Moore of the Royal College of New York in America]" "IN. LUMINE. TUO. VIDEBIMUS. LUMEN [In Your Light We Shall See Light]" "1st PET. 11.1.2&c." and EXIMIO. JUVENI PROPTER. INSIGNES. IN. ARTIBUS. PROGRESSUS [To an Outstanding Youth on account of Noteworthy Progress in the Arts]"

Museum of the City of New York, Gift of Mrs. Robert Le Roy

This fine academic medal is among the earliest American examples known. In 1762 John Sargent, an English merchant and member of Parliament, asked Benjamin Franklin to offer two gold medals that would be presented by the College and Academy of Philadelphia (now the University of Pennsylvania), to two students for their essays. A decade later, Lord Botetourt, the royal governor of Virginia, had gold medals produced in London that were to be presented to students at the College of William and Mary.[117] In 1766 a society was formed at King's College (now Columbia University) to encourage literary excellence.[118] Its distinguished membership included: Sir Harry Moore, the colony's governor; General Thomas Gage, the commander of Britain's troops in North America; and the Reverend Dr. Myles Cooper, the King's College president. On 17 May 1767 the Literary Society's minutes book records a purchase from the engraver Elisha Gallaudet of four silver medals for the sum of eight pounds sterling.[119] In May 1768 the society presented to Benjamin Moore, who the previous year had been awarded a gift of books "for his diligent attendance, good Behavior and General Improvement since his Entrance into College," one of these silver medals, the handsome example illustrated here. Moore graduated at the head of his class and eventually became president of his alma mater and New York's second Episcopal bishop.

47. Tankard, c. 1726 *(cat. no. 27)*

Paul Revere, Sr. (1702–1754), Boston. Marked on the bottom, and to the left of the handle "PR" in a shield with a crown above. Silver, h. 8 in. (20.4 cm.)

Inscribed "The gift of Capt. Henry Lovebond In building the Ann Gally 1726" and "I^W R" on the handle

Private collection, on loan to The Fine Arts Museums of San Francisco

Usually the silver presented to American captains commemorates a valiant maritime engagement, as, for example, the superb covered cup presented to Richard Spry by Boston merchants (fig. 57) or the punch bowl that the merchants and insurers of New York gave to Lieutenant Bill (fig. 48). In this seemingly unique instance during the colonial period, the presentation appears to have been made before the ship was even launched. At present nothing is known of either Captain Henry Lovebond or the galley *Ann*. Identification, never easy during a period when written information was scanty, is further hampered by the broad definition of the type of vessel called galley.[120] In 1722, four years earlier than the date engraved on this tankard, Paul Revere was an apprentice working in the shop of John Coney.[121] The Lovebond tankard must represent one of Revere's earliest, if not his first, major commission. Although he never attained the reputation that Coney long enjoyed in the craft, he clearly was a competent craftsman and passed those qualities on to his famous son, namesake, and apprentice.

48. Punch bowl, 1748 *(cat. no. 28)*

George Ridout (active c. 1745–c. 1751), New York. Marked "GR" in a rectangle four times on the underside. Silver, diam. 10 1/2 in. (26.7 cm.)

47

THE GIFT OF
The Insurers and Merch.ts of the
City of New York
To Capt. John Bill of the Roy. Catharin
Privateer for His Gallant Behavior at the Taking the
Le Mars a French Privateer off Sandy Hook
Fourth of June A Dom 1748

48

Inscribed "THE GIFT OF The Insurers and Merch^ts of the CITY OF NEW YORK To LIEU^t John Bill OF THE ROY^al CATHARIN PRIVATEER FOR HIS GALLANT BEHAVIER AT THE TAKEING THE LE MARS A FRENCH PRIVATEER OFF SANDY HOOKY^e Fourth of June ADom 1748"

The Metropolitan Museum of Art, New York, Lent by Mr. and Mrs. Samuel Schwartz, 1967

The threat posed by the French to England's American territories was constant during the 1740s. To protect the colonies as well as maritime commerce, the British navy patrolled the northern waters, as did privateers hired by the American merchants and insurers. In June 1748 Captain John Burgiss and his crew were acclaimed throughout New York City for their daring victory over the French privateer *Le Mars*. The *New-York Gazette* announced that "the principal Merchants of this City set on Foot a Subscription for two Pieces of Plate, to be presented to him and his Lieutenant, as an Acknowledgement of the signal Service done.[122] This little punch bowl, inscribed for Lieutenant John Bill, must be one of the two pieces of plate that the newspaper mentions. The second piece, presented to Captain Burgiss, is not known to survive. In New York Burgiss was awarded the freedom of the city, although he did not receive a gold box containing its seal. The minutes of the Common Council, describe the engagement:

Captain John Burgiss Commander of the privateer Snow or Vessell of Warr Called the Royall Catharine did on the fourth Day of this Instant month of June on his return in the said snow from a Successfull Cruize meet on this Coast (about Six Leagues from Sandy Hook) a ffrench privateer Brigantine Called Le Mars of Considerable force and having on board near three times the Number of his Men[;] which Brigantine gave Chase to and engaged the said John Burges and in that Engagement attempted Severall (198) Times to Board and take him[;] which he the said John Burgiss by his prudence Conduct and Valour not only prevented but also did Vanquish Overcome take and bring the said french privateer into this Port and Harbour of New York.[123]

49

49. Two-handled bowl, c. 1699 *(cat. no. 29)*

Jesse Kip (1660–1722), New York. Marked "IK" in a rectangle. Silver, diam. handle to handle 8½ in. (21.6 cm.)

Inscribed "I^VDM" on the side (for Jacob and Mary Van Dorn) and "1699" on the opposite side

From the Collections of the Henry Ford Museum and Greenfield Village, Dearborn, Michigan

In 1700 Colonel Lewis Morris complained that the residents of Middletown, New Jersey, maintained little or no religious conviction: "they are p'haps the most ignorant and wicked People in the world, their meetings on Sundays is at the Public house, where they get their fill of Rum, and go to fighting & running of races."[124] This fine bowl commemorates one of the races run at Middletown the year before Morris was provoked to denounce such pastimes. Engraved on the side are the initials of Jacob and Mary Van Dorn, in whose family the bowl descended until this century. Writing about the Van Dorn family in 1906, John E. Stillwell discussed the bowl along with other heirlooms.[125] He recounted family history, in which it was claimed that the bowl was won by one of the household slaves, who trained a colt and ran it in the race.

The bowl is one of a group marked by New York and Albany silversmiths.[126] They are patterned after a Dutch form called "brandewijnskom" (brandywine bowl). In the Netherlands they were brought out on special occasions and filled with raisins soaked in brandy. In America these bowls were probably produced as early as the 1680s and as late as the mid-eighteenth century, clearly demonstrating the persistence of Dutch traditions long after New York had become an English colony.

50. Punch bowl, c. 1743 *(cat. no. 30)*

John Inch (1720–1763), Annapolis, Maryland. Marked "II" three times on the bottom. Silver, diam. of the rim 7^5/16 in. (18.5 cm.)

Inscribed "Annapolis Subscription Plate 4.^d May 1743" around the rim

The Baltimore Museum of Art, Gift of Sarah Steuart Hartshorne and Alice Key Montell

This diminutive punch bowl has long been regarded as the earliest known major work by a Maryland silversmith. The engraved inscription provides tangible evidence of a long tradition of horse racing in the colony.[127] In Maryland the practice of presenting silver racing trophies can be dated as early as 1721, when the Annapolis town officials commissioned Cesar Ghiselin to make a dozen spoons.[128] Although these are not known today, one other colonial Maryland trophy, an unmarked punch bowl with paneled lobes, has survived. It was presented to a Virginian, William Fitzhugh, for his mare Kitty Fisher, the winner of the Maryland Jockey Club sweepstakes in 1773.[129]

John Inch is believed to have been born in Annapolis, where he may have apprenticed to Philip Syng, Sr. Like so many other colonial goldsmiths, Inch is known to have supplemented his income by practicing a series of related, as well as unrelated, professions. The diversity of these activities is suggested in an advertisement placed by Inch's widow, who assured their clients that "the Silversmith's Business, Tavern Keeping and Boats to go up and down the Bay, are carried on as usual by Jane Inch."[130] This punch bowl may well represent the first major commission that Inch received after completing his apprenticeship. Notable for its simplicity and purity of design, the late-Baroque bowl has a high flared foot—an appealing departure from the more typical interpretation. The inscription indicates that it was purchased with funds raised through a subscription, a practice frequent during the period.[131]

According to family tradition, the Annapolis Subscription Plate punch bowl was won by Dungannon, a horse owned by Dr. George Stewart of Annapolis. Dr. Stewart was born in 1700 in Perthshire,

Scotland. Having emigrated to Maryland, in addition to practicing medicine he held several provincial offices and was elected to the Assembly. About 1743 he married Anne, the daughter of Charles Digges of Warburton, and the bowl descended in their family until two of their great-great-granddaughters presented it to the Baltimore Museum of Art.

51, 52. Punch bowl, c. 1750 *(cat. no. 31)*

Adrian Bancker (1703–1772), New York. Marked "AB" in an oval. Silver, diam. 7 in. (17.8 cm.)

Inscribed on the bottom "A^GE" (Andrew and Elizabeth Gautier) and outside at the base "This Hapen'd Feby. 23. 1749/50" and on the bottom "17 1/2 oz."

The Metropolitan Museum of Art, New York, Anonymous loan

No other example of colonial American presentation silver includes such a graphic vignette of the event that it commemorates as Andrew Gautier's punch bowl. According to a newspaper account published 26 February, just a few days after the fire:

Friday Morning last about 4 o'Clock, a violent Fire broke out in the new Free-School-House, Kept by Mr. Joseph Hildreth, Clerk of Trinity Church in this City; which got to such a Height before it was discovered, as to render it impossible to save it from being entirely destroyed; . . . and tho' it stood at a considerable Distance from the Church, yet the Flames ascended so high, and carried with them such Abundance of live Coals, as to put the Church in imminent Danger, particularly the Steeple; which was set on Fire five several Times, almost at the Top, what little Wind there was setting directly on it; notwithstanding

which, by the good Providence of God, and the Diligence and Activity of a few Persons within who broke Holes through, it was happily extinguished, and preserved: . . . There was scarce any Thing saved out of the house, from the Fury of the Fire; and we are assured, besides a great deal of Furniture and other Things, the Records of the Church are entirely consumed. The whole Loss Sustain'd, is supposed to be near Two Thousand Pounds Value.[132]

That same day the vestry set up a committee to investigate the catastrophe and prepare a record. In less than a week they reported their findings and voted that a committee be established to extend their appreciation to Gautier and to the others who helped bring the fire under control. The committee was given fifty pounds to apportion among the heroes of the occasion.

Shortly thereafter Gautier used his share of the reward money to commission Adrian Bancker to fashion this fine punch bowl. Though he was the one who ordered the bowl, in his will Gautier bequeathed it to his eldest son, describing it as if it had actually been presented to him: "My silver bowl, which was presented to me by Trinity Church of New York, for my asistance at the fire of the school house and church."

52

51

53

53. Punch bowl, c. 1751 *(cat. no. 32)*

Unknown maker, New York. Silver, diam. 9¹⁵/₁₆ in. (25.2 cm.)

Inscribed "This, Plate Won By A Horse, Calᵈ, Old Tenor Belonging To Lewis Morris, Junʳ, Octᵇʳ, yᵉ, 11, 1751"

The Metropolitan Museum of Art, New York, Gift of Mrs. Lewis Morris

Lewis Morris, Jr. (1726–1798), whose horse Old Tenor won this handsome punch bowl in 1751, was one of colonial America's foremost racing enthusiasts. Morris was born at Morrisania, the family manor in Westchester County, New York. He completed his education at Yale in 1746, the same year his father became lord of the manor. Following his graduation, Lewis returned to Morrisania to assist his father with the management of the family estates. In 1749 his wealth was significantly augmented by his marriage to Mary Walton, the daughter of Jacob and Maria (Beekman) Walton. Married and settled at Morrisania, he enjoyed the comfortable life of an aristocratic landholder. Morris developed one of the finest stables in the colonies, and by the time he reached the age of twenty-four, one of his horses had won the New York Subscription Plate.[133] A notice announcing this 1751 race, although not specifying the punch bowl as a trophy, was published shortly before its running:

On the Eleventh of October next, the New-York Subscription Plate will be Run for, by any Horse, Mare or Gelding, bred

in America, that never won a Plate before on this Island, . . . Horses that are intended to run for this Plate, are to be entered the Day before the Race, with Adam Van Denberg, living on the Church Farm, paying Two Dollars each, and at the Post the Day of Running, paying Four.[134]

Little is known about this bowl. It was commissioned, as its engraved inscription indicates, with funds from the race's subscribers or sponsors. Because of their contribution they would not have been charged admission to the grounds. The fact that the bowl was not marked by its maker is unusual, especially since such a piece of silver would have made a fine advertisement for his skills. The engraving was probably executed by the silversmith himself, since it does not display the competence that one would expect from a professional engraver. Whoever engraved the bowl based his depiction of a galloping horseman on a published design, since a similar figure embellishes an Irish racing trophy bearing the same date as this punch bowl.[135] As relations with England deteriorated, Morris's idyllic style of life came to an end. In 1776 he signed the Declaration of Independence and assumed the position of brigadier general in the Westchester County militia.

54. Ladle, 1762 *(cat. no. 33)*

Paul Revere, Jr. (1735–1818), Boston. Marked "•Revere" in a rectangle on the inside of the bowl. Silver, wood, l. 15 in. (38.1 cm.)

Inscribed "Nᵒ 1 The Gift of Bʳ Samˡ Barrett to Sᵗ Andrew.s Lodge Nᵒ 82 1762"

The Lodge of Saint Andrew, Boston

55. St. Andrew's Lodge Notification, 1784. Paul Revere, Jr. (1735–1818). Engraving, 9½ x 7¾ in. (24.1 x 19.7 cm.). American Antiquarian Society, Worcester, Massachusetts

This elegant Rococo-style ladle is one of a pair presented to the Masonic Lodge of St. Andrew, Boston, by Samuel Barrett, a sailmaker who had been inducted in 1760.[136] Freemasonry was the most widespread of all idealistic and philosophical societies during the eighteenth century. Introduced to America in 1731, by the

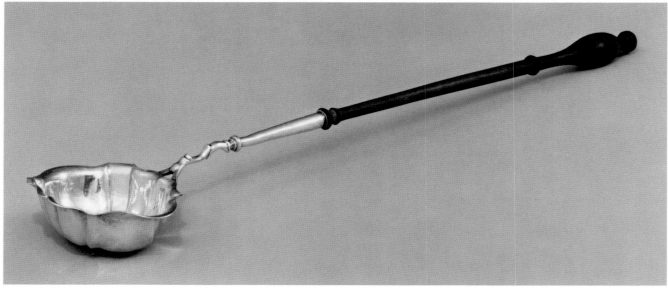

54

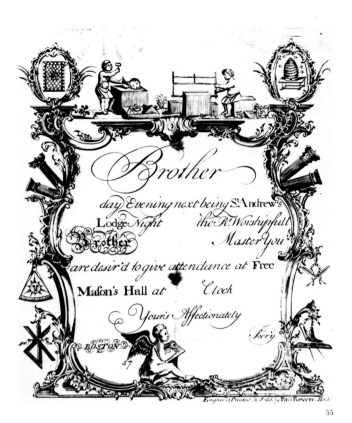

55

56

time of the American Revolution it was established throughout the Thirteen Colonies. During this early period the Masons often met at coffee houses and taverns. Usually following degree work they would gather for refreshment. Like the punch bowls, glasses, bottles, flasks, decanters, and other vessels decorated with Masonic symbols, this punch ladle was undoubtedly used at convivial lodge receptions, where such well-known patriots as Joseph Warren, John Hancock, and Paul Revere, who later engraved a notification or "summons" for the lodge (fig. 55), might be found lifting a glass with their associates. In 1762 Barrett ordered the ladles from Revere, and according to the silversmith's daybook they were completed on 19 November. On 30 November the lodge thanked Barrett for his donation of "two genteel silver ladles."[137] Evocative of St. Andrew's historic past, the Barrett ladles, which remain in use to the present day, symbolize the vigorous role played by the lodge two centuries later.

56. Tankard, c. 1733–34 *(cat. no. 34)*

Samuel Vernon (1683–1737), Newport, Rhode Island. Marked "SV" in a heart-shaped reserve with a fleur-de-lis below, on the lip, the cover, and the handle. Silver, h. 8⁹/₁₆ in. (21.7 cm.)

Engraved with the coat of arms of Rhode Island

Yale University Art Gallery, New Haven, Connecticut, Mabel Brady Garvan Collection

In 1731 the Rhode Island General Assembly approved a proposition to reach a boundary settlement with the Massachusetts Bay Colony. The Massachusetts General Assembly approved the proposal and appointed a group of commissioners from Connecticut to represent them. In turn, the Rhode Island Assembly selected as their representatives Colonel William Willett, Colonel Isaac Mix, and James Jackson—all of New York. The matter dragged on, but

at the October 1733 session the boundary lines were at last agreed upon:

> *Which being duly considered, be it enacted by the General Assembly of this colony, . . . that His Honor, the Governor, procure forthwith three silver tankards, of the value of £50 each, . . . with the arms of the government handsomely engraven on each of them; and for defraying the charges thereof, to draw money out of the general treasury; and as soon as the said tankards are made and finished, that His Honor, the Governor, send one of them to each of our said commissioners, with the acknowledgment of this General Assembly, for their assistance in endeavoring to reconcile and put an end to the dispute between the two governments.*

This tankard, which descended in the Willett family, is believed to be one of the assembly's gifts. It is interesting to note that this tankard (perhaps the other two as well), which was crafted by Samuel Vernon, an elected assistant of the General Assembly— arguably a conflict of interest—could have embroiled the state in yet another dispute.[138]

57. Two-handled covered cup, 1744 *(cat. no. 35)*

Jacob Hurd (1702/3–1758), Boston. Marked "Jacob Hurd" on two lines in a shaped cartouche on the bottom and "HURD" in a rectangle twice on opposite sides of the bezel. Silver, h. 13⁷/₈ in. (35.3 cm.)

Inscribed "TO Richard Spry Eqʳ Commander of yᵉ COMET BOMB For his gallant Behaviour & Singular Service Done Yᵉ TRADE in taking a french Privateer This Piece of Plate Is Presented By Several of yᵉ Merchants in Boston NEngᵈDecʳ 21, 1744"

Private collection

The magnificent Comet-Bomb cup, given to Richard Spry (1715–1775), a captain in the British navy, reflects the establishment in America of the custom of presenting silver objects to military heroes. Spry's victory was celebrated enthusiastically in Boston: "On Friday last several of the Merchants of this Town made an Entertainment for Capt. *Richard Spry*; Commander of his Majesty's Sloop the *Comet-Bomb*, and presented him with a handsome Piece of Plate, in Gratitude for his gallant Behaviour and good Conduct in taking a French Privateer Ship, commanded by Capt. *Le Grotz*, from Cape Breton, which had for some Time infested our Coast."[139]

The Comet-Bomb cup is one of the great pieces of American late-Baroque silver. Hurd's design evinces his understanding and mastery of the style, which, in its best examples, is characterized by complex but balanced organization. The molded foot introduces a lightness that John Burt's cup for Samuel Browne does not display (fig. 43), but the sweeping handles, bold body, and domed cover with its turned finial are fully Baroque. Also in 1744 Hurd made a similar cup that was given to Edward Tyng, commander of the *Prince of Orange*, following his victory over a French privateer,[140] but the Tyng cup is elaborately engraved with a cartouche composed of cannon, guns, swords, halberds, and banners, all symbolic of the victorious encounter. The Comet-Bomb cup is also engraved with an elaborate scrolled cartouche, but the engraver, who is clearly not the same individual who engraved the Tyng cup, used a more conventional late-Baroque design. On the reverse of the Comet-Bomb cup is engraved a second cartouche, which incorporates some naturalistic motifs in an asymmetrical arrangement. While essentially late Baroque, this engraving also has elements of the Rococo style, which would appear in a fully developed version on the teapot Hurd made for the Fayerweather family in 1745.[141]

Of all colonial silver, no form is more closely associated with presentation occasions than the two-handled covered cup. Contrary to their appearance these cups, like all colonial presentation silver, were utilitarian as well as ritualistic. For example, after Tyng received his cup, it was filled with "bishop," a punch composed of wine, sugar, and citrus juices mixed with mulled and spiced port.[142]

58. Gorget, c. 1760 *(cat. no. 36)*

Joseph Richardson, Sr. (1711–1784), Philadelphia. Marked "IR" in a rectangle twice at the sides of the eyelets. Silver, w. 5¼ in. (13.3 cm.)

Historical Society of Pennsylvania, Philadelphia

Indian trade silver was an extensive and lucrative business for colonial silversmiths. For example, in a four-year period Joseph Richardson recorded making 240 rings, 84 wristbands, 96 arm bands, 374 crosses, 1,472 brooches, 216 ear bobs, 48 hair bobs, 252 hair plates, 48 moons, and 30 gorgets—a total of 2,860 objects for the Indians.[143] Richardson's production seems prolific, and yet records document an equally extensive output by other American silversmiths, as well as a quantity of imported English ornaments. Most Indian presentation silver was given by representatives of the European governments with territorial claims in America, for the purpose of maintaining peaceful relations and encouraging military alliances. Yet at least one organization, formed in 1757 by the Quakers in Philadelphia, encouraged peaceful coexistence between the two cultures. This was the Friendly Association of Regaining and Preserving Peace with the Indians by Pacific Measures.[144] Joseph Richardson was a

58

member of the standing committee. This handsomely engraved ornament marked by Richardson is the finest of the few pieces of surviving Indian presentation silver. Although this gorget or "half moon," as they were sometimes called, is devoid of any engraved inscription, its vignette of a Quaker seated beneath a tree offering a peace pipe to an Indian seated opposite him indicates that it was presented by the Friendly Association.

59, 60. Medal, 1764 *(cat. no. 37)*

Daniel Christian Fueter (active c. 1754–c. 1776), New York. Marked "DCF" in an oval stamp and "N:York" in two lines. Silver, diam. 2⅛ in. (5.4 cm.)

Inscribed on the back "Happy While United" and "1764" and on the front "Georgius III D G M Bri Fra et Hib Rex FD [George III by the grace of God King of Great Britain, France and Ireland, Defender of the Faith]"

Yale University Art Gallery, New Haven, Connecticut, Mabel Brady Garvan Collection

61. Presentation certificate, April 1770 (1946 restrike). Henry Dawkins (active 1753–1776), Philadelphia. Engraving, 10 x 9½ in. (25.4 x 24.1 cm.). The New-York Historical Society, New York City

The earliest American-made medals commemorating the colonists' military victories over the Indians, as well as the earliest Indian peace medals, were cut by Edward Duffield and struck by Joseph Richardson in 1756 and 1757.[145] Shortly thereafter, Daniel Christian Fueter, the New York silversmith, produced two sets of Indian peace medals for Sir William Johnson, the Superintendent of Indian Affairs. The first of these medals were awarded to the chieftains who joined the British in the successful attack against the French at Montreal in 1760.[146] About four years later, Fueter produced the medal illustrated here. It depicts an Indian and a British officer pledging friendship between their two peoples, and on the reverse is a bust of King George III, yet another reminder of allegiance due the crown. This medal was presented after the defeat of Pontiac's Conspiracy to those chiefs pledging

59

60

By the Honourable Sir William Johnson Bart. His Majesty's sole
Agent and Superintendent of Indian Affairs for the Northern Department of North America. Colonel of the Six United Nations
their Allies and Dependants &c. &c.

To

Whereas I have received repeated proofs of your Attachment to his Britanic Majesty's
Interests, and Zeal for his service upon Sundry occasions, more particularly

I do therefore give you this Public Testimonial thereof as a Proof of his Majesty's Esteem & Approbation, Declaring you the said   to be a   of Your
                    and recommending it to all his Majesty's Subjects and faithfull Indian Allies
to Treat and Confide you upon all occasions agreable to your Character, Station, and Services.___

Given under my Hand and Seal at Arms at Johnson hall
the   day of   17

By Command of Sir W: Johnson.

61

their loyalty to Britain. A few years later, Johnson had the Philadelphia engraver Henry Dawkins prepare a copper plate and two
hundred blank certificates illustrated with a picture of Johnson
presenting a group of chiefs with medals (fig. 61). These he also
gave to the allied leaders.[147]

62, 63. Tea urn, 1774 *(cat. no. 38)*

Richard Humphreys (1750–1832), Philadelphia. Engraved by
James Smither (1741–1797). Marked "R. Humphreys" in
script in a rectangle on the lid, base, and, twice, on the bezel.
Silver, h. 21½ in. (54.6 cm.)

Inscribed "the Conti¹ Congress TO Chaˢ Thomson Secʳʸ in Testimony of their Esteem and Approbation 1774"; "Smither
Sculp"; and "NIL DESPERANDUM [Never Despair]"

Philadelphia Museum of Art, Purchased with funds given by the
Dietrich Brothers' Americana Corporation

The great tea urn presented by the first Continental Congress to
Charles Thomson (1729–1824) marks a turning point in the
American colonies, artistically as well as politically. Thomson
was well known throughout the colonies and possessed the respect
and confidence of the most influential men. He later recounted his
appointment as secretary to the Continental Congress, four days
after he married his second wife. On Monday, 5 September 1774,
while on his way to call on her family, he was stopped and given a
message that Peyton Randolph, president of the congress, wanted
to see him. Upon Randolph's asking him to accept the position,
Thomson bowed to the president and then, as he said, sat down at
his desk and remained in that post for nearly fifteen years (he
resigned in 1789, following Washington's first inaugural).

Less than two months after Thomson had assumed the secre-
taryship, on 25 October 1774, Samuel Ward, a representative
from Rhode Island, entered into the congressional record:
"ordered a piece of plate for the Secretary, £50 sterling."[148] The
commission was given to Richard Humphreys, a twenty-four-
year-old silversmith who had left Wilmington, Delaware, for Philadelphia two years earlier. There, he advertised, he took "the
house in which Philip Syng lately dwelt" and established his goldsmith's business.[149]

Humphreys's tea urn is an early example of the American neoclassical style, but it is also notable for its close relation to contemporary English silver.[150] Its design must have been derived
from an imported English tea urn, such as the one ordered by
George Washington or a member of his family from the London
silversmith John Carter at some time after May 1774.[151]
Humphreys's urn is much lighter in appearance than the covered
two-handled cups produced earlier in the century by Coney, Burt,
and Hurd (figs. 39, 43, 57). The form as well as the ornament is
drawn from classical antiquity. Humphreys embellished the urn

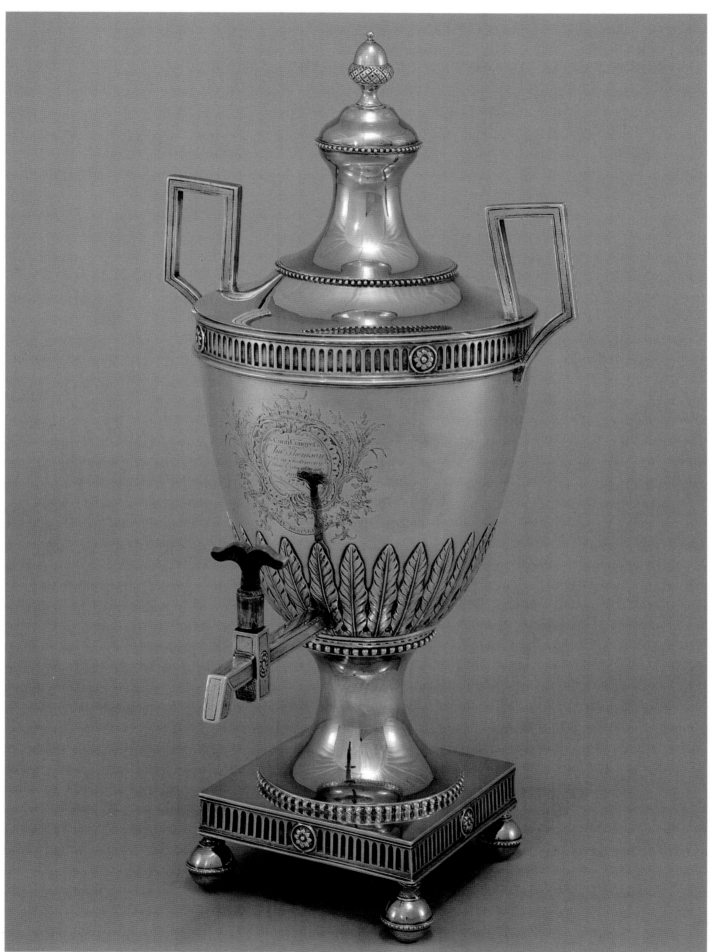

with a range of neoclassical decoration, including beading, fluting, and applied rosettes and acanthus leaves. Its place in the vanguard of design is affirmed by a comparison with the engraved Rococo cartouche framing the inscription. Here Humphreys drew upon the expertise of James Smither, undoubtedly because he lacked the skill necessary to execute the work himself. English-trained, Smither was working in the colonies by 1768, when he first advertised in the Philadelphia press.[152] According to William Dunlap, he "undertook all kinds of engraving, and probably stood high in public opinion; he was the best, for he stood alone."[153] Unlike Humphreys, Smither maintained his political ties to England and turned his skills to the enemy's advantage by engraving plates to counterfeit Pennsylvania currency.[154]

The Thomson tea urn is evocative of both a political and a design revolution. Yet, surprisingly, following the success of the former, the design revolution never really achieved great heights. Certainly America adopted the neoclassical style, but her craftsmen continued to draw upon English work. Few examples of American silver in the antique style were produced that can rival in richness the Thomson tea urn.

64, 65. Salver, c. 1675–91/92 (cat. no. 39)

Timothy Dwight (1654–1691/92), Boston. Engraving attributed to John Coney. Marked "T•D" in a heart-shaped reserve three times on the rim. Silver, diam. of dish 11⁵/₁₆ in. (28.7 cm.)

Inscribed "T^{B}M" (Thomas and Mary Barton) on the rim

Museum of Fine Arts, Boston, Gift of Mr. and Mrs. Dudley Leavitt Pickman

The captivating engraving that encircles the broad rim of this salver is composed of images that may be symbolic of courtship and marriage (compare fig. 66) and probably make reference to the wedding of Mary Willoughby to Thomas Barton in 1710.[155] The salver, which was introduced during the second half of the seventeenth century, was "a new fashioned peece of wrought plate broad

and flat, with a foot underneath, . . . used in giving Beer or other liquid thing, to save the Carpit and Cloathes from drops." This is the earliest known American example of the form,[156] but for whom it was made is not known. Mary and Thomas Barton's initials were engraved over the first owner's, and the original plumage surround was virtually obliterated by the richly engraved floral and animal figures, probably added at the same time as the Barton initials.

By 1710 the Boston silversmith John Coney had wrought no fewer than seven pieces of silver for Mary Willoughby's "maiden plate": a tankard, salver, pair of canns, spoon, and matched fork and spoon. This impressive array of silver was not beyond the means of a granddaughter of Francis Willoughby, the Massachusetts Bay Colony's deputy governor, for when he died, in 1671, he left an estate estimated to exceed four thousand pounds. Coney was engaged by the Bartons after their marriage to produce at least three more pieces of silver: a porringer and an unusual pair of can-

dlesticks. It therefore seems likely that Coney was the craftsman commissioned by the Bartons to reinitial this salver and execute its compelling engraved decoration. This attribution is further substantiated by a similarly engraved plate marked by Coney.[157]

The Barton salver's decoration recalls the forms and designs that were embossed on English silver of the second half of the seventeenth century. Many of the engraved flowers and fanciful animals are symbolic of marriage. The carnation symbolizes love as well as marriage, and frequently appears along with the tulip as decoration on tin-glazed earthenware chargers and carved and painted furniture, as well as in portraits. The lion and the unicorn frequently represent conjugal union: the lion as a symbol of male strength and courage, the unicorn of virginity and virtue. The other animals may represent some attributes desirable in a marriage: the camel, dignity and obedience; the elephant, strength, fidelity, wisdom, and conjugal felicity.

66, 67. Sugar box, 1680–1700 *(cat. no. 40)*

John Coney (1655/56–1722), Boston. Marked "IC" with an amulet between and fleur-de-lis below in a heart-shaped reserve once on the bottom and twice in the matting on top, indistinctly on the molding of the rim. Silver, h. 4^{13}/$_{16}$ in. (12.2 cm.)

Inscribed "The gift of Grandmother Norton to Anna Quincy born 1719"; added after 1837 "Joanna Quincy (Thaxter) Loring Sophia (Loring) Whittemore Anna Quincy (Thaxter) Cushing Mary (Cushing) Churchill. 1900"

Museum of Fine Arts, Boston, Gift of Mrs. Joseph Richmond Churchill

This magnificent sugar box, which John Coney fashioned for the Norton family, represents the culmination of the Mannerist style in seventeenth-century America. The form had been introduced in Boston at least by 1638, when Elizabeth Glover brought with her from England "a great siluer trunke with 4 knop to stnd on the table and with suger."[158] A small group of American examples, of which this is possibly the earliest, must have been patterned after an English sugar box. The inscription, "The gift of Grandmother Norton to Anna Quincy born 1719," appears to have been added at the time the box was presented. Although there are no earlier initials, there can be little doubt that the box was made by Coney for the Reverend John and Mary (Mason) Norton.[159] John Norton (c. 1651–1716) attended Harvard College and was graduated, like Samuel Sewall, in the class of 1671. Seven years later he was ordained and took the pulpit at Hingham. Shortly thereafter, it became apparent that the congregation required a new meeting house and during his pastorate a new one was constructed, in 1681/2. That meeting house, known as the Old Ship, is the only one surviving from the seventeenth century in New England.

The sugar box is symbolic of courtship, marriage, and procreation. Treatises published in the seventeenth century attribute to sugar passionate as well as fecundating properties. The form, similar to the mid-sixteenth-century Italian *cassone*, or chest given to newly married couples, as well as the foliate and animate decoration, further evoke such themes.[160] While it would have been possible, and certainly appropriate, for Coney to fabricate this sugar box when John Norton married Mary Mason in 1678, it seems doubtful that so young a goldsmith could have executed so elaborate a box. Perhaps it commemorates the birth of one of their children, possibly Elizabeth in 1695/96, to whose daughter, Anna, Mary Norton presented it in 1719.[161] The sugar box descended in the family of Anna Quincy Thaxter and, according to the family tradition, was given to the eldest daughter in each successive generation until 1913, when it was presented to the Museum of Fine Arts, Boston.

68, 69. Spoon, c. 1684 *(cat. no. 41)*

Cornelius van der Burch (c. 1653–1699), New York. Marked "CV" over "B" in a heart-shaped reserve on the back of the bowl. Silver, l. 6³/₈ in. (16.2 cm.)

Inscribed "OS V Cortlt obᵗ Aᵒ 1684: Apʳ: 4" and "OS" flanking the Van Cortlandt arms; "PA" (probably for Pieter Abrahamszen Van Deursen) on the handle

Yale University Art Gallery, New Haven, Connecticut, Mabel Brady Garvan Collection

The custom of presenting a spoon as a funeral gift is a practice that in America is most closely identified with the Dutch culture of New York. This presentation tradition is recorded as early as 1637, at a funeral in New Amsterdam, and it continued to be

68

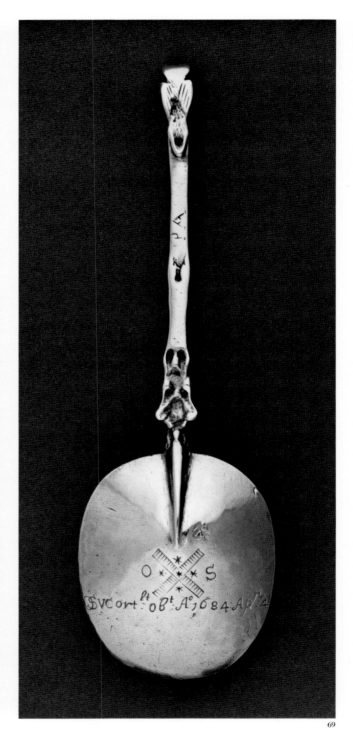

69

observed at least through the first quarter of the nineteenth century.[162] This particular spoon, as its engraved inscription indicates, commemorates the death of Oloff Stevenszen Van Cortlandt (1600–1684). The elaborate cast handle and engraved bowl, with its memorial inscription and then Van Cortlandt arms, attests to the importance of this elderly man who had held several public offices, including burgomaster, or mayor. Van Cortlandt amassed one of the largest fortunes in New York and became the progenitor of one of the most prominent families in colonial America. This spoon design, with its distinctive cast, scrolled handle, is derived from Dutch examples. In the Netherlands this type of spoon is reserved for use on holidays or family occasions, when it is set out with the brandywine bowl (fig. 49).

70, 71. Spoon, c. 1686 *(cat. no. 42)*

Jesse Kip (1660–1722), New York.

Marked "IK" in a rectangle on the back of the handle. Silver, l. 7¼ in. (18.4 cm.)

Inscribed "Cornelia Dúÿcken Vereert Door haeroom en Compeer Johannis Abeel Anno 1686 den 25 Agusty"

The New-York Historical Society, New York City, Gift of Mr. Edmund Astley Prentis

Since the seventeenth century in America, the spoon has been a customary form of silver to present infants and young children.

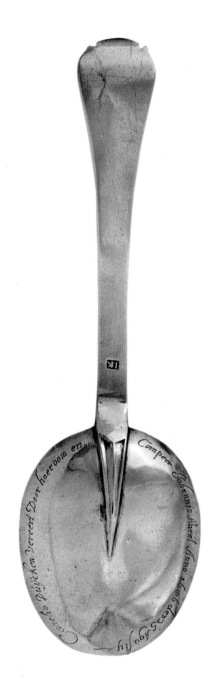

This tradition has both English and Continental antecedents, although in this instance the antecedents are clearly Dutch. This trifid-handled spoon is similar to English and European examples of approximately the same date.[163] Encircling the rim on the back of the bowl is the precisely engraved inscription in Dutch, which translates as, "Cornelia Duycken, Gift of her uncle and godfather Johannis Abeel, 25 August 1686." Cornelia Duyckinck was the daughter of the early New York portrait artist Gerrit Duyckinck, and her uncle Johannis Abeel was an early mayor of Albany. Whether the spoon commemorates a specific occasion or was simply a gift to the young girl is not clear. However, since her baptism was recorded eight months earlier, on 25 December 1685, it clearly cannot have been a birth or baptismal gift.

72. Whistle, coral, and bells, 1761–65 *(cat. no. 43)*

Daniel Christian Fueter (active c. 1754–1776), New York. Marked "DCF" in an oval and "N: York" in two lines on the underside of the mouthpiece. Gold, coral, l. 5³/₁₆ in. (13.2 cm.)

Inscribed "THE GIFT OF MRS MARY LIVINGSTON TO HER GRANDDAUGHTER MARY DUANE"

Yale University Art Gallery, New Haven, Connecticut, Gift of Mrs. Francis P. Garvan, James R. Graham, Walter M. Jeffords, and Mrs. Paul Moore

73

73. *Portrait of Mrs. Jacob Hurd (Margaret Brown) and Child*, c. 1765. William Johnston (1732–1772). Oil on canvas, 30 x 25 in. (76.2 x 63.5 cm.). The Metropolitan Museum of Art, New York, Anonymous Gift

This peculiar little object—a whistle and bells fashioned in gold, with a piece of coral attached—was both a toy and a baby's teether; it was also an amulet, for coral in colonial times was thought to have a protective, medicinal quality.[164] The portrait shown in figure 73, believed to be of Margaret Brown Hurd— daughter-in-law of the silversmith Jacob Hurd—and one of her infant children, includes a depiction of such a toy.[165] Perhaps that coral and bells, in which the child appears to be less interested than in the embroidered fabric of its mother's gown, was made some years earlier by Jacob Hurd, who died in 1758, or by one of his sons, Nathaniel and Benjamin, or his son-in-law, Daniel Henchman, all of whom were silversmiths.

The Duane whistle and bells is one of only four American examples in gold, all of them marked by New York silversmiths.[166] This is the most richly ornamented of the four and the only one engraved with a presentation inscription, which identifies it as a gift from Mary Tong (Maria Thong) Livingston (1711–1765), the wife of Robert Livingston, the third proprietor of the Livingston manor, to Mary Duane (b. 1761), her granddaughter.[167]

In this diminutive, frivolous object Fueter has created one of the most beautiful and sophisticated expressions of the Rococo style in American art. The swirling movement of the gadrooned bands, the lavishly chased scrolls, the naturalistic ornament, and the playful putto reveal a sensitivity rarely encountered in the work of American artists and artisans of this period.[168] Fueter's mastery of his craft must have been achieved during his appren-

ticeship and employment in his native Switzerland. There he surely had access to the published sketches of such masters as Meissonier, the great French designer and silversmith. In 1749 Fueter fled Bern, having been sentenced to death for plotting to overthrow the provisional government. By December 1753 he was working in London but by the following year he had departed for New York.[169] He remained there until about 1776, when he received a pardon from the Swiss government. He left behind a rich body of work and made an important contribution to the evolution of design in American silver.

74–76. Tankard and teapot, 1763 *(cat. nos. 44, 45)*

Benjamin Burt (1729–1805), Boston. Engraved by Nathaniel Hurd (1729/30–1777), Boston. Marked "BENJAMIN BURT" in two lines in a cartouche. Silver, wood, h. of tankard $8^{13}/_{16}$ in. (22.5 cm.); h. of teapot $5^{7}/_{16}$ in. (13.8 cm.)

Tankard engraved with the Brown family arms and crest. Teapot inscribed "OB to AB" and engraved with the Brown family arms

Tankard lent by J. Carter Brown, Trustee for Elissa L. R. Brown. Teapot lent by Museum of Fine Arts Boston, Gift of Jane Bortman Larus in honor of Mrs. Laura Bortman

77. *Portrait of Nathaniel Hurd*, c. 1765. John Singleton Copley (1738–1815). Oil on canvas, 28³/₄ x 24¹/₂ in. (73 x 62.2 cm.). Memorial Art Gallery of the University of Rochester, Marion Stratton Gould Fund

Silver was a traditional material for wedding gifts during the colonial period, as it is today. Such gifts commemorate the union between a man and a woman and provide the couples with the utensils they require to establish a household. Recently an extensive order of silver for the 1764 marriage of Moses Brown of Providence to his young cousin Anna has been identified.[170] Several pieces from this commission survive, as does a series of letters between Brown and Benjamin Burt, the Boston silversmith he patronized. These papers offer a rare insight into the business aspect of the silversmith's craft.

In 1762 the wealthy Providence merchant Obadiah Brown died, having willed that his estate should be divided into fifths, one for each of his four daughters and the remaining fifth for his nephew Moses Brown, whose upbringing he had overseen. On 1 January 1764, Obadiah Brown's daughter Anna married her cousin Moses. A few months before the wedding, on 19 August 1763, Brown wrote to Benjamin Burt, ordering "one Silver Tankard, 6 porringers, Teapots, point canns, Cream pott, pepper Caster, 1 doz Table & 1 doz teaspoons and 1 pr Tea Tongs." Brown wrote again on 2 September:

75

76

77

Please add to ye former Memo. One Mustard. The arms a cheveron between Three Lyons Paws Erected with in a brodure and an Eagle display'd and the same as that Mr. N. Hurd Ingravd on a Seal for me Some time past. That ye arms be adornd in ye most beautiful & best manner & ye plate to be mark'd OB to AB.

Moses Brown's letter documents a common but rarely recorded practice: the silversmith employed a professional engraver, in this case Nathaniel Hurd (fig. 77), to engrave a completed work. He also specifies that the silver should bear the initials of the deceased Obadiah Brown. Clearly this silver represented in Moses' mind a dowry or wedding gift from Anna's late father. Moses outlived Anna, as well as his second and third wives, dying in 1836 just before his ninety-eighth birthday. Even at the end of his life he regarded the silver as the gift of his uncle. Among his bequests was one to "Anna Arnold, daughter of the late Thomas Arnold, one silver porringer which was the gift of her grandfather to her Aunt Anna Brown, for whom she was named, marked O.B. to A.B."

The Brown silver, which commemorated an eighteenth-century marriage and became a familial bequest in the nineteenth century, has recently been presented as a christening gift to a member of the Brown family's newest generation.

78. Mourning ring, c. 1763 *(cat. no. 46)*

Houghton Perkins (1735/36–1778), Boston and Taunton, Massachusetts. Marked "H•P" in a rectangle on the inside of the band. Gold, diam. ³/4 in. (1.9 cm.)

Inscribed "E:Quill, Ob 1 July 1763 AEt 22"

78

This ring's engraved inscription memorializes Elizabeth Harris Quill. It is a reminder of the display that characterized colonial mourning practices. These practices, established in the seventeenth century, continued well into the eighteenth century. For instance, in 1752, when Sarah Dennie died in Boston, her funeral expenses included charges from Jacob Hurd and Knight Leverett for gold rings, and even a charge for "Negroe's Cloaths for mourning." In all, the funeral expenses totaled more than £600, the equivalent of thirty percent of the Dennie estate.[171] At various times the Massachusetts legislature attempted to limit these extravagances, but were never completely successful.

Elizabeth Harris had married John Quill less than a year before her death. She was buried from Trinity Church in Boston, and this ring was presented at the time to a member of the clergy or one of the more prominent mourners.[172] Unfortunately the name of the original recipient of the ring is not known, but it does bear the mark of its maker, Houghton Perkins. Jacob Hurd was Perkins's uncle, guardian, and probably his master as well. In fact, Perkins's ring was embossed with a winged skull using a swage similar to those on rings marked by Hurd and his son Nathaniel.[173]

79

79. Shoe buckle, 1765–95 *(cat. no. 47)*

Myer Myers (1723–1795), New York. Marked "MM" in a rectangle on the back of each end. Gold, steel, l. 2⁵/16 in. (5.9 cm.)

Inscribed "The Gift of Robt. Arcdeckne Esqr. to Danl. McCormick"

AMICITIÆ PIGNUS PRO BENEFICIIS RECEPTIS

In Testimony of Exemplary Justice & As a Small Acknowledgement
For Kindnesses Receiv'd, This Plate Is Humbly Presented To Theo. Van Wyck
By His Frinds, Sam.ˡ Schuyler Will.ᵐ Lupton & Corn.ˢ Swits

GRATIOR AMICO VENIENS IMMOBILE VIRTUS

One of the most beautifully developed American objects in the Rococo style, this graceful shoe buckle evidences the high level of luxury that existed for a select few in the American colonies.[174] These gold shoe buckles must have been worn on very grand occasions, perhaps to complement a heavily brocaded suit incorporating gold threads and a richly embroidered silk vest. On the buckle's reverse is the engraved presentation inscription identifying it as a gift to Daniel McCormick from Robert Arcdeckne. McCormick (1742–1834) was a prosperous New York merchant who presented a basin to the First Presbyterian Church in New York.[175] Nothing is known about Arcdeckne or why he made this gift. Was it to signify friendship, or did it, perhaps, represent a bribe? Putting supposition aside, the buckle makes an important artistic and cultural statement. It demonstrates as well as any example of Myers's work his fine sense of design and his adroit craftsmanship. He has imbued a mere shoe buckle with the playful, carefree aesthetic of the Rococo.

80. Salver, c. 1768 *(cat. no. 48)*

Myer Myers (1723–1795), New York. Marked "Myers" in script on the front. Silver, diam. 12 in. (30.5 cm.)

Inscribed "Amicitiae Pignus Pro Beneficiis Receptis [A pledge of friendship for kindnesses received] In Testimony of Exemplary Justice & As a small Acknowledgement For Kindnesses Receivd. This Plate is Humbly Presented To Theo[rs]: Van Wyck By His Friends Saml. Schuyler. Will[m] Lupton & Corn[s]. Swits. Gratior Amico Veniens Immobile Virtus [Steadfast virtue coming more welcome to (than?) a friend]"

Philip Van Rensselaer Van Wyck

The Van Wyck salver depicts an interpretation of Psalms 34:15, "The eyes of the Lord are upon the righteous, and his ears are open unto their cry." The presentation inscription is enclosed within an asymmetrical scrolled and foliate surround. Myers was aware of the work of English silversmiths during this period.[176] In fact, a similar gadroon-edged salver bearing the date-letter 1763–64 was made for the Philipse family of New York by Richard Rugg of London.[177] The salver was fabricated by Myers about 1768, as its engraved inscription indicates, for Samuel Schuyler, William Lupton, and Cornelius Swits. These three men were relatives of Theodorus Van Wyck (1718–1776), a New York merchant and alderman. Schuyler was Van Wyck's nephew, and Lupton and Swits were the husbands of his nieces Johanna and Catherine Schuyler. When Brandt Schuyler, their father, died, in 1752, Theodorus Van Wyck assisted his sister in raising her young son and daughters. In 1760 Margretta Van Wyck Schuyler remarried, and it is believed that her brother continued to shoulder his familial responsibilities until her children reached adulthood. The salver was probably commissioned after the two older Schuyler daughters had married.[178] It magnificently conveys the feelings of respect, appreciation, and affection that the Schuyler children bore for their uncle. It remains in Theodorus Van Wyck's family, having descended to the present generation.

From the New Republic to the Centennial

David B. Warren

During the century following the Revolution, the democratization of America proceeded apace. At the same time, precious metals became much more widely available. For both these reasons, during the nineteenth century presentation silver became extremely popular, taking a variety of forms and filling a diversity of purposes. Examples ranged from lavish commissioned services honoring national heroes to mundane, ready-made cups given in recognition of the best two-year-old mule. In style, presentation silver followed the prevailing fashions, from the neoclassical of the Federal period to the diverse revival styles that flourished at the time of America's Centennial celebration. Across the country, silversmiths evolved from self-employed craftsmen to large urban firms that filled diverse orders, including presentation silver, from all regions of the nation. Several companies eventually dominated the industry. Fletcher and Gardiner of Philadelphia were preeminent throughout the decades between 1810 and 1830. During the 1830s and 1840s, the Ames Manufacturing Company of Massachusetts began to emerge as the leading manufacturer of swords, an important presentation genre. By the 1850s Tiffany and Company of New York and the Gorham Manufacturing Company of Providence had begun to establish the hegemony over silver production that they still maintain today.

At the end of the eighteenth century, the nonutilitarian trophy made its debut (figs. 93, 111), but for the most part presentation forms reflected developments in domestic silver as pitchers, matching tea sets, large trays, and other types were introduced. The most common forms remained cups, beakers, and goblets—the latter often presented in pairs with pitchers. In 1854 the New Orleans firm of Hyde and Goodrich advertised, "Plain or rich silver tea and coffee sets, urns, ornamental vases or pitchers for presentations. Water and milk pitchers, goblets and cups suitable for regatta shooting and agricultural prizes."[1] Tiffany and Company advertised "presentation services" and were "prepared to manufacture presentation yachting, racing and special articles in solid silver from original and fresh designs."[2]

When the century opened, the leaders who were steering the grateful infant nation through dangerous military and political waters captured America's heart and imagination. The outpouring of presentations to the heroes of the War of 1812 marks a quantitative and qualitative high point for American silver. As early as the 1820s, however, a new American hero made an appearance— the businessman—and by 1876 the silver given to the captains of industry eclipsed in importance, originality, and excellence of design that given to military and political heroes. Presentation silver on the themes of war, industry, and progress predominated, and the most innovative, sophisticated, and valuable pieces were made in these categories until the end of the era, when leisure-time and elective activities began to occupy the attention of a significant number of Americans. As in the colonial period, silver continued to be presented to churches, educational institutions, teachers, friends, and family, but these commissions did not receive the same sort of energy as the others.

A slim body of contemporary description records some of the ways in which silver was presented. An object might be bestowed on the recipient by a small committee on behalf of the donors; often the gift was accompanied by a letter of transmittal (fig. 92). Occasionally an object was exhibited to the public before or after presentation (figs. 96, 131, 138). In other instances the silver testimonial was presented at a large public reception or dinner held specifically for the occasion (figs. 96, 104).

RELIGION AND EDUCATION

The ancient tradition of presenting silver to churches continued in the years that followed the Revolution, but the total number of pieces donated immediately after 1775 dropped by approximately one-third and did not reach prerevolutionary levels until about 1825. Undoubtedly, the general social upheaval and cost of the war explain this decline, but the Anglican churches suffered in addition for their pro-English sympathies and did not enjoy donations on the prewar scale until after 1800.[3] Church presentations also seem to have lost the prestigious associations that they had held in the eighteenth century. This trend is reflected in the rather average quality of most of the surviving examples, which are primarily modest beakers and cups. The donors of these lesser pieces tended to be individuals, whereas the more ambitious examples seem to have been presented by groups of donors.

Some gifts were made to new churches or to new church buildings. In 1812 the ladies of St. Paul's Episcopal Church in Edenton, North Carolina, donated a communion dish made by Hugh Wishart of New York.[4] The communicants of St. Paul's Church in Baltimore commissioned Isaiah Wagster to make a neoclassical covered cup for the new structure that in 1793 replaced an earlier building.[5] In Detroit, then on the frontier, the silversmith Victor Rouquette made and presented a chalice to his parish church of St. Anne when it was rebuilt after the great fire of 1805 (fig. 86). In two instances, high-style Gothic-revival church plate, which seems to be associated primarily with the Episcopal church, was given to chapels of ease by their respective parishes: Christ Church, St. Michael's, Maryland, about 1840, and Trinity Church, New York City, in 1855 (figs. 87, 88).

Occasionally the date of making and the date of bequest or presentation are decades apart. A Boston tankard with bright-cut ornament made about 1790 realized a bequest made in 1751 but not fulfilled until the death of the donor's widow.[6] In the 1790s, the Brattle Street Church in Boston reused silver from a 1707 gift for a neoclassical communion cup made to match three others (fig. 84). There are other instances in which silver was reused. A 1694 London-made flagon and chalice given by King William III to Trinity Church in New York was cut down and altered to match new church silver made by Garrett Eoff in 1824. Some of the Eoff silver was given to Trinity Chapel in 1855.[7]

The presentation of silver by students to their teachers, a practice almost exclusively associated with Harvard College, virtually ended before the Revolution. The cessation of this custom at Harvard (the last known example was given in 1770) probably reflects a change in the teaching structure: young tutors closely associated with individual classes were about this time replaced by professors who had less intimate contact with their students. The practice continued sporadically, however, in some frontier and rural settlements. In 1842 the students of an anatomical class in Kentucky presented Dr. James M. Brush with a pitcher made by Edward Kinsey.[8] In Salem, North Carolina, S. A. Sleeper received a small cup engraved, "A token of love from her pupils Dec. 25 1853."[9] Small medals recognizing academic excellence are the most ubiquitous form of education-related presentation silver. In his will Benjamin Franklin established such an award, and beginning in 1793 fourteen Franklin medals were given to outstanding students in four Boston Schools.[10] There are examples of nineteenth-century academic medals in several American museums. The gold medals received by Victorine du Pont from Miss Rivardi's School in Philadelphia in 1807 and by Lydia Reynolds from the Albany Academy in 1829 are in the collections of the Winterthur Museum and the Yale University Art Gallery, respectively.[11]

INDUSTRY AND PROGRESS

Americans who advanced the standard of living in their new nation and found practical solutions to its problems became the recipients of a new category of presentation silver. Achievements in agriculture, improved transportation, better city services, advances in banking, and new forms of communication all were recognized by grateful citizens with a gift of silver. The pride inherent in these presentations is reflected in their lavish design and in their usually high cost—an exception being the awards for agricultural excellence, which tended to be simple cups and beakers of relatively modest price. Agricultural societies, established for the improvement of livestock and farming practices, burgeoned during the early nineteenth century. Often these organizations awarded to the best entry in specific classes at the annual autumn fair premiums or prizes whose dollar value was established (figs. 100, 101). An 1820 tract, outlining the procedures for setting up such a society, admonishes, "Have all your premiums in silver plate with appropriate devices on the article" and conveniently illustrates what those premiums should be (fig. 82). Numerous examples survive.[12]

The perils of the sea are a pervasive theme in presentations of this era. Grateful shipowners, insurers, and passengers conveyed their appreciation to skillful captains in the form of silver gifts. In 1779 shareholders in the privateer brig *General Pickering* noted the achievement of Jonathan Harraden in bringing captured cargo safely home (fig. 89). Nathaniel Garland, who in 1823 fought pirates intent on capturing his cargo of specie, was praised by the two companies that carried the insurance and presented with a pair of pitchers to commemorate the event (fig. 95). Captain Thomas Bennett received a tea set from grateful passengers of the packet ship *New York* in 1827, and Captain D. D. Porter of the U.S. mail steamer *Georgia* received a pitcher and tray from his New-York–to–New-Orleans passengers in 1851.[13]

Better facilities for transportation meant flourishing commerce, and grateful citizens recognized those responsible for such improvements with some of the century's most ambitious silver. In this category the pièce de résistance is undoubtedly the superb pair of vases presented to De Witt Clinton in 1825 upon the completion of the Erie Canal (fig. 96). These vases not only rival War of 1812 presentation silver in size and elegance but also herald the advent of the businessman as hero. To the south, proprietors of the Chesapeake and Delaware Canal in 1830 recognized the services of their president, James C. Fisher, with a large urn.[14] The completion in 1786 of the Charles River Bridge, which linked the city of Boston to the North Shore, generated presentations from proprietors of the bridge company (fig. 91). In 1840 the citizens of Boston recognized the contribution of Samuel Cunard's newly established packet line between Boston and Liverpool with a large two-handled cup.[15] In 1851 Edward K. Collins was presented with a solid-gold tea and coffee set valued at $5,000 marking the establishment of transatlantic service for New York City. It utilizes the same design as the service presented to Marshall Lefferts (fig. 104) and was conceived by the same craftsman—John Chandler Moore. The occasion of the completion of the transcontinental railroad in 1869 was marked with gold replicas of the final spike hammered into place. One of these was presented to Leland Stanford.[16]

Among the many improvements in city services during the nineteenth century, none was more important than the assurance of a plentiful supply of potable water. The Water Works of Philadelphia, begun in 1799, became a model of its kind, and the contributions of Frederick Graff, chief engineer and supervisor, were publicly recognized in the 1820s with presentation silver (fig. 94). In 1832 Thomas Seetrel, a mason, was given a pitcher to mark his achievement in constructing Providence's first aqueduct; in the 1850s Nicholas Dean received a pitcher and two goblets for his work on New York City's Croton Aqueduct; and in 1853 Montgomery Meigs was presented with a teakettle on stand in recognition of his contributions to the Washington, D.C., aqueduct (fig. 105).[17]

Pioneers in the field of community health were not overlooked. In Philadelphia, Dr. Benjamin Rush was presented with a silver tray as tribute for his services during a yellow fever epidemic in 1798. In 1854 the citizens of Adams County, Mississippi, thanked Dr. L. P. Blackburn for his "rigid and successful enforcement" of a quarantine by presenting him with a pitcher.[18]

The telegraph was one of the most important advancements in communication in the nineteenth century. Marshall Lefferts, who organized the New York and New England Telegraph Company, was presented by his appreciative stockholders with a magnificent service of plate in 1850 (fig. 104). In 1858 Cyrus West Field was given a gold box by the City of New York in recognition of his initial effort to lay an ocean cable, and upon the successful completion of the Atlantic link Field was presented with a large service by the international banker George Peabody (fig. 106).

82. *Recommended Design for a Premium Cup.* From Elkanah Watson, *History of Agricultural Societies on The Modern Berkshire System*, 1820

PURSUITS OF LEISURE AND AVOCATION

During their first century as a nation, Americans of all classes spent their leisure time in a wide variety of activities, ranging from membership in volunteer societies to involvement in outdoor sports. Increased interest in volunteer fire companies and horse racing and a new passion for yachting generated a variety of occasions to mark achievement and new sorts of presentation silver.

The urban volunteer fire company, an institution that was born in the middle of the eighteenth century, reached its height in the first half of the nineteenth. The activities of the firemen, their valor, and their contests are reflected in an interesting body of presentation silver. One of the most distinctive forms is the fireman's trumpet, which had its origins in the utilitarian horn used by a company leader to call out the cadence as his team of men created water pressure by hand-pumping the fire engines. Silver ceremonial trumpets were presented not only to leaders of the fire companies. In 1852 James Mount of New York, at the risk of his own life, rescued two women and two children trapped in the second story of a burning house. The event is carefully depicted on a trumpet presented to him by a committee of grateful citizens.[19] Heroism of a similar nature was recognized in 1811, when Isaac Harris received a pitcher for saving

83. Urn, 1822. Harvey Lewis. *See pages 88–89*

the Old South Church in Boston (fig. 114). Pursuit of the most efficient and swiftest service engendered fierce rivalries between individual fire companies. Confirmation of excellence was often sought through contests between the rivals. In 1846 Fire Company Number Six of Mobile, Alabama, won a cup for throwing water the greatest distance through one hundred feet of hose;[20] ten years later, the Torrent Fire Company of Providence, Rhode Island, bested the Phoenix Fire Company in a similar contest and was awarded a trumpet (fig. 118). The paramilitary and clublike aspects of membership in a volunteer fire company were paralleled in local militia groups, among which contests were also held. In 1827 the Irish Volunteers of Charleston, South Carolina, pre-

sented a silver harp-shaped medal as a premium for the best shot.[21] In 1838 the Independent German Yagers of Baltimore commissioned a cup for "dem besten Schutzen," and a similar cup was awarded in 1848 to the best shot by the Independent Grays, also of Baltimore.[22] In 1828 the newly founded, exclusive United Bowmen of Philadelphia commissioned a club bowl, to be awarded yearly to the best shot in archery (fig. 113).

The presentation of silver premiums or trophies to the victors in horse races, a practice dating back to the seventeenth century, continued in the nineteenth century. The large nonutilitarian racing cup appeared early in the nineteenth century. The prize won by Wade Hampton's Vingt-Un in 1803 (fig. 111) is a modest twenty-one inches in height; by 1860 the Woodlawn Racing Association of Louisville had commissioned a thirty-four-inch cup weighing twenty-nine pounds.[23] Equally monumental was the cup commissioned by August Belmont in 1897 (fig. 198). In Kentucky, where horse racing became a way of life, the most popular form of racing trophy was a silver pitcher (fig. 116). These pitchers became the possession of the winning stable, unlike the challenge trophy which was retained for only one year.

The pleasure boat or yacht was introduced to America by George Crowninshield of Salem, Massachusetts, when his sloop *Jefferson* was built in 1801. Crowninshield's oceangoing yacht *Cleopatra* was built in 1817. The boat club, with its regattas and prizes, had its origins in England in 1775, when the duke of Cumberland offered a silver cup to the winner of a sailing race and the Cumberland Sailing Society was established.[24] Although a Knickerbocker Boat Club was established in New York in 1811, it was short-lived; not until mid-century did yacht clubs become firmly established in Boston (1835), New York (1844), and New Orleans (1849).[25] The early yachting trophies were modest in scale and domestic in form. In 1846 a small pitcher was awarded by the New York Yacht Club in its fall regatta (fig. 117). An octagonal water pitcher was the first prize at the 1849 Mobile, Alabama, Regatta Club meet.[26] In the years following the Civil War, yachting trophies began to evolve into an important and specific genre of presentation silver— commissioned pieces, large of scale and loaded with maritime and yachting iconography (fig. 120).

POLITICS AND THE MILITARY

While the theme of heroism pervades presentation silver, at no time was it more important and inspiring than in the first quarter of the nineteenth century. The tradition of saluting military valor with the gift of a sword began in America at the time of the Revolution, when Congress made presentations to outstanding leaders. The practice was taken up by states, cities, and groups of private citizens, and reached an apex during the Mexican War (an event that inspired few other types of presentation silver). One of the most remarkable presentation swords was awarded to General Grant in 1863 (fig. 140). By the end of the Civil War, however, the tradition had begun to decline.

The military presentation silver produced during the relatively short period between 1812 and 1818 is among the most monumental and superb ever made in America. The major commissions came from the citizens of the large seaport cities, led by Philadelphia, with Baltimore a close second. Most typically, these presentations consisted of either a large urn (at the time invariably characterized as a vase) or an extensive service of tableware. Oliver Hazard Perry and Stephen Decatur were the recip-

ients of both types of gifts. Examples of the services they received are illustrated in figures 128 and 131. The response of the citizenry to the inspiring victories of their military leaders was amazingly quick. Philadelphians resolved to honor Isaac Hull less than three weeks after his triumph over the *Guerrière* in August 1812. He received a large silver vase.[27] Though it took more than two weeks for word of Oliver Hazard Perry's Lake Erie victory to reach Boston, the project to organize a presentation began the same day the news arrived. Not only naval heroes were recognized. Following a long-standing tradition (fig. 121), the City of New York honored General Jacob Brown with a gold box (fig. 130). Colonel George Armistead received a cannonball-shaped vase from the citizens of Baltimore (fig. 132), and General Andrew Jackson was presented with a large urn by the ladies of South Carolina in 1817.[28]

Military presentation silver made after 1820 is not as a rule as ambitious in either scale or stylishness, but the custom continued throughout the century. In the 1840s General George Cadwalader was given an urn by his friends and fellow citizens of Philadelphia. In 1855 Commodore Matthew Perry was presented with a tea service in recognition of his services in negotiating the treaty with Japan. The visit of the great revolutionary-war hero Lafayette stirred the patriotism of all Americans in 1824–25. Each day the newspapers chronicled his every action. Congress voted him a gift of $300,000. In Baltimore he was presented with a gold medal (fig. 133), and in Charleston, South Carolina, he received a silver map case engraved with a sketch of his route through America. In 1832 New Yorkers gave him a gold medal similar to the one he had received earlier in Baltimore.[29]

Important figures in the political arena were also recognized. In 1835 Daniel Webster was given a large urn which, like De Witt Clinton's vases (fig. 96) was inspired by the antique Warwick vase found at Hadrian's villa at Tivoli.[30] Activity in the Whig party prompted a number of presentations to party leaders, including Henry Clay, who received two large urns in the 1840s (fig. 139). Indian leaders, too, received silver gifts. As part of official policy in dealing with the Indians, the government commissioned silver medals, armbands, and other objects to be given to important Indian chiefs (figs. 123, 129). Clearly this silver was highly valued by the recipients: an armband made in Philadelphia in the 1790s was found a century later in a burial mound in Michigan.[31] Slavery became a major political issue in the nineteenth century, and those who worked for abolition were recognized with presentation silver. In 1817 the Manumission Society of New York presented a pair of pitchers to John Curtis, marking his efforts in expediting the passage of New York's manumission act.[32] David Paul Brown, a noted abolitionist, received a pair of pitchers with salvers from "the disfranchised citizens" of Philadelphia in 1841 (fig. 137).

RITES OF PASSAGE AND FRIENDSHIP

Between the American Revolution and the Centennial, a great deal of silver was presented in a private context but, like church silver, it was not nearly as remarkable as pieces made for presentation to men and women in the public eye. Americans recorded the deaths of family members in schoolgirl embroideries and mourned the death of George Washington in every conceivable kind of textile, ceramic, and wallpaper, but they no longer as a matter of course memorialized the deaths of family members and friends with presentation silver. There were exceptions. Remarkable in any age would be Elizabeth De Lancey's nota bene of her own death, in 1784: an étui engraved, "This Memorial was bequeathed by the best of Mothers to her Son Oliver De Lancey."[33] A survival of seventeenth-century Dutch practice is the 1808 Albany spoon that marks the passing of Colonel Philip Pietersen Schuyler.[34] In 1800 Martha Washington presented a lock of her deceased husband's hair to the Grand Lodge of Masons in Boston, and the Masons commissioned a neoclassical gold urn to contain the lock.[35] An apparently unique silver urn, also of Boston origin, is inscribed in memory of Miss Abigail Cazneau and dated 1802 (fig. 145). Death is touched upon tangentially in the 1815 presentation by Lady Houstoun of Savannah to the lawyer who assisted her in settling the estates of her husband and brother-in-law (fig. 147). Similar sentiments are embodied in the 1876 presentation of an ewer and tray to George Townsend Adee by the heirs of William Timson in recognition of his fidelity as a trustee and guard.[36]

Birth also received scant recognition in other than modest form. In 1828 John Quincy Adams presented a cup to his first grandchild, Mary Louise, and in North Carolina a silver snuffbox marked the fiftieth birthday of E. Pfohl in 1825. Exceptional is the gold porringer and spoon presented in 1852 to Mary Phoenix Warren as a gift from her parents commemorating the birth of her daughter Mary Ida Warren.[37]

Silver was presented on the occasion of a marriage throughout the period, but generally the presentation is not documented by an accompanying engraving. Fortunately for posterity, Elizabeth Willing Powel of Philadelphia believed in inscribing her gifts; several enormously stylish pieces presented by her as wedding presents to young family members during the 1810s and 1820s are known today (figs. 150, 152). In Galveston, Texas, at the 1868 marriage of Mr. and Mrs. J. M. Hayden, three of the groom's regular dining companions presented the bride with a large silver pitcher engraved "from the Mess."[38] In 1869 Tiffany and Company advertised "a great variety of fancy articles in cases for wedding presents, presentation services. Special articles made to order."[39]

Silver-wedding anniversaries were observed at least as early as 1869. In April of that year, General and Mrs. Wallen of Governor's Island at Port Columbus, New York, celebrated their twenty-fifth year of marriage and were presented with "a service of massive silver beautifully designed and appropriately engraved."[40] Presentations in honor of men going into retirement became increasingly important during the period. A pitcher presented to the Reverend Joseph McKean in 1804 by his late parishioners in Milton, Massachusetts, is an early example (fig. 146). A relatively modest urn was presented to Henry M. Dobbs of New Orleans upon his stepping down from the presidency of the Mechanic Society in 1831, but Wendel Bollman, chief engineer of the Baltimore and Ohio, received a large and elaborate tea and coffee service complete with large coffee urn and tray when he left the railroad in 1859 (figs. 154, 159).

The bond of friendship both within and outside the family circle was frequently celebrated with a gift of silver during the nineteenth century. A small but exquisitely engraved beaker made in New York is inscribed "This gift is to my son . . . by his father Samuel Samuel" (fig. 144). Walter Channing of Boston received a tea service from his sister's family when he retired in 1817 (fig. 149). John Livingston of New York gave his son-in-law a pair of Gothic-style pitchers and goblets in 1845 (fig. 155). While these three gifts celebrate personal friendships, presentation silver also recognized more public relationships between individuals. Thomas Jefferson's friendship with Camilla Franzoni, wife of the Italian sculptor who was working on the United States Capitol, is marked by a surviving sugar bowl suitably inscribed and dated 1808.[41] The marquis de Lafayette presented a pair of goblets and a spoon to Washington hotel-keeper David Williamson in 1824 (fig. 153). Occasionally groups of people, describing themselves as "friends," would join together to present silver to an individual. The *New York Herald* on 18 June 1850, carried an account of an evening party at which the friends of Mr. Justice Osburn, in testimony of the esteem in which they held him, presented him with "a splendid service of silver . . . two pitchers, two goblets and a salver all beautifully engraved." G. W. Lester received a similar goblet inscribed "from a few of his Southern friends, N. Orleans, June, 1853."[42] While many such presents from "friends" were undoubtedly given altruistically, clearly some of them represent what Gerald Ward has characterized as "the dark side" of presentation silver, the intent to influence.

84. Two-handled covered cup, c. 1790–1800 *(cat. no. 49)*

Joseph Loring (1743–1815), Boston. Marked "J Loring" under the foot. Silver, h. 11³⁄₈ in. (28.9 cm.)

Inscribed "The Gift of Mr. William Johnston to Brattle Street Church, Boston 1707"

Museum of Fine Arts, Boston, Gift of the Benevolent Fraternity of Churches

This neoclassical cup is one of a set of four commissioned at the end of the eighteenth century.[43] Whereas the other three are engraved "Property of Brattle Street Church Boston," the inscription on this cup acknowledges a gift that dates only eight years after the founding of the church, in 1699. That difference suggests that this cup, which Joseph Loring made to match the other three, was fabricated of silver from the 1707 gift. Were it not for the inscription, it would be impossible to differentiate this piece from a sugar bowl in domestic use, which indicates that the Protestant church continued to use nonliturgical forms.

85. Communion dishes, c. 1800 *(cat. no. 50)*

Paul Revere, Jr. (1735–1818), Boston. Marked "REVERE" in a rectangle on the back of each plate. Silver, diam. 13³/₈ in. (34 cm.)

Inscribed "The property of the First Church in Beverly purchased by the pastor, Dean Benjn Cleaves, and Dean Robert Roundy, 1801"

Anonymous lender

The First Parish Church in Beverly, Massachusetts, was founded in 1667. As early as 1754, silver was purchased through a two-fold effort that included both a subscription by the parishioners and the sale of church stock. In 1798 a flagon made by Paul Revere, Jr., was bought with funds generated by the sale of church stock and selected by a committee of three: the pastor, Deacon Benjamin Cleaves, and Deacon Robert Roundy.[44] The inscription on the plates illustrated here, acquired three years later from the same silversmith, mentions the same purchasers. Probably these plates, too, were bought with church funds and selected by the pastor and the two deacons. The form, which is relatively rare, has often been called an alms dish, but there is strong evidence that these plates were intended for use during Communion service.[45]

86. Chalice, 1819 *(cat. no. 51)*

Victor Rouquette (active 1818–1824), Detroit, Michigan. Marked "VR" inside base. Silver, gilt, h. 10¹/₂ in. (26.7cm.)

Inscribed "Fait et donné par Victor Rouquette à l'église de Ste. Anne du Detroit à l'honneur de la très Sainte Vièrge Marie en Avril 1819"

Archives of the Archdiocese of Detroit

Detroit was founded by Antoine de la Mothe Cadillac in 1701 as a French fortress and fur-trading post. The Church of Ste. Anne, founded at the same time, was dedicated on 26 July, the feast day of Saint Anne. During the eighteenth century, St. Anne's was housed in several successive buildings, the last erected in 1798. A disastrous fire on 11 June 1805 completely destroyed Detroit. Following this calamity, the citizens determined that they would rebuild their city according to plans drawn up by Pierre L'Enfant, the French-born architect who laid out Washington, D.C., on a plan of sweeping boulevards. Unfortunately for the parish, Jefferson Avenue, one of the proposed grand boulevards in the new Detroit plan, ran straight through the hallowed site of the city's oldest church and burial ground. Although an alternate site offered by the city was acceptable to the parish priest, Father Gabriel Richard, many of his parishioners were upset by the proposed desecration of their burial ground. The parish became bitterly divided, and the controversy raged until 1816, when Bishop Carroll of Baltimore intervened to settle it. The cornerstone for the new stone church was laid on 18 June 1818 by Bishop Joseph-Octave Plessis. That same year, Father Richard advertised that he would purchase stone and lime.[46] To help erect the church, parishioners pledged either a one-fifth tithe or building materials.[47] Victor Rouquette's chalice, as the inscription indicates, was made for the new church and given by the silversmith. It is entirely possible that it represented his offering in lieu of a tithe or materials. The strong residual French influence in Detroit, which is suggested by the inscription, is confirmed by the style of Rouquette's chalice, which with its wide-spreading foot and large ovoid knop recalls the design of late-seventeenth-century French plate and early-eighteenth-century French Canadian plate.[48]

87. Communion set, c. 1840 *(cat. no. 52)*

Andrew Ellicott Warner (1786–1870), Baltimore. Marked "AEW 11" on the bottom. Silver, h. of flagon 10½ in. (26.7 cm.)

Inscribed "St. John's Chapel St. M.P."

Christ Episcopal Church, St. Michael's Parish, St. Michael's, Maryland

The colony of Maryland, dominated by the Roman Catholic Calvert family, did not have an established Anglican church until 1692, when the Maryland Assembly established three parishes, St. Paul's, St. Peter's, and St. Michael's.[49] St. Michael's was established in Talbot County. While attendance at church was an expected thing, it often was difficult for parishioners to get there, particularly when faced with such natural barriers as rivers or with unusually bad weather. The solution was a so-called chapel of ease situated in a more convenient location for parishioners from outlying areas. St. John's Chapel, located on the Miles River, was a chapel of ease of St. Michael's parish. This set was presented to the chapel by the parent church. The design of the communion vessels echoes the cluster columns of medieval Gothic architecture, adding an ecclesiastical symbolism to the forms.

88. Chalice, c. 1855 *(cat. no. 53)*

Francis W. Cooper and Richard Fisher, New York City (active 1855–1862). Engraved by Henry B. Horlor. Chased by William J. Seely. Marked on the bottom "COOPER & FISHER" and "131 AMITY St., N.Y." Silver, parcel-gilt, enamel, h. 9¾ in. (24.8 cm.)

The Parish of Trinity Church in the City of New York

On 2 November 1850, the parishioners of Trinity Church, New York, adopted a resolution to erect a chapel of ease on West Twenty-fifth Street, near Broadway, to accommodate the parishioners who had moved uptown to the center of the city. Richard Upjohn, the noted Gothic-revival architect who had rebuilt the parent church a few years before, was retained to design the new chapel. The plain brownstone structure was dedicated on 17 April 1855.[50] This elaborate Gothic-style chalice reflects the High Church taste of Upjohn, who lined the interior of the chapel with rich Caen stone and closed the nave with an elaborate chancel arch. Trinity Church records indicate that the new chapel was provided with two chalices, two patens, a credence paten, and an alms basin, as well as a smaller chalice and paten and five other alms basins, all by Cooper and Fisher.[51]

88

89, 90. Tankard and pair of canns, 1780 *(cat. no. 54)*

Benjamin Burt (1729–1805), Boston. Marked "Benjamin Burt" twice on the side of the tankard and once on the bottom of each cann. Silver, h. of tankard 9¼ in. (22.9 cm.)

Inscribed on the side of each object "The gift of the owners of the ship Pickering" and the cipher "JH"

Peabody Museum of Salem, Salem, Massachusetts

During the Revolution, the town of Salem, Massachusetts, licensed a fleet of privateers to prey on enemy shipping. Under the established system, after deducting the costs of outfitting the vessel the owners took a half share of captured prizes. The captain

90

89

and crew divided the remaining half on a sliding scale according to rank. On 29 September 1778, George Williams, on behalf of himself and others, petitioned the legislature of Massachusetts that Jonathan Harraden be commissioned as commander of the brigantine *General Pickering*.[52] The *Pickering*, with sixteen guns, set sail from Salem in 1780. On 20 May she engaged and defeated a twenty-gun English man-of-war and captured a fourteen-gun schooner on 1 June. Four days later, the *Pickering* escaped the attack of a large frigate, *Arquilles*, and set sail for her home port bearing her valuable booty. Portraits of the *Pickering* are engraved on the three pieces of silver crafted by Benjamin Burt and presented to Harraden by the grateful owners.

91. Teapot, 1786 *(cat. no. 55)*

Zachariah Brigden (1734–1787), Boston. Marked "Z Brigden" on the bottom. Silver, h. 4³/₄ in. (12.1 cm.)

Inscribed "Presented to Capt. David Wood by the proprietors of CHARLES RIVER BRIDGE, in testimony of their entire Approbation of his faithful Services as a special director of that Work, begun A.D. 1785, and perfected A.D. 1786"

Museum of Fine Arts, Boston, Gift of Miss Penelope Barker Noyes in memory of her father, James Atkins Noyes

On 2 February 1785, the town of Charlestown chose a committee to represent them at the General Court and to support a petition by Boston citizens to build a toll bridge, which would replace the existing ferry across the Charles River. David Wood was a member of that committee.[53] It was generally conceded that the bridge would provide a valuable road link from the somewhat isolated city of Boston, located on a peninsula, to the rest of the state. The petition was granted the same year; a corporation was established; and construction was begun. Wood became a director of the newly formed Charles River Bridge Corporation. The bridge was completed and opened 17 June 1786 amid great festivity and celebration.[54] The proprietors showed their appreciation to those who had supervised the construction by presenting them with silver engraved with views of the bridge. This handsome teapot by Zachariah Brigden is also engraved with bright-cut borders and floral swags.

91

92

92. Bowl, c. 1800 *(cat. no. 57)*

Hugh Wishart (active 1793–1837), New York City. Engraved by
William Rollinson. Marked "WISHART" at the base of the
engraving. Silver, diam. 13½ in. (34.3 cm.)

Inscribed "Presented by the President and Directors of the New
York Insurance Company to Captn. Wm. D. Seton as a testi-
mony of the high sense which they entertain of his gallant con-
duct in defending his ship the Northern Liberties against the
French privateer Malartic of superior force in the Bay of
Bengal. 13 Decr. 1799"

Museum Purchase, William H. Noble Bequest Fund, The Fine
Arts Museums of San Francisco

On 9 December 1800, at a general meeting of the board of directors of the New York Insurance Company, those present resolved
unanimously to communicate their thanks to Captain William D.
Seton for his meritorious service in, nearly a year before, eluding
capture by a French privateer. Such attacks were costly, and
Seton, in safely returning both his ship and its cargo, clearly
deserved the thanks of the owners and insurers of the merchant
vessel. They determined, therefore, to present him with a piece of
plate valued at one hundred pounds. James Scott and Augustus
H. Lawrence, both directors of the company, were appointed as a
committee to implement the resolution. By 5 January 1801, less
than a month later, the silver punch bowl and ladle were apparently ready, for they are described in a letter of that date written to
Seton by Charles McEvers, president of the New York Insurance
Company, that was intended to accompany the presentation.
McEvers relates that the beautiful marine scene which was
engraved on the bowl by William Rollinson, is emblematic of
Seton's generous action. Seton's letter of acceptance, written from
Norfolk, Virginia, is dated 26 January 1802.[55] Rollinson, a prom-
inent New York engraver, also decorated medals presented by the
government to Indian chiefs. Punch bowls were widely used in
American homes, almost exclusively for celebrations; Scott and
Lawrence chose the form, perhaps, because it has ceremonial
connotations, though it is not a trophy.

supercargo of the vessel in a letter to the owners written several weeks later.[56] Three men were lost, and Captain Anderson was wounded in the chest by a musket ball. However, the attack was warded off, and the cargo and ship were saved. The urn that the grateful insurers presented to Anderson is notable as an early departure, in both sizes and design, from a domestic form to a nonutilitarian presentation piece.

94. Urn, 1822 *(cat. no. 58)*

Harvey Lewis (active c. 1811–1825), Philadelphia. Marked "Harvey Lewis" in a rectangle on the bottom. Silver, h. 13³/₈ in. (34 cm.)

Inscribed "This vase is presented on behalf of the city of Philadelphia by the Watering Committee of the Council to Frederick Graff to express their admiration of the taste, judgement and fidelity, with which he arranged, superintended and assisted in prosecuting to a conclusion the Public Works at Fair Mount"

Historical Society of Pennsylvania, Philadelphia, Gift of Miss Henrietta Graff, June 13, 1906

Recognizing the need for an improved water supply, the rapidly growing city of Philadelphia turned in 1798 to the architect Benjamin Latrobe. The resultant Philadelphia Water Works became a model civic improvement. Frederick Graff, a native Philadel-

93

93. Urn, 1799 *(cat. no. 56)*

Joseph Lownes (1758–1820), Philadelphia. Marked "J. Lownes". Silver, h. 18 in. (45.7 cm.)

Inscribed "To Capt. W. Anderson of the ship *London Packet* from the Marine Insurance Office. We regard your valor"

Philip H. Hammerslough Collection, Wadsworth Atheneum, Hartford, Connecticut

As a result of the increasing threat to American shipping by foreign privateers, especially vessels under the French flag, the U.S. Department of the Navy was established in 1798 under Benjamin Stoddert, who rapidly enlarged the fleet. On 10 September 1799, the American ship *London Packet*, built in Baltimore in 1790, was engaged by a French privateer of sixteen guns. The battle, which lasted an hour and three-quarters, was vividly described by the

94

phian who worked as a draftsman under Latrobe, became the superintendent of the Water Works in 1804 and continued in that capacity until 1847. During his tenure, Graff enlarged and improved the facility with a new steam-powered works in 1815 and water-powered mills in 1819.[57] The Philadelphia Water Works became an enormous source of civic pride, and the open land surrounding them was gradually taken in as the city's Fairmount Park. Graff's contribution was recognized by the members of the Watering Committee with this sophisticated urn, which is engraved on one side with a view of the Water Works; later, in 1828, he received an equally sophisticated pitcher.[58] This urn, with its winglike handles, resembles French silver, which was influential both generally in Philadelphia and specifically in the work of Lewis (fig. 148). It brings to mind a decidedly French tea set made by Anthony Rasch (fig. 134).

95. Pair of pitchers, 1823 *(cat. no. 59)*

John B. Jones (active 1816–1822), Boston. Marked "J. B. Jones" on the center bottom. Silver, h. 9¼ in. (23.5 cm.)

Inscribed on the lid of one pitcher "Presented by the Salem Commercial Insurance Company to Captain Nathaniel Garland of the Schooner Tatler In Testimony of their high sense of his heroic conduct in defending the Vessel & Property under his Command against a piratical assault of his crew on the seventeenth of September AD 1823" and on the lid of the other pitcher "Presented by the Marine Insurance Company to Captain Nathaniel Garland of the Schooner Tatler In Testimony of their high sense of his heroic conduct in defending the Vessel & Property under his Command against a piratical assault of his crew on the seventeenth of September AD 1823"

Peabody Museum of Salem, Salem, Massachusetts

The 16 October 1823 issue of the *Essex [Massachusetts] Register* heralds the return to Salem from Philadelphia of the schooner *Tatler* and explains that Captain Garland remained behind to testify in the trial of two men charged in the recent murder and mutiny. The mutiny occurred off Delaware Bay as *Tatler* was en route from Baltimore carrying a valuable load of specie. Garland, who was attacked and wounded in the incident, wrote a full account of the events after he was put ashore at Lewes, Delaware.[59] The cargo was insured by the Marine Insurance Company, Salem's oldest, established in 1803, and the Salem Commercial Company, established in 1818. On 17 November 1823, the directors of the Marine Insurance Company voted that a piece of plate with a suitable inscription be presented to Garland. The letter of conveyance is dated 1 December, suggesting that the presentation piece described in the local press as "an elegant Pitcher . . . of the value of about seventy dollars" was a stock item.[60]

97

96–99. Vase, 1824 *(cat. no. 62)*

Thomas Fletcher and Sidney Gardiner, Philadelphia (active 1811–1825). Marked "FLETCHER & GARDINER, PHILA. 1824". Silver, h. 23¾ in. (60.3 cm.)

Inscribed "The Merchants of Pearl Street, New York, to the Hon. DeWitt Clinton whose claim to the proud title of "Public Benefactor" is founded on those magnificent works, the Northern and Western Canals"

The Metropolitan Museum of Art, New York, Purchase, Louis V. Bell and Rogers Funds; Anonymous and Robert G. Goelet Gifts; and Gifts of Fenton L. B. Brown and of the grandchildren of Mrs. Ranson Spaford Hooker, in her memory, by exchange, 1982

The economic importance of the Erie Canal to the city of New York was recognized by a group of ten prominent merchants. They formed a committee and launched a competition for the design of suitable plate to be presented to Governor De Witt Clinton, who was the motivating force behind the construction of the canal. On 17 January 1824, Fletcher and Gardiner were announced as the winners of the competition.[61] Their monumental design for the pair of vases was of sufficient interest to the general public that a full and detailed description appeared in the New York press when the vases were exhibited there in March 1825, prior to the presentation to Governor Clinton. The form of the vases, an article in the *New York Commercial Advertiser* related, was copied from "the celebrated antique vase found among the ruins of the Villa of Adrian, and now in the possession of the Earl of Warwick. The handles and some of the ornament are also similar to those on that beautiful specimen." The ornament, which is rich in both allegorical representation of the arts and sciences and actual scenes along the canal's route, was also described in minute detail. The vases, the description went on, each of which weighed about four hundred ounces, were made by Messrs. Fletcher and Gardiner and designed by Thomas Fletcher. The presentation took place on 19 March 1825 at a reception held at the governor's mansion in Albany. An address was delivered by Isaac S. Hone, chairman of the committee of Pearl Street merchants.[62] In his acceptance speech, Clinton praised the vases highly. "I receive these splendid fabrics with the highest gratification," he said. "In design and execution they reflect honor on the taste, skill and ingenuity of our artists." He described the donors as "the representatives of the most important section of the most commercial city in the Western world." Because of its proximity to the ocean and new connection to the most fertile regions of the interior, New York enjoyed preeminent advantage, he concluded. After the ceremony Clinton acceded to the request of the citizens of Albany that the vases be exhibited locally; they were taken to Knickerbocker's Hall and placed on view.[63]

98

99

100

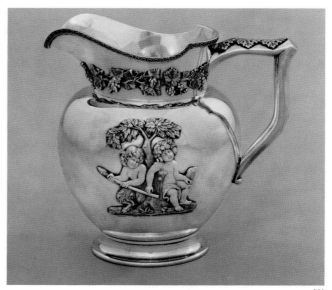

101

102

100. Cup, 1823 (cat. no. 60)

Horace and Allyn Goodwin, Hartford, Connecticut (active 1821–1825). Marked "Goodwin" and "Hartford" in rectangles, Silver, h. 4½ in. (11.4 cm.)

Inscribed "Hartford County Agricultural Society Premium, to Frederick Oakes for the best cultivated farm, A.D. 1823"

Philip H. Hammerslough Collection, Wadsworth Atheneum, Hartford, Connecticut

The Hartford County Agricultural Society was established in 1817 for the "promotion and improvement of agriculture and rural economy." Among the classes recognized annually was the best cultivated farm—one of not less than forty acres, improved at the least expense. The first prize was a silver cup valued at forty dollars. Although the West Hartford farm of Frederick Oakes, a Hartford silversmith, businessman, and gentleman farmer, was first viewed by the Agricultural Society's visiting committee in 1821, it was not until 1823 that he won the prize, at the October fair. From 1825 to 1830 Oakes served as treasurer of the Agricultural Society. He was also a member of the visiting committee in 1825 and 1826.[64]

101, 102. Pitcher, c. 1823–30 (cat. no. 61)

Edward Lownes (1792–1834), Philadelphia. Marked "E. LOWNES" four times on the bottom. Silver, h. 8⅛ in (20.6 cm.)

Inscribed "Presented to Col. John Hare Powel by the Penna Agril Socy not only in testimony of their personal regard, but of their high respect for his talents, zeal and liberality in promoting the agricultural interests of his country"

Historical Society of Pennsylvania, Philadelphia, Gift of Robert Hare Powel, June 30, 1949

The Pennsylvania Agricultural Society was founded in 1823 to continue the traditional Philadelphia interest in developing agricultural resources and upgrading livestock.[65] John Hare Powel

(1786–1856), one of the organizers, served in 1823 and 1824 as corresponding secretary. A prominent Philadelphian and gentleman farmer, Powel was the author of numerous papers for agricultural periodicals and of the 1827 tract *Hints for the American Husbandman*.[66] Powel also introduced the English breeds of Durham Shorthorn cattle and Southdown sheep to America. At the October 1824 Pennsylvania Agricultural Society fair, Powel was awarded a forty-dollar premium for an imported thoroughbred horse.[67] This pitcher, which would have cost more than forty dollars, is not the premium but rather recognizes Powel's overall contribution to the society. The form of the pitcher reflects English earthenware examples, as does the banding of grapes, which, like the reliefs on either side, underscores the agricultural theme.

103. Pitcher and salver, c. 1825 (cat. no. 63)

Stephen Richard (active 1802–1839), New York City. Marked "S. Richard Maker NY" on the bottom of the salver. Silver, h. of pitcher 13¼ in. (33.7 cm.)

Inscribed "The Phenix Bank of New York to Charles Bancroft Esqr."

Private collection

103

In 1815 Charles Bancroft moved from New York to Montreal, where he became a member of the banking house Gates and Nephew. The firm had been important in the United States during the War of 1812, serving both as an agent and as an expediter of commerce between southern Canada and the United States. Apparently Gates and Nephew continued to have important ties with America. They served the Phenix Bank by purchasing silver dollars and forwarding the hard currency to New York, where it was in demand among merchants in the China trade. Bancroft was married to the niece of Horatio Gates, a partner in the firm. The Phenix Bank presented identical pitchers, goblets, and salvers, to Gates and Bancroft.[68]

104. Teakettle on stand, 1850 (cat. no. 64)

Designed by John Chandler Moore (active 1827–1851) for Ball Tompkins and Black (active 1839–1851), New York City. Marked on the underside "BALL TOMPKINS & BLACK/NEW YORK/J.C.M/22". Silver, h. 17 5/16 in. (43.9 cm.)

Inscribed on one side "To Marshall Lefferts, Esq., President of the New York and New England and New York State Telegraph Companies" and on the other "From the stockholders and Associated Press of New York City as a token of his advancing the cause and credit of the Telegraph System, the noblest enterprise of this eventful age. New York, June 1850"

The Metropolitan Museum of Art, New York, Gift of Mrs. F. R. Lefferts, 1969

The telegraph, invented in 1835 by Samuel F. B. Morse, would prove an important means of disseminating news in the latter half of the nineteenth century, but at first the generally unreliable service provided by a multitude of small telegraph companies made it difficult for individual newspapers to send and receive news. Then in the 1840s Marshall Lefferts perfected and patented a telegraph system with an automatic plan of transmission, and on 19 April 1849 the New York and New England Telegraph Company, a conglomerate of smaller companies, was established with Lefferts as president.[69] Lefferts's reliable company proved a great boon to the fledgling Associated Press, established by six New York newspapers in 1848 to facilitate collection and dissemination of news by telegraph. This kettle is part of a large service presented as a surprise to Lefferts at a dinner given to celebrate the completion of a new section of line. The presentation consisted of the large urn shown here and two pitchers with a four-piece tea set, according to an account of the event in the *New York Herald* for 26 June 1850.[70] The service was, the *Herald* relates, "manufactured for the occasion." John Chandler Moore personalized this Rococo-revival teakettle by adding a finial in the form of Zeus holding lightning bolts. Moore used the same design, without Zeus, for at least three other presentation teakettles.[71]

From
the Stockholders
and Associated Press
of New-York City;
Viz., Courier & Enquirer,
Journal of Commerce, Express,
Herald, Sun and Tribune,
a token of the satisfaction and
confidence inspired by his efficient
services in advancing the cause and credit
of the Telegraph System, the noblest
enterprise of this eventful age.
New-York, June 1850.

105

105. Teakettle on stand, c. 1853 *(cat. no. 65)*

Galt and Brothers (1802 to the present), Washington, D.C. Marked "M.W. GALT & BRO." and with three pseudo hallmarks (one an eagle and two unidentified). Silver, h. 21 in. (53.3 cm.)

Inscribed "Presented to Captain Montgomery C. Meigs by the Corporation of Washington with a resolution of thanks approved 12th March, 1853 for his effort on the Washington Aqueduct"

National Museum of American History, Smithsonian Institution, Washington, D.C. Gift of General Montgomery C. Meigs

In the 1850s Montgomery C. Meigs, an 1836 graduate of West Point, was assigned to supervise both the survey of a new aqueduct for Washington, D.C., and the building of new wings and a dome on the Capitol. The proposed aqueduct would carry most of Washington's water supply from the Great Falls of the Potomac to the city. On 12 March 1853, the Corporation of Washington passed a resolution of thanks to Meigs and approved his report on the aqueduct.[72] The teakettle was presented to Meigs on 9 June 1854 by a committee consisting of Mayor John W. Maury, Joseph Burrows of the board of aldermen, and A. W. Miller of the corporation. The rich vocabulary of aquatic detail—stone arches, dolphins, shells, and serpent—was obviously chosen for this specific commission.

107

1166. FRUIT STAND. No. 164.
Av. Wt. 84 oz.
Hight 16 in.
Diam 10 in.

108

106. Fruit stand, 1866 *(cat. no. 66)*

Gorham Manufacturing Company (active 1831 to the present), Providence, Rhode Island. Marked on the bottom with a lion passant, anchor, and Gothic "G/164". Silver, h. 16³/₄ in. (42.6 cm.)

Inscribed "George Peabody to Cyrus W. Field in testimony and commemoration of an act of very high commercial integrity and honor. New York, 24 Nov. 1866"

Museum of the City of New York, Gift of Newcomb Carlton

107. Working drawing for Fruit Stand Number 164. Design Department Archives, Gorham Textron

108. Photograph of Fruit Stand Number 164. In Photograph Scrapbook Number One, c. 1865–83. Design Department Archives, Gorham Textron

"We arrived here at 9 o'clock this morning, all is well, Thank God. The cable has been laid and is in perfect working order." These historic words were sent to New York by Cyrus West Field from the port of Heart's Content in England on 28 July 1866. The headlines of the *New York Times* for 30 July read, "The Atlantic Cable/ Successful Completion of the Great Work/The Old and New Worlds Joined Together." Subsequent issues of the *Times* headlined the European news with the new description, "By Ocean Telegraph." As early as 1854, Field, a New York merchant and financier, had begun to promote a transatlantic telegraph cable. He put together a $1.5 million syndicate to fund the project. In 1858 a cable was laid from Trinity Bay in Newfoundland to Valencia in Ireland, but it broke almost immediately.[73] Although Field recapitalized, the Civil War delayed the completion of the cable until 1866.

George Peabody, who presented this fruit stand to Field, made his fortune in the wholesale grocery firm of Riggs and Peabody in Baltimore. Later he moved to England, where he established the banking house of George Peabody and Company. Clearly the transatlantic cable was of enormous benefit to Peabody's business. The inscription may refer to the fact that Field repaid those who had lost money in the 1858 project. This stand, part of a large service, is personalized with cast portrait-medallions of Field and Peabody; however, records of the Gorham Company and surviving drawings indicate that the service was made up of stock items (figs. 107, 108).

109. Cigar case, 1868 *(cat. no. 67)*

Browne and Spaulding (active c. 1868), New York City. Marked inside the original leather presentation box, "Browne & Spaulding 560 & 570 Broadway, N.Y." Gold, l. 5¹/₂ in. (14 cm.)

Inscribed "To Commodore Vanderbilt from a stockholder in Hudson River, Harlem, New York Central Rail Roads, Jan 1, 1868"

Harold Stirling Vanderbilt Collection. The Jean and Alexander Heard Library. Vanderbilt University, Nashville, Tennessee

In the mid-1860s Cornelius Vanderbilt needed space on the west side of Manhattan to build a freight yard for his newly acquired Hudson River Railroad. St. John's Park, an urban square fashionable in the eighteenth century but down at the heel by 1865, was the ideal site. Vanderbilt bought the square, demolished all the houses surrounding it, and built a huge three-story brick freight

109

111

110

ond Boston Theatre, designed by Charles Bulfinch and opened to the public on 26 December 1796, and a representation of that building is engraved on the side. A bill from Revere indicates that this was one of four punch urns ordered by the proprietors.[75] Samuel Brown was a Boston merchant involved in the China trade. In 1790 he and Charles Bulfinch were co-investors in a ship.[76]

house. The St. John's Park Freight Station, depicted on this box sent to Vanderbilt by a grateful stockholder, provided a huge terminal close to the mercantile center of the city where loading and unloading could be accomplished indoors.[74]

110. Punch urn with cover, 1796 *(cat. no. 68)*

Paul Revere, Jr. (1735–1818), Boston. Marked "REVERE" to the right of the left handle. Silver, h. 11⅝ in. (29.5 cm.)

Inscribed "The proprietors of the Boston Theatre to Samuel Brown, Esqr., one of their trustees, 1796"

Rosalinde and Arthur Gilbert

In 1792 the long-standing prohibition against the public staging of plays in Boston was lifted by repeal of a law of 1750. The next year a group of Bostonians interested in drama organized themselves, and the first Boston Theatre was completed in 1794; however, the company went bankrupt in 1795. This urn commemorates the sec-

112

111, 112. Trophy, c. 1803 *(cat. no. 69)*

Charles A. Burnett and Thomas Rigden, Georgetown, D.C. (active 1800–1806). Marked "BURNETT & RIGDEN" on the four sides of the pedestal base. Silver, h. 21½ in. (54.6 cm.)

Inscribed around the oval engraving of a horse and rider at a starting gate "Washington Cup won by Vingt-un Novr 11th 1803"

Private collection

Colonel Wade Hampton of Columbia, South Carolina, was a distinguished revolutionary-war hero who left his military career to serve in Congress in 1795. Having left Congress to run unsuccessfully for president in 1801, he returned to Washington in 1803 as a representative from South Carolina. The fall 1803 meeting of the Washington Jockey Club was announced in the local press on 10 September. The races were to take place during a five-day period on a course that was described as well-prepared and enclosed with a post-and-rail fence. All horses, mares, and geldings were subject to the rules of the club and required to carry jockeys of specific weights. The prizes ranged from purses valued at $200 to a sweepstake of $1,600. On the fourth day of the meet, however, the prize was "a 50 guinea silver cup."[77] The meet commenced on 8 November, and on 11 November ten subscribers at five guineas each entered the race for the silver cup. The report of the race one week later in the *National Intelligencer and Washington Advertiser* notes that Colonel Hampton's bay Vingt-Un, by the imported horse Diomed, was the winner. The mention of imported horseflesh, with the intimation of improved breeding, is an interesting

footnote, anticipating the message of the Belmont Memorial Challenge Cup (fig. 198). This two-handled cup, although large in scale, is like a sugar bowl in form and thus is related to a sugar bowl awarded by the nearby Tappahannock Jockey Club in June 1800.[78] Certainly the bright-cut ornament here is similar in style and placement to that found on domestic silver. Clearly, however, this piece was intended to be a trophy. First, it is explicitly described as a cup in the newspaper accounts. Second, it is engraved with two equine scenes, one depicting two horses racing, the other a portrait of Hampton's Vingt-Un engraved within an oval inscribed "Washington Cup." This is one of the earliest American examples of the two-handled sporting trophy, which had its origins in eighteenth-century England.

113. Bowl, 1828 *(cat. no. 72)*

Thomas Fletcher (1787–1866), Philadelphia. Marked "T. FLETCHER" and "1828" on one side of the pedestal. Silver, h. 13½ in. (34.2 cm.)

Inscribed "Instituted Sept. 3 1828, this bowl is the absolute property of the United Bowmen"

Lent by The Club of the United Bowmen of Philadelphia, Established 1828. On permanent deposit with The Historical Society of Pennsylvania, Philadelphia

"Feeling the want of out door exercise and disliking billiards ten-pins, etc., a few friends joined in choosing archery before breakfast and a walk in the country." These words describe the genesis of the United Bowmen of Philadelphia, founded in 1828 by Franklin Peale, Titian R. Peale, Robert E. Griffith, M.D., Samuel P. Griffitts, Jr., and Jacob G. Morris and still in existence.[79] Initially a member, the portraitist Thomas Sully did not actively participate and was not, therefore, awarded founding-member status. Membership in the group grew to approximately thirty and was held to that number. Candidates were accepted only on the death of members. Club members met socially on a monthly basis, but the most important meetings were the archery contests. The constitution of the club not only spelled out the rules and regulations but described the uniforms to be worn for club events. It also provided that each year on the second Saturday of June, four prizes would be shot for by members of the club. "The first prize shall be the club bowl, and the club shall within the month after each and every annual shooting, append a medal to the bowl on which shall be inscribed the name of the successful competitor, with the date, and the winner of the same shall, within one year from the receipt of it have added thereto ornamental work, according to the design adopted by the club." Thus, the leaf ornament on the body of the bowl is applied in sections and does not extend all the way around. Thomas Fletcher's design, which is similar to that of the De Witt Clinton vases (fig. 96), had a more exaggerated rim, presumably to accommodate the medals that would be appended over the years. The second prize, a silver cup valued at fifteen dollars made according to a design approved by the club, is a goblet with a stem in the design of an arrow. The third prize is a smaller cup of the same design valued at ten dollars, and the fourth prize is a silver arrow.

114. Pitcher, 1811 *(cat. no. 70)*

Ebenezer Moulton (1768–1824), Boston. Marked "MOULTON" in a rectangle at the left of the handle. Silver, h. 8¼ in. (21 cm.)

Inscribed "To Mr. Isaac Harris for his intrepid and successful exertions on the roof of the Old South Church when on fire December 29nth 1810. The Society present this token of their gratitude, Boston, January 29nth 1811"

Museum of Fine Arts, Boston, Gift of the Heirs of Isaac Harris through Mrs. Edward Wyman

On 29 December 1810, a fire broke out in a stable on Milk Street in Boston. It reached such raging proportions that the entire district was in danger of being destroyed. Volunteer firemen came from the neighboring towns of Medford, Charlestown, Roxbury, Cambridge, and Cambridgeport. Their efforts were recognized with special public thanks from the fire wards of Boston.[80] Isaac Harris was a mastmaker whose business was located in Washington Street near the Old South Church, in the area of the fire. The engraved scene on the side of this pitcher shows Harris's ladder leaning on the church and Harris on the roof, the smoke and flames swirling in the background. The barrel-shaped pitcher is a fairly standard form in the early nineteenth century, but clearly extra efforts were expended to record the details of Harris's heroism for the presentation one month after the fire.[81]

115. Tray, 1826 *(cat. no. 71)*

Stephen Richard (active 1802–1839), New York City. Marked "S. RICHARD" in a serrated rectangle with rounded corners. Silver, l. 25⁷/₁₆ in. (64.6 cm.)

Inscribed "Presented by the Corporation of the City of New York to Charles Rhind Esqr. Jany. 1st 1826"; "Reception of Majr. Genl. La Fayette A.D. 1824"; "Grand Canal Celebration A.D. 1825"; and "Engd. by I. D. Stout"

The Metropolitan Museum of Art, New York, Lent by Mr. and Mrs. Samuel Schwartz, 1967

Charles Rhind, born in Aberdeen, Scotland, began his mercantile career in New York City as a ship chandler about 1810. His business expanded, and by the mid-1820s he was engaged in trade with the Russian port of Smyrna and was also agent for the North River Steam Boat Company. Rhind's avocation apparently was organizing and participating in public celebrations. At the two most important social and political events in early-nineteenth-century New York, Rhind held positions of leadership. He was chairman of the reception committee that greeted Lafayette on his arrival in New York in 1824, and the next year was admiral of the New York Fleet at the harbor festivities following the opening of the Erie Canal. To honor Rhind, the City of New York commissioned this tray and a footed basket from Richard, and a teapot, sugar bowl, creamer, and waste bowl from Garrett Eoff. The present location of all but this tray is unknown.

114

116

116. Pitcher, c. 1845–51 *(cat. no. 73)*

George Stewart (active 1843–1852), Lexington, Kentucky. Marked "G W STEWART LEX K." on the side of the base. Silver, h. 13¼ in. (33.7 cm.)

Inscribed under the spout "B.U.S."

Private collection

The Lexington Jockey Club was established at Postlethwaite's Tavern in 1797. In 1838 John Brennan, proprietor of the Phoenix House, as the tavern was then known, offered a silver pitcher valued at one hundred dollars as a prize bearing his name.[82] The Brennan Stake, awarded to the winning three-year-old in the Kentucky Racing Association's spring meet, was the first named competition established by the association. A similar pitcher was donated each year by Brennan and later by John Garland Chiles, who had purchased the hotel. Beginning in 1851 the association purchased the prize. Pitchers were a common and popular presentation form in Kentucky, and the racing trophies made in Lexington are often unusually rich in repoussé ornament. The fortunate winner of this example, enriched with a depiction of the race, did not inscribe the details of the victory. Another pitcher by Stewart, engraved with the identical scene, was awarded at the Brennan Stake in 1844.

117. Pitcher, 1846 *(cat. no. 74)*

William F. Ladd (active 1829–1886), New York City. Marked "Wm. F. LADD" on the bottom in a rectangle and "New York" in a serrated rectangle. Silver, h. 9¼ in. (23.5 cm.)

117

Inscribed "New York Yacht Club Subscription Stakes October 7th 1846"

The New-York Historical Society, New York City

The New York Yacht Club was organized on 30 July 1844 by John Cox Stephens at a meeting with eight other men held on Stephens's schooner *Gimcrack*.[83] In the autumn of 1846 the Club organized a regatta in which the crews of the yachts were club members rather than paid hands as had been customary until that time. A regatta of amateurs is called a Corinthian—in reference to the amateur status of the sailors of ancient Corinth. This first Corinthian regatta in America was held on 7 October over a special course within New York Harbor. Six boats started; the race was won by *Maria*. This small trophy is based on domestic silver both in scale and in form. The silversmith was careful, however, to incorporate marine ornament, and the cartouche is enriched with a trident, gaff, and shells. The cast dolphin spout and conch-shell thumb-piece are bold and hint at the riches to come in later yachting trophies.

118, 119. Fire trumpet, 1856 *(cat. no. 75)*

Albert L. Lincoln and Charles M. Foss, Boston (active 1848–1857). Marked "LINCOLN FOSS PURE COIN FOSTER" on the inside of the lip. Silver, h. 18⅞ in. (47.9 cm.)

Inscribed on the flared bell "Torrent No. 5 built by Wm. Jeffers Pawtucket, R.I." and on the back "Won from Phoenix Fire Company no. 6, A. Kelly, foreman tho having c[h]allenged Torrent Fire Company no. 5, M. Hines, foreman"

Historic Mobile Preservation Society, Mobile, Alabama

The volunteer fire company had its origins in Philadelphia, when Benjamin Franklin established the Union Fire Company in 1736. By the early nineteenth century, every able-bodied male Ameri-

118

119

can citizen was expected to take part in volunteer community affairs, either the militia or fire fighting. The companies were organized along paramilitary lines, with foremen (or captains) and ranks. Before the invention of steam-powered engines, firemen were required to build up water pressure with hand pumps, which were stroked to cadences called by their foremen through speaking trumpets. By mid-century the fireman's trumpet had become a distinctive and popular form of presentation silver. The presentations recognized leadership, individual heroes, and, like this example, victory in a contest with rival companies. While a detailed description of a contest and repoussé depiction of a fire engine are not unusual on such presentations, the freestanding wheels lend a rare note of verisimilitude.

120. Commodore's Ocean Challenge Cup, 1872 *(cat. no. 76)*

Tiffany and Company (1837 to the present), New York City. Marked "TIFFANY & CO" on the front of the base between two dolphins. Silver, gilt, h. 36 in. (91.4 cm.)

Inscribed on the medallion on the back "Commodore's Ocean Challenge Cup Rambler vs Madelaine Won by Rambler July 27, 1872 Madelaine vs. Rambler Won by Rambler September 20 1872 Sandy Hook Light Ship to Brenton's Reef Light Ship and Return July 27, 1876 Idler Seawanhaka Yacht Club, American Boston Yacht Club, Wanderer New York Yacht Club, Tidal Wave, New York Yacht Club, Countess of Dufferin, Royal Canadian Yacht Club won by Idler Commodore S.J. Colgate 32 Hrs. 18 M. 16 Sec."

New York Yacht Club, New York City

In 1871 Commodore James Gordon Bennett, Jr., presented this trophy to the New York Yacht Club as a challenge cup. The gift, which was valued at $1,000, came with explicit instructions concerning the conditions under which the cup could be held, including provisions for its return should the yacht holding the cup be sold from the club. The first challenge took place on 27 July 1872, when James Forbes's *Rambler* of the Eastern Yacht Club, Boston, raced and beat Jacob Voorhis's *Madeleine* of the New York Yacht Club.[84] *Rambler* was again victorious in a rematch on 20 September. Following the first race, the cup was illustrated in *Harper's Weekly*, where it was described as "a beautiful urn-shaped piece . . . the handles are elegantly and appropriately ornamented with naval emblems . . . and the whole piece is surmounted by the figure of an ancient mariner, who may represent Columbus, pointing to a globe."[85]

120

121. Box, 1784 *(cat. no. 77)*

Samuel Johnson (baptized 1720–d. 1796), New York City. Engraved by Peter Maverick (1755–1811), New York City. Marked "SJ" in a rectangle on the inside of the bottom. Gold, l. 3¼ in. (8.3 cm.)

Inscribed on the cover "Presented by the Corporation of the City of New York with the freedom of the City"

Yale University Art Gallery, New Haven, Connecticut, Mabel Brady Garvan Collection

In 1784 the Common Council of New York, wishing to recognize the achievements of various revolutionary-war heroes, voted to present the freedom of the city to Governor George Clinton, General Washington, John Jay, the marquis de Lafayette, and Baron

121

Friedrich Wilhelm von Steuben. Each presentation included a gold box containing the seal of the city and a document outlining the recipient's particular contribution to the victory and conveying the freedom of the city. Steuben's box, which was engraved by Peter Maverick with the arms and motto of New York City, is illustrated here. It reflects the city's long-standing tradition of presenting gold boxes to those it wished to honor. In his will Steuben left the American portion of his estate to his former aides-de-camp Benjamin Walker and William North. In a specific bequest to North, Steuben left his silver-hilted sword and "the gold box given me by the city of New York."[86] Thus, this box became for a second time a presentation object.

1788 John Penn, Sr., purchased two identical tankards from Joseph Anthony and had them inscribed to Charles Jarvis and Gunning Bedford.[88] Bedford, a prominent Philadelphia attorney, acted as the Penns' agent in the settlement of the land claims. The Penn family arms, ironically adopted by the new Commonwealth, appear in the neoclassical shield on the front of the newly fashionable barrel-shaped tankard.

GEORGE WASHINGTON
PRESIDENT.
1792.

123

122

122. Tankard, c. 1788 *(cat. no. 78)*

Joseph Anthony, Jr. (1762–1814), Philadelphia. Marked "I Anthony" in script in a rectangle twice on the underside of the cover. Silver, h. 6⅞ in. (17.4 cm.)

Inscribed "Presented by John Penn. Junr. and John Penn. Esqrs. to Mr. Gunning Bedford as a respectful acknowledgement of his services 1788"

Philip H. Hammerslough Collection, Wadsworth Atheneum, Hartford, Connecticut

Since 1681 the family of William Penn had held valuable rights to vast lands that had been granted in a charter from Charles II. The Revolution presented a threat to those rights, and as early as 1779, the cousins John Penn, Sr., and John Penn, Jr., were maneuvering to keep their hereditary property.[87] By 1787 it was clear to the Penns that they might lose everything, and they petitioned the Representatives of the newly established Commonwealth of Pennsylvania for a settlement on their lands. In February

124

104   POLITICS AND MILITARY

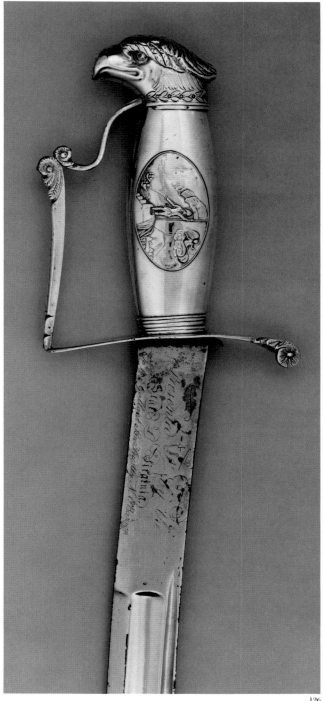

123, 124. Medal, 1792 *(cat. no. 79)*

Unknown maker. Silver, h. 6³/4 in. (17.2 cm.)

Inscribed on the front "George Washington President 1791" and on the back "E Pluribus Unum"

Buffalo and Erie County Historical Society, Buffalo, New York

125. *Portrait of Sagoyewatha (Known as Red Jacket)*, c. 1828. Charles Bird King (1785–1862). Oil on panel, 17¹/2 x 13³/4 in. (44.5 x 34.9 cm.). Albright-Knox Art Gallery, Buffalo, New York. Gift of the Seymour H. Knox Foundation, Inc., 1970

The practice of presenting silver medals to the Indians had its origins in the European tradition of presenting medals to negotiators of treaties and visitors of distinction. After the Revolution, the presentation of medals became an important part of the government's American Indian policy. When the tribes shifted their allegiance from the English to the Americans, they often exchanged their English medals for new American ones.[89] The first examples were made in New York in 1789, and a new, larger series was produced in 1792. That year this medal was presented by President Washington to the Seneca chief Red Jacket in Philadelphia. Red Jacket apparently valued the medal highly and wore it on all occasions; it hangs around his neck in the well-known portrait by Charles Bird King in the Albright-Knox Art Gallery, Buffalo (fig. 125).

126. Sword, c. 1810 *(cat. no. 81)*

Reuben Johnson and James Reat, Richmond, Virginia (active c. 1804–1815). Marked "Johnson & Reat". Silver, gold, l. 38³/16 in. (97 cm.)

Inscribed on the front of the blade "Presented by the State of Virginia to her gallant son Priestly [*sic*] N. O'Bannon" and on the reverse "Assault & conquest of the City of Derna in Africa April 27, 1805"

On loan from the United States Navy Marine Corps Museum, Washington, D.C.

In 1805 the United States retaliated against piratical raids on American shipping by vessels of the dey of Tripoli. Among the sites chosen for attack was the city of Derna, located in present-day Libya, between Tobruk and Bengazi. First Lieutenant Presly O'Bannon of the U.S. Marine Corps led a mixed army of Arabs and mercenaries overland to Derna.[90] A heroic and successful charge ensued, and reputedly O'Bannon raised the American flag over the conquered fortress. The success of the American forces in the Tripolitan wars generated a flurry of presentation swords in the 1820s. This presentation is unusual, however, in being close in date to the event and coming from a state rather than from Congress.[91] With its eagle-headed pommel, it represents a type usually made in Philadelphia.

127. Tea service, 1799 *(cat. no. 80)*

Paul Revere, Jr. (1735–1818), Boston. Marked "REVERE" on the bottom inside and twice on the bottom outside. Silver, h. of teapot 7¼ in. (18.4 cm.)

Inscribed on the teapot, pourer's side, "EH" and on the other side "To Edmund Hartt, Constructor of the Frigate Boston, presented by a number of his fellow citizens as a memorial of their sense of his ability, zeal & fidelity in the completion of that ornament of the American Navy, 1799"

Museum of Fine Arts, Boston, Gift of James Longley

Recognizing the need for an established navy, in 1794 President Washington ordered Secretary of War Henry Knox to arrange for the design and construction of new vessels. One of those vessels, the later-legendary *Constitution*, was built in the Boston shipyard of Edmund and Edward Hartt. In 1798 the rising threat of trouble with France made the need for ships urgent once again. The mer-

chants whose ships were under attack were the chief sufferers, and Congress devised a clever scheme to subsidize the construction of new vessels to defend the American merchant-marine fleet. An act of 30 June 1798 provided that ships built by public subscription would be accepted by the navy.[92] The citizens of Boston rallied to the cause and raised funds to build a new frigate. *Boston*, the third American naval ship to bear that name, had twenty-eight guns and was designed by Edmund Hartt and built in the Hartt shipyard. Paul Revere, by then also involved in the copper business, provided copper sheathing for *Boston*'s hull.[93] A group of grateful Bostonians commissioned Revere to execute this teapot, cream pitcher, and sugar bowl for Hartt. The frigate was launched on 20 May 1799 and during the ensuing year conducted a successful tour of the West Indies. In 1801 she carried Robert Livingston to France, where he served as ambassador, and went on to the Mediterranean to defend American shipping against the Tripolitan pirates. In 1802 she returned to Washington, D.C., badly damaged from action off Tripoli. She never sailed again, and her hulk was burned in 1814 to preclude capture by the British.

128

128. Cooler, 1813–14 *(cat. no. 82)*

Jesse Churchill and Daniel Treadwell, Boston (active 1805–1814). Marked "CHURCHILL & TREADWELL" on the base and on the bottom of the inner basket. Silver, h. 9 in. (22.9 cm.)

Inscribed "Sepr. 10th, 1813, signalized our first triumph in squadron, a very superior British force on Lake Erie, was entirely subdued by Com. O.H. Perry, whose gallantry in action is equalled only by his humanity in victory" and "Presented in honour of the victor, by the citizens of Boston"

Mead Art Museum, Amherst College, Amherst, Massachusetts, Bequest of Herbert L. Pratt, '95

On 29 September 1813, Boston was greeted with the banner head-line, "Great Naval Victory On Lake Erie, Federalists 'Won't Give Up the Ship'—Most Glorious Achievement." The body of the article relates that the victory cheered the hearts of every American and that Commodore Perry "wears the first garland which the history of our nation will claim."[94] The same paper carried a notice that those citizens desirous of presenting to Perry either a sword or some other appropriate token of respect should meet at the Hall of the Exchange Coffee House. Bostonians met and appointed John Coffin Jones as chairman of the committee to pursue the presentation. On 6 October 1813 the committee reported that an elegant sword accompanied by a piece or pieces of plate suitably engraved and inscribed was planned. When completed, the silver, which was presented to Perry in Newport, Rhode Island, on 17 May 1814, was minutely described in the Boston press and characterized as of the most elegant order. Included were "Two *Ice Pails* or decanter *Coolers* barrel shape and hooped 'round."[95]

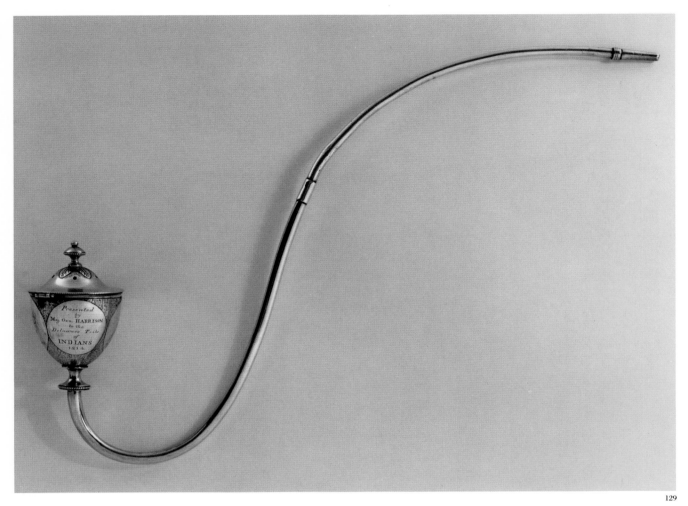

129. Peace pipe, 1814 *(cat. no. 83)*

Unknown maker. Silver, l. 21 in. (53.3 cm.)

Inscribed "Presented by Maj. Gen. Harrison to the Delaware Tribe of Indians 1814" and "peace and friendship".

National Museum of Natural History, Smithsonian Institution, Washington, D.C.

During the War of 1812, unsettled relations with the Indians along America's northern and western frontiers underscored the importance of the government's program of presenting silver gifts. On 1 July 1814, a presidential commission signed a treaty with the northwest Indian tribes at Greenville, Ohio. One of the commissioners was General William Henry Harrison. On 8 July Harrison presented the Wyandot, Seneca, Delaware, and Shawnee chiefs each with a large silver pipe engraved with symbols of protection and peace: clasped hands and a depiction of Harrison shaking hands with a pipe-holding chief. The purpose of the gift was both an acknowledgment of past support and an expression of hope for support in the future. The gesture was apparently successful as the Wyandot chief immediately turned over his English medals.[96]

130. Box, c. 1814 *(cat. no. 84)*

Retailed by Stolenwerck and Brothers (active 1803–1818), New York City. Unidentified French marks. Gold, l. 3¼ in. (8.3 cm.)

Inscribed "The Corporation of the City of New York to Major General Jacob Brown in testimony of the high sense they entertain of his valour & skill in defeating the British forces superior in number, at the battles of Chippawa and Bridgewater on the 5 and 25 of July 1814"

National Museum of American History, Smithsonian Institution, Washington, D.C., Gift of Mrs. Susan Brown Chase

In the spring of 1814 it became vital for the U.S. army to defeat the British on the Canadian front before the enemy could transfer troops from Europe following the defeat of France in March. Major General Jacob Brown was appointed commander on that front. He

constructed a bridge over the Chippewa River and on 5 July attacked the main British force, which had retreated for safety across the river. The battle was a success for Brown's forces and the British battery was captured. The victory was notable on two counts: it marked the first time that well-drilled American regulars, as opposed to militia, engaged and defeated the British, and it was, as Brown wrote to Secretary of War John Armstrong, the first victory gained in face-to-face combat on a plain.[97] Brown's important victory captured the imagination of the American public and soon along with Lake Erie and New Orleans became a legendary subject of toasts. Minutes of the New York Common Council for 10 October 1814 record a resolution that "the freedom of the City be presented in a gold box to General Jacob Brown." A 9 January 1815 entry records a payment of $265 to "Stolenwerck and Brothers gold box Gen'l Brown." The box was presented in Common Council 28 January 1815.[98] The marks on the box, currently unidentified, are not those of Stolenwerck. Stylistically, the piece is closer to French examples, suggesting that Stolenwerck may have been simply the retailer.

131. Tureen, 1817 *(cat. no. 86)*

Andrew Ellicott Warner (1786–1870), Baltimore. Marked on the bottom in a rectangle "ANDW E WARNER BALT"; Baltimore assay marks for 1817 on the bottom. Silver, h. 12 in. (30.5 cm.)

Inscribed "The citizens of Baltimore to Commodore Stephen Decatur, Rebus gestis insigni: Ob virtutes dilecto"

The Museum of Fine Arts, Houston, The Bayou Bend Collection, Museum purchase with funds provided by the Theta Charity Antique Show in honor of Betty Black Hatchett

"Tribute to Valor. We learn that a rich and tasteful service of plate of Baltimore workmanship intended for presentation by the Citizens of Baltimore to Commodore Stephen Decatur is now finished and will be exhibited for the gratification of the citizens for a few days at Mr. F. Lucas, No. 138 Market-Street."[99] These words herald the completion of the service presented on 29 September 1817 to the great naval hero Stephen Decatur. The service, for which

131

Andrew Ellicott Warner was paid $6,000, consisted of a candelabrum, two ice pails, two tureens (of which this is one), two twenty-three-inch oval dishes, two sixteen-inch oval dishes, four sauce tureens, and one vase.[100] Presentation was made by Richard Caton, Isaac McKim, and John Hoffman. This trio of prominent Baltimoreans represented the group of energetic and prosperous men who were leading Baltimore to a position of economic importance. Caton and Hoffman were prominent merchants. McKim owned a fleet of Baltimore clipper ships and was later a founder of the Baltimore and Ohio Railroad. It was logical that with civic pride they should turn to a local silversmith for the presentation service.

132. Punch bowl, tray, ladle, and cups, c. 1816 (cat. no. 85)

Thomas Fletcher and Sidney Gardiner, Philadelphia (active 1811–1825), and Andrew Ellicott Warner (1786–1870), Baltimore. Marked under the base of the punch bowl "Philada/ Fletcher & Gardiner" and engraved on top of the base of the punch bowl in script "Fletcher & Gardiner fecerunt/Philadelphia" and "A.E. Warner"; Baltimore assay marks for 1816 on the bottom of the cups; "A.E.W." and Baltimore assay marks for 1816 on the ladle. Silver, h. of bowl 15³/₁₆ in. (38.5 cm.)

Inscribed "Presented by the citizens of Baltimore to Lieut. Colonel George Armistead for his gallant and successful defense of Fort McHenry during the bombardment of a large British force, on the 12th and 13th September 1814 when upwards of 1500 shells were thrown, 400 of which fell within the area of the Fort and some of them the diameter of this vase"

National Museum of American History, Smithsonian Institution, Washington, D.C., Gift of Alexander Gordon, Jr.

In the fall of 1814, the defense of Fort McHenry in Baltimore's harbor and the gallantry of Colonel George Armistead, fort commander, captured the hearts and minds of all Baltimoreans.[101] Although greatly outnumbered by the besieging enemy force and heavily bombarded, as the inscription on this punch bowl indicates, Armistead carefully husbanded his cannonballs, occasionally firing to keep the enemy at bay, though he knew that his powder magazines were not bombproof. His bravery and subsequent victory spared the city of Baltimore from bombardment by the British naval forces. The anniversary of the victory became a local holiday, the mayor and city council asked Armistead to sit for his portrait in 1816, and at his untimely death, in 1818, the commander was buried with enormous ceremony. "The proces-

133

sion," the press reported, "was the largest ever witnessed in this city on a similar occasion."[102] The respect felt for Armistead by the people of Baltimore and their gratitude for his achievement are reflected in the design chosen for this unique example of presentation silver. Not only is the inscription unusually detailed, the design of the bowl is emblematic of the circumstances of the defense. The globular cannonball design is without parallel in punch bowls. The fact that the beakers were produced by Warner and not Fletcher and Gardiner is another unusual aspect of this service.[103] The unmarked tray may be a later addition.

133. Medal, 1824 *(cat. no. 88)*

Charles Pryse (active Baltimore 1824, Washington, D.C., 1834). Engraved by John Sands (active Baltimore 1824–1827). Marked on the reverse "October/1824/C. Pryce Fecit/J. Sands Sc." Gold, h. 3³/₃₂ in. (7.9 cm.)

Inscribed on the front "America our gratitude, October 19th 1781" and on the back "Presented to Genl Lafayette by A. Denmead, W. Smith, J. W. Miller, W. H. Miller, M. H. Kenna, G. Dunan, J. A. Roche, F. B. Booth, E. Duffy, J. P. Redding, O. C. Osborne, R. E. France, A. W. Barnes, W. S. Branson in behalf of the young men of Baltimore. October 1824"

Courtesy of the Museum of Early Southern Decorative Arts, Winston-Salem, North Carolina

At the invitation of President Monroe, the marquis de Lafayette made a triumphant and sentimental visit to America in 1824–25. One of the scenes of his glory nearly half a century earlier was Baltimore, where during 1781 he had charmed the local ladies into sewing uniforms for his troops. In anticipation of Lafayette's October 1824 visit to Baltimore, a notice appeared in the local press on 21 September, advising young men from seventeen to twenty-one years of age of a meeting to make arrangements for presenting a medal to the distinguished guest.[104] The medal was completed in a relatively short time, for on 9 October, the day of Lafayette's arrival, a notice in the same newspaper related that it was on view at the shop of Samuel Kirk. In his welcoming address, the chairman of the Lafayette Committee spoke of those present who had served with the marquis and then described the new generation who were eager to honor the hero. During the festivities a special pavilion was erected at Light and Baltimore streets. There, a group of young men in the De Kalb Cadets presented Lafayette with scrolls inscribed with their sentiments of gratitude.[105] Like the De Kalb Cadets, the fourteen young men whose names are engraved on the back of this medal represented the new generation. The medal may have been presented at the same ceremony. While in Baltimore Lafayette visited the local agricultural society fair and distributed to members premiums described as "the trophies of their industry and skill."[106] Pryse's cast medal is rich in iconographic references to America. The bald eagle with arrows and olive branch perches on a terrestrial globe that prominently features America. The central reserve, framed with cornucopia, was engraved by Sands with the figure of Justice, ships, and barrels suggesting the burgeoning of commerce under the just American government.

135

134. Tea and coffee service, 1818–19 *(cat. no. 87)*

Anthony Rasch (active 1807–1857), Philadelphia and New Orleans. Marked "A. RASCH" on the sugar bowl in a rectangle. Unidentified marks on the waste bowl. Silver, h. of coffeepot 11 1/8 in. (28.3 cm.)

Inscribed "In grateful remembrance of the gallantry of Captain Johnston Blakely late of the U.S. Navy who during a short cruise in the sloop of war *Wasp* in the year 1814 captured the two British sloops of war *Reindeer* and *Avon* and was afterwards lost at sea. This plate is presented to his daughter Udney Maria Blakely by the State of North Carolina"

North Carolina Museum of Art, Raleigh, Gift of Mr. and Mrs. Charles Lee Smith, Jr., in honor of Dr. Robert Lee Humber

136

134

135, 136 (opposite top, center). *United States Sloop of War WASP Sinking HM Sloop REIN-DEER and Putting Part of Her Crew on Board a Portuguese Bay*, and *The Commencement of the Action between HMS Avon and the USS Wasp. The Castilian Convoy in the Distance*, c. 1820. John Christian Schetky (1778–1874). Watercolor on paper, 15 x 19¼ in. (38.1 x 48.7 cm.). The Museum of Fine Arts, Houston, The Bayou Bend Collection, Gift of Miss Ima Hogg

The exploits of USS *Wasp* in the War of 1812 quickly became legendary. Built in Newburyport in 1813 by the shipyard of Cross and Merrill, *Wasp* was designed as a ship-sloop, a type of war vessel whose mission was to harass enemy shipping. Upon her commissioning, Johnston Blakely was assigned command. In July 1814 *Wasp* successfully captured the two British vessels *Avon* and *Reindeer* (see figs. 135, 136). Shortly thereafter she was lost with all hands. In 1818 the sentiments of the nation were expressed by Henry Brackenridge: "The return of this vessel after her brilliant cruise was for a long time fondly looked for by our country; but all hope has vanished."[107] Blakely, a native of Ireland who had emigrated to America at an early age, was a 1797 graduate of the University of North Carolina. At his death, his orphaned daughter Udney Maria became the first ward of the state of North Carolina.

Utilitarian rather than ceremonial silver was an appropriate choice for presentation to a young woman, yet the inclusion of large eagle finials and crossed anchors, which are engraved on the back of each piece, both suggest Captain Blakely's naval background and indicate that this is no ordinary tea and coffee set. This extremely stylish service, made by Rasch in Philadelphia before he moved to New Orleans in 1822, represents the acme of French-inspired silver. The swan handles of the sugar bowl recall those of Harvey Lewis's 1822 urn (fig. 94).

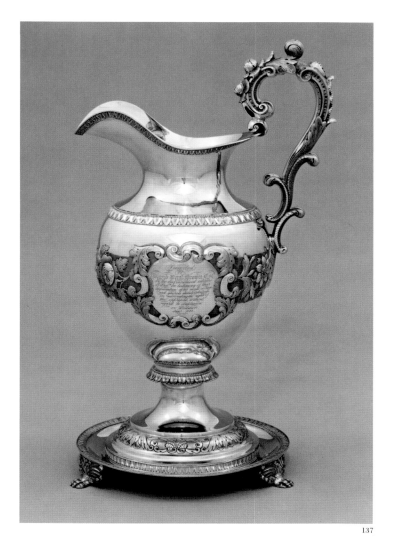

137

137, 138. Pitcher on stand, 1841 *(cat. no. 89)*

Conrad Bard and Robert Lamont, Philadelphia (active 1841–1845). Engraved by John Sartain (1808–1897). Marked "BARD & LAMONT" on the bottom of the stand. Silver, h. of pitcher 16½ in. (41.9 cm.)

Inscribed "Presented to David Paul Brown Esqr. by the disfranchised citizens of Phila. in testimony of their appreciation of his moral courage, and generous disinterestedness, in advocating the rights of the oppressed, without regard to complexion or condition Jany 1841"

The Detroit Institute of Arts, Founders Society Purchase, Beatrice Rogers Bequest Fund

David Paul Brown, a distinguished lawyer, was noted for his eloquence, particularly in support of abolition. In 1841 his efforts on behalf of the oppressed were recognized by the gift of a pair of pitchers with salvers. The presentation, which took place in Bethel Church, Philadelphia, before an audience that filled the building, was described in detail by an eyewitness:

> *Last fifth day afternoon we had the pleasure of witnessing the presentation of a pair of elegant silver pitchers to David Paul Brown by a large number of the colored people of this city, in testimony of their gratitude for his services to the cause of freedom and humanity in his many gratuitous efforts as advocate before the Councils for those whom the oppressors claimed as fugitives from the southern house of bondage. . . . On the altar stood the shining gift—the richly wrought pitchers of burnished silver, massive, of tasteful form and elegant finish. They were placed on slightly*

138

> *elevated silver stands made to correspond with them. On one side of each was an appropriate and most beautifully executed device, a slave kneeling in graceful attitude with hands clasped before the breast and face turned upwards as in supplication. This one understood was the gratuitous work of one of the finest artists in this country, the amiable and gifted I. Sartain and it is not unworthy even of his high and well deserved reputation. On the other side done also in admirable style was [the inscription].[108]*

Speeches of presentation and acceptance followed, and the ceremony closed with a prayer. John Sartain was a noted Philadelphia mezzotint engraver and magazine illustrator.

139

139. Urn, 1846 *(cat. no. 90)*

Tennessee State Museum, Nashville

William Gale and Nathaniel Hayden, New York (active 1846–1850). Retailed by Thomas Gowdey and John Peabody, Nashville, Tennessee. Marked on the rim of the base "GALE AND HAYDEN"; in a rectangle with clipped corners "G&H"; in a diamond "1846". Marked on the bottom of the bowl "GOWDEY & PEABODY" and "G&H". Silver, h. 32 in. (81.3 cm.)

Inscribed "Presented to Henry Clay, the gallant champion of the Whig cause by the Whig Ladies of Tennessee. A testimonial of their respect for his character, of their gratitude for his patriotism, and public services, and their admiration for his talents, and his high and noble bearing under all the trying circumstances of his eventful life. The historic muse will cherish, defend and perpetuate his reputation. Detur digniori"

The Whig party was founded in 1836 as part of an anti-Jackson movement. The coalition, led by Henry Clay, was interested in protecting national manufactures, establishing a national bank, and ensuring economic self-sufficiency for America. These goals were to be achieved through protective tariffs and improvements such as roads and canals to unite markets. Clay retired from the Senate in 1842 and two years later ran for president as a Whig candidate against James Knox Polk. Despite Clay's defeat, his supporters remained loyal and committees in various cities expressed their support by the presentation of lavish silver.[109] This monumental urn is rich in engraved rhetoric and in pictorial symbolism pertaining to Clay's life and political views. The portrait of Clay is based on a painting by John Neagle commissioned by the Whigs of Philadelphia.

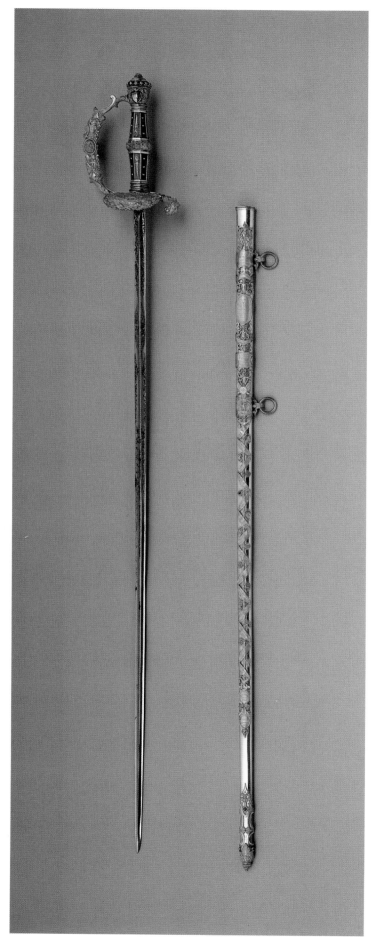

140, 141. Sword and scabbard, 1863 *(cat. no. 91)*

Designed by John Quincy Adams Ward (1830–1910), executed by Ames Manufacturing Company, Chicopee, Massachusetts (1829–1935). Marked in script on riccaso of blade "Ames Mfg. Co. Chicopee Mass." and on the reverse of the scabbard "Made by Ames Mfg. Co. Chicopee Mass." Steel, gold plate, diamonds, tortoiseshell, l. 37⁷/16 in. (95 cm.)

Inscribed on scabbard "Palo Alto, Resaca de la Palma, May 9th, 1846; Monterey, Sept. 19, 20, 21, 1846; Vera Cruz Siege, Mar. 7 to 27, 1847; Cerro Gordo, Apr. 18, 1847; San Antonio. Aug. 20, 1847; Churubusco, Aug. 20, 1847; Molino del Rey, Sept. 8 1847; Chapultepec, Sept. 13, 1847; Garita, San Cosmo, September 14, 1847; City of Mexico, September 14, 1847; Belmont, Nov. 7, 1861; Fort Henry, Feb. 6, 1862; Fort Donelson, Feb. 13, 14, 15, 16, 1862; Shiloh, Apr. 6, 7, 1862; Corinth Siege, Apr. 22 to May 30, 1862; Iuka, Sept. 19, 1862; Corinth, October 3, 4, 1862; Hatchie, Oct. 5, 1862; Tallahatchie, Dec. 1, 1862; Port Gibson, May 1, 1863; Raymond, May 12, 1863; Jackson, May 14, 1863; Champion Hill, May 16, 1863; Black River Bridge, May 17, 1863; Vicksburg, July 4, 1863; Chattanooga, Nov. 23, 24, 25, 26, 1863"

142

National Museum of American History, Smithsonian Institution, Washington, D.C., Grant-Vanderbilt Collection

This remarkable sword represents the culmination of a tradition that began in America at the end of the eighteenth century, when Congress presented swords to revolutionary-war heroes. In this superb example—a gift to General Ulysses S. Grant—the work of a leading manufacturer and the design of a prominent sculptor are combined.[110] The donors, citizens of a rural county in northwestern Illinois, expressing the sentiments of the grass-roots Northern states, spent $2,000 on their gift, a considerable sum at that time.[111]

Founded in 1829, the Ames Company became the most prolific producer of swords in America. At first, established firms such as Fletcher and Gardiner offered keen competition, but an 1834 commission from the state of South Carolina to produce presentation swords honoring War of 1812 heroes made Ames a leader in this category of production. Similar belated patriotism on the part of the states of New York and Virginia soon assured Ames's preeminence. At the end of the 1840s and into the 1850s, commissions for swords to honor veterans of the Mexican War flooded in.

Emblematic themes and allegorical figures were always an important feature of the ornament of presentation sword hilts and blades, and the Grant sword is no exception. On the grip, emblematic heads are interspersed among the panels of tortoiseshell and gold, while the guard is formed by miniature implements of war arranged in trophies. The scabbard is engraved with the names and dates of the great military engagements in which Grant saw action.

142. Sugar bowl, 1862–65 (cat. no. 92)

Tiffany and Company (1837 to the present), New York City. Designed by Edward C. Moore (active 1848–1891). Marked on the bottom "TIFFANY & CO./1000/ENGLISH STERLING/925–1000/8392/550 BROADWAY" with a Gothic "M" on each side. Silver, h. 6 in. (15.2 cm.)

Inscribed "Presented to Alban C. Stimers Ch Engr. USN to commemorate important services rendered to his country on board the *Monitor* before and during her memorable conflict with the *Merrimac*, in Hampton Roads, March 9th 1862"
The New-York Historical Society, New York City

The *Monitor* was an innovative ironclad vessel designed by the Swedish-American naval architect John Ericsson in 1862. On 9 March 1862, she engaged CSS *Virginia*, formerly USS *Merrimac*, in a historic battle off Hampton Roads, Virginia. Although the battle was inconclusive, it was important to the future of naval warfare as the first engagement between ironclads and because the gun turret was then established as standard equipment.[112] Alban Stimers was a prominent naval engineer who had served on the *Merrimac* before her capture by the Confederates. During the historic engagement, Stimers was on board the *Monitor* as an observer and actually operated the turret during the conflict.[113] The sugar bowl presented to Stimers by Ericsson is rich with nautical references. Rope borders the cartouche and the lid, a banding of anchors ornaments the body, and Neptune heads are applied to the handles. The finial includes a cannon and a Watts-type centrifugal governor.

143

144

143. Vase, 1869 *(cat. no. 93)*

Tiffany and Company (1837 to the present), New York City. Designed by Edward C. Moore (active 1848–1891). Marked on the bottom "TIFFANY & CO./2179/QUALITY/925–1000/3824/550 BROADWAY" with a Gothic "M" on each side. Silver, silver-gilt, h. 15 in. (38.1 cm.)

Inscribed "Thirty six members of the Union League Club unite in presenting this vase to Thomas Nast as a token of their admiration of his genius and of his ardent devotion of that genius to the preservation of his country from the schemes of rebellion, April 1869"

The Metropolitan Museum of Art, New York, Gift of Mrs. Thomas Nast, 1907

The Union League Club was founded in New York in 1863 by members of the Union Club who were angered and concerned that loyalty to the Union and support of abolition were not being sufficiently emphasized. They were especially outraged that Judah P. Benjamin had been allowed to resign prior to taking his post in the Confederate cabinet, rather than being expelled. In April 1869, Tiffany advertised that they made presentation-silver articles "from original and fresh designs."[114] This vase, with gilded and matte silver surfaces, is richly ornamented with cast emblems. At the shoulder, two putti wield charcoal-holders, emblems of Thomas Nast's trade as a political cartoonist. They fend off fanciful batlike creatures, just as Nast with his political drawings defended the Union.

144. Beaker, 1778 *(cat. no. 94)*

Daniel Christian Fueter (1754–1779), New York City. Marked "DCF" in an oval and "N: YORK" in a shaped rectangle. Silver, h. 3³/₁₆ in. (8.1 cm.)

Inscribed "This gift is to my son R. . . . Samuel by his father Saml Samuel N. York, 14 March 1778" and "I wish they were all hang'd in a rope, the Pretender Devil and the Pope, three mortal enemies remember the Devil Pope and the Pretender, most wicked damnable and evil the Pope Pretender and the Devil"

Courtesy, The Henry Francis du Pont Winterthur Museum, Winterthur, Delaware

This small beaker is distinguished by its elaborate engraved ornament. A nearly identical beaker made in St.-Malo, France, in 1707–8 and engraved about 1750 in New York City with exactly the same scenes and words may have served as the prototype for this example.[115] The pictures and inscriptions express fervent anti-Jacobite and anti-Roman Catholic opinions. It is not surprising that they were felt in staunchly Protestant New York. The initials of the original owner, "IDM," are engraved on the bottom. While the identities of Mr. Samuel and his son are not known, there is every reason to suspect that the father was responsible for the engraving recording his gift. The beaker may have been intended to serve as a reminder from an old man to a young one.

145. Urn, 1802 *(cat. no. 95)*

Robert Evans (1768–1812), Boston. Marked "EVANS" in a rectangle at the edge of the foot. Silver, h. 6¹/₄ in. (15.9 cm.)

Inscribed "In memory of Miss Abigail Cazneau, died December 8th, 1802, and now o'erpast the awful bound, thou pilgrim sweet! with blessing crown'd, enjoyest virtues doom" and on the opposite side "Born July 27, 1769"

Museum of Fine Arts, Boston, Gift of George Blaney, Alice B. Holmes, and Marguerite B. MacLean in memory of Hannah Cazneau Blaney

The theme of mourning is widespread in the American decorative arts following the Revolution, but personal mourning is most commonly expressed in schoolgirl embroideries, in which the urn is frequently a major motif. No other silver urn like this one seems to have survived. However, the inscription and the sentiments expressed are similar to those commonly found in embroideries. Abigail Cazneau was a member of a Boston family of Huguenot extraction who became loyalists.[116]

145

Inscribed "Presented to the Revd. Joseph McKean by a number of his friends late parishioners of Milton as a testimonial of their affection and to hold in remembrance how deeply they regret his separation from them. 1804"

Courtesy, The Henry Francis du Pont Winterthur Museum, Winterthur, Delaware

Joseph McKean graduated from Harvard in 1794 and pursued a career as a teacher until he completed his theological studies at the Berwick, Massachusetts, Academy in 1797. That same year he was ordained the fourth minister of the First Congregational Church in Milton. In 1804, suffering from ill health, McKean traveled southward to Charleston and Savannah. Apparently his health was not improved by the change of scene and rest, and, having returned to Milton, he formally requested relief from his duties as pastor on October 4.[117] The diary of the Reverend William Bentley of Salem suggests that there was more to the departure than ill health, noting that McKean was an excellent man but somewhat uncomplying in his temper, and that he left his charge in Milton after some controversy.[118] McKean went to the West Indies to recover, and in 1808 he was appointed professor of oratory at Harvard. In form, Revere's pitcher is based on contemporary Liverpool earthenware models.

147. Pitcher, 1815 *(cat. no. 97)*

Thomas Fletcher and Sidney Gardiner, Philadelphia (active 1811–1825). Marked "PHILADA" and "F&G" in rectangles on the base. Silver, h. 13³/4 in. (34.9 cm.)

Inscribed "Lady Houstoun presents this pitcher to Colonel Johnston with her grateful thanks for his attention in settling the estates of Sir Patrick and Sir George Houstoun"

The Museum of Fine Arts, Houston, The Bayou Bend Collection, Gift of Mrs. James P. Houstoun, Jr. in memory of Mr. James P. Houstoun, Jr.

Patrick and George Houstoun were sons of Sir Patrick Houstoun, the fifth baronet, who had come to Georgia with General James Oglethorpe. During the Revolution the State of Georgia confiscated the lands of both brothers, who were loyalists, and revoked their citizenship. In 1782 George and Patrick, who had in 1762 succeeded his father as the sixth baronet, were petitioning for the restoration of their property and rights.[119] Patrick, who died childless in exile in England, was succeeded in 1785 by George as the seventh (and last) baronet. Although Sir George died in 1795, the vast size of his estate and the confusing claims stemming from the revolutionary-war confiscations delayed the settling of both estates for many years. Ann Moodie, Lady Houstoun, the widow of Sir George, was left with the task of executing the wills. She found support in the person of James Johnston, Jr., a lawyer who was married to her daughter, Ann Marion Houstoun. Desiring to give Johnston some token of her thanks for his services, Lady Houstoun looked beyond Savannah for an appropriate piece of plate. As there were strong patterns of trade between Savannah and Philadelphia, it was natural that she should turn to Fletcher and Gardiner, who had only moved to Philadelphia in 1812 but were well on their way toward establishing a national reputation as the designers and makers of the finest and most up-to-date presentation silver. While more modest than the great urns being produced for the War of 1812 heroes, Lady Houstoun's pitcher, for which she was billed by the silversmiths on 15 November 1815, is in the most current French-inspired taste.

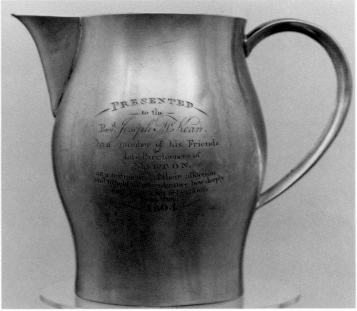

146

146. Pitcher, 1804 *(cat. no. 96)*

Paul Revere, Jr. (1735–1818), Boston. Marked "REVERE" in a rectangle on the bottom. Silver, h. 6¹/2 in. (16.5 cm.)

148

148. Inkstand, 1815 *(cat. no. 98)*

Harvey Lewis (active 1811–1825), Philadelphia. Marked "H. LEWIS" in a serrated rectangle twice on the bottom. Silver, h. 3⁷/₁₆ in. (8.7 cm.)

Inscribed "In evidence of the cherished love and esteem of Elizth Powel for her favorite Sophia H. Olis"

Yale University Art Gallery, New Haven, Connecticut, Mabel Brady Garvan Collection

Elizabeth Willing Powel (1742–1830) the wife of the prominent merchant and mayor of Philadelphia Samuel Powel, became Federal Philadelphia's grande dame. Although childless, Madame Powel, as she was known, was a generous benefactress to young friends and family. This extraordinary inkstand represents French-influenced Philadelphia silver at its very best. It is sad that nothing is known about Elizabeth Powel's favorite, but to date Sophia Olis's identity has remained elusive. The unusual surname does not appear anywhere in Philadelphia records, suggesting that Sophia lived elsewhere. Elizabeth Powel's fondness for gifts of silver, evident from this and other surviving examples, is clearly indicated in a letter she wrote on 4 July 1812: "My dear Young Friend, as it is the anniversary of our Independence it cannot be ill timed to test your patriotism by begging your acceptance of a silver asparagus tongs."[120]

149. Tea set, 1817 *(cat. no. 99)*

Thomas Fletcher and Sidney Gardiner, Philadelphia (active 1811–1825). Marked outside the bottom of the teapot "PHILA."; outside the bottom of the sugar bowl "Fletcher & Gardiner, Phila."; and outside the bottom of the creamer "Fletcher & Gardiner". Silver, h. of teapot 9¹/₄ in. (23.5 cm.)

Inscribed on all pieces "From the family of George Gibbs to Walter Channing, 1817"

Charles V. Swain

The Rhode Island Gibbs and Channing families were related both by blood ties and by business associations. The Newport shipping firm of Gibbs and Channing was formed by George Gibbs II (1735–1803) and his brother-in-law Walter Channing (1759–1827). Although they began originally as flour merchants, their business expanded into shipping in the West Indian trade. Walter Channing, having led the firm by himself following the death of Gibbs in 1803, retired and moved to Boston in 1815.[121] The firm had connections in Philadelphia. That fact and the renown of Fletcher and Gardiner may explain why the Gibbs family looked southward for the silver they presented to Walter Channing upon his retirement.

149

150, 151. Tea caddy, 1817 *(cat. no. 100)*

Philip Garrett (1780–1851), Philadelphia. Marked in a rectangle twice on the bottom "P. GARRETT". Silver, h. 3⁷/₁₆ in. (8.7 cm.)

Inscribed "A bridal gift from Elizth Powel to Abigl Griffitts, March 1817"

Yale University Art Gallery, New Haven, Connecticut, Mabel Brady Garvan Collection

Abigail Griffitts was the daughter of Mary and Samuel Powel Griffitts, a prominent Philadelphia physician. Abigail's brother was a founding member of the United Bowmen (see pages 99–100). The bride's grandmother, Abigail Powel Griffitts, was a sister of Samuel Powel and the sister-in-law of the donor of this wedding present. The Griffitts family were Quakers, and the records of the Philadelphia Monthly Meeting note that Abigail Griffitts married Michael Waln Wells at the Mulberry Street Meeting House on 3 April 1817. From the inscription, we conclude that the tea caddy was a bridal gift and that it was presented the month before the wedding. Stylistically this tea caddy, with its boat-shaped form, reeded handle, and bright-cut engraving, would seem to date at least two decades earlier than 1817.

152. Cake basket, c. 1823 *(cat. no. 101)*

Harvey Lewis (active 1811–1825), Philadelphia. Marked twice on the bottom. "HARVEY LEWIS". Silver, w. 15³/₈ in . (39.1 cm.)

Inscribed "A bridal gift, from Elizabeth Powel to her beloved great niece Anne Francis with sincere wishes that each succeeding year of her union, may add to her happiness"

Private collection

Anne Francis was the granddaughter of Elizabeth Powel's sister Ann Shippen Willing Francis, and daughter of Elizabeth's cousins Thomas Willing Francis and Dorothy Willing Francis. Anne was therefore related to the donor of this cake basket through both her parents. The gift celebrates Anne's marriage to James Ashton Bayard on 8 July 1823. Bayard, a prominent Delaware Federalist, had served as one of the commissioners to Ghent, where a peace treaty had been signed between Great Britain and the United States in 1814. The cake basket was a relatively new form, and this example by Lewis is extremely stylish and rich in cast ornament. Lewis was apparently a favorite silversmith of the generous Elizabeth Powel. In addition to the inkstand she presented to Sophia Olis some years before (fig. 148), she purchased other items by Lewis, which are listed in an inventory of 1830.[122]

153. Pair of goblets, 1824 *(cat. no. 102)*

Samuel Kirk (1793–1872) Baltimore. Marked once on each goblet "KIRK"; Baltimore assay mark for 1824 once on one goblet and twice on the other goblet. Silver, h. 5³/₈ in. (13.7 cm.)

Inscribed "Presented to David Williamson by Genl. La Fayette 1824" on the side of each goblet

The Maryland Historical Society, Baltimore

152

When the marquis de Lafayette was on his triumphal visit to America in 1824–25, he was widely feted and many times presented with silver in recognition of his valor and as tribute to the affection with which he was regarded in the United States. A gold medal (fig. 133) presented to him by the young men of Baltimore in October 1824 was exhibited in the shop of Samuel Kirk prior to the hero's arrival. Lafayette continued his progress southward, but by the year's end he was in Washington. There on 1 January 1825, he was entertained at David Williamson's hotel at "a sumptuous and elegant dinner prepared in Mr. Williamson's best style."[123] These cups, possibly ordered by Lafayette while he was in Baltimore, represent the French nobleman in a new role: the popular recipient of so many trophies as the donor of a handsome piece of presentation silver. Although Williamson has been elsewhere identified as a prominent Baltimorean, his name does not appear in the city directories. It seems logical, therefore, to identify him with the well-known Washington hotelier.

154. Urn, c. 1831 *(cat. no. 103)*

Henry Harland (1789–1841), New Orleans. Marked "HARLAND" in a scroll with a star in a circle and "D" in a rectangle at each end. Silver, h. 9^{15}/$_{16}$ in . (25.2 cm.)

Inscribed on one side of the bowl over a device of the craftsman's insignia "To H M Dobbs president of the New-Orleans

153

Mechanic Society" and on the other side of the bowl "Presented by the members in testimony of respect for 25 years faithful service Jany 22d 1831"

Yale University Art Gallery, New Haven, Connecticut, Mabel Brady Garvan Collection

Henry M. Dobbs, Sr., by trade a watchmaker, founded the New Orleans Mechanic Society in 1806. The purpose of this tradesmen's organization was "to relieve the wants, comfort the sufferings and promote the happiness of our fellow creatures." Henry Dobbs served as president of the society from its establishment until his retirement a quarter of a century later. Henry Harland was the tenth tradesman to take a membership in the Society.[124] Harland's urn, which makes clear references both to antique vases and to the contemporary silver presented to national heroes, has a monumentality that belies its relatively small size. Its diminutiveness would preclude its use as a wine cooler, underscoring the ceremonial intent of the presentation piece.

155. Pitcher and goblet, c. 1845 *(cat. no. 105)*

Zalmon Bostwick (active 1845–1852), New York. Marked "Z Bostwick" and "NEW YORK" twice on the pitcher. Silver, h. of pitcher 11 in. (27.5 cm.)

Inscribed on the pitcher "John W. Livingston to Joseph Sampson 1845" and on the goblet "J.W.L. to J.S. 1845"

Virginia Carroll Crawford Collection, High Museum of Art, Atlanta

Zalmon Bostwick advertised that he made silver in the best style.[125] In this example, he has translated into metal the interpretation of Gothic frequently found in contemporary English Staffordshire pitchers. While the Gothic style was chosen with some frequency for furniture—especially that purchased for libraries—it is relatively uncommon in American silver, rare, even, in nonliturgical silver. John W. Livingston was a distinguished naval officer. Joseph Sampson, his son-in-law, was a New York City auctioneer. The choice of the Gothic style may have had a particular significance—unfortunately forgotten today—for the donor, the recipient, or for both of them. The matching pitcher and goblet are in the collection of the Brooklyn Museum.

156. Urn, 1835 *(cat. no. 104)*

Colin van Gelder Forbes and John W. Forbes, New York City (active 1808–1838). Marked "FORBES & SON" in a rectangle twice on the outer rim of the base. Silver, h. 20 in. (50.6 cm.)

The collection of Gerard L. Eastman, Jr., on loan to the Museum of the City of New York

Although by trade a grocer, John De Grauw was deeply involved in the activities of New York's volunteer fire companies. By his own description he was born a fireman, having a father, two uncles, and three brothers who were also members of Engine Company

156

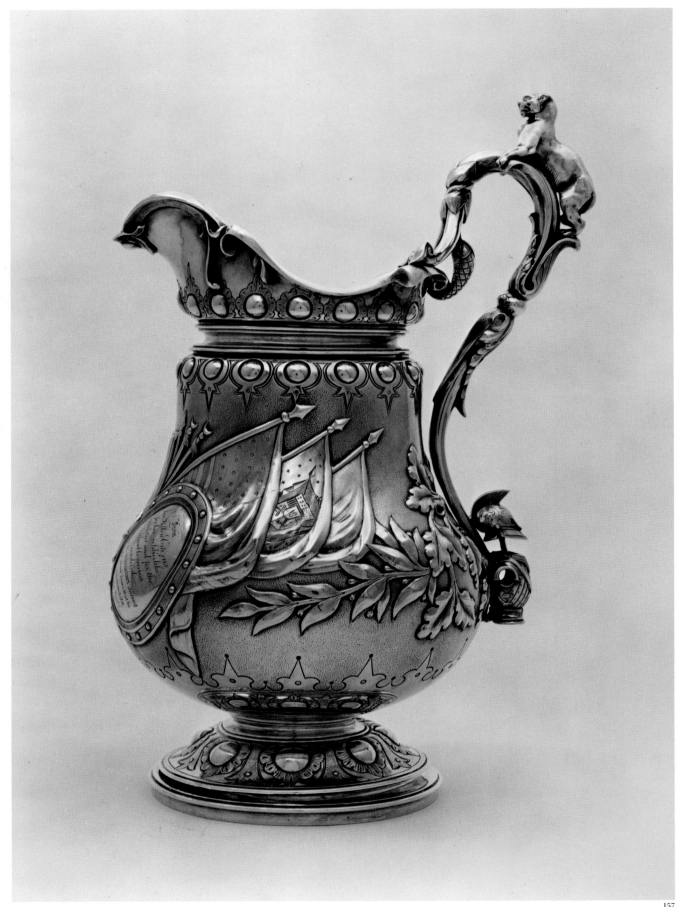

157

RITES OF PASSAGE AND FRIENDSHIP

158

Number 16.[126] De Grauw was a member of the company for twenty-one years and served as its foreman. To be a fireman, De Grauw in his later years observed, "one must have a love for arduous duty . . . and the pleasantest thing about being a fireman was to have a big fire and to go to work and put it out." After the great New York City fire of 1835, De Grauw organized two new hose companies and raised $1,700 to purchase apparatus for them. For many years he served as chairman of the board of trustees of the New York Fire Department and was presented with this Rococo-revival urn upon his retirement from that post. In the center of the repoussé scene is a standing man, presumably De Grauw, receiving a scroll from a seated allegorical figure, possibly the personification of New York.

157. Pitcher, 1859 *(cat. no. 106)*

Tiffany and Company (1837 to the present), New York City. Designed by Edward C. Moore (active 1848–1891). Marked on the base "Tiffany & Co./1004/English Sterling/925–1000/6248/550 Broadway" with a Gothic "M" on each side. Silver, h. 14-3/4 in. (37.5 cm.)

Inscribed "To Col. A. Duryee this testimonial is presented on his retireing from the Colonelcy of the Seventh Regiment National Guard as a mark of high appreciation from his fellow citizens for his soldierlike qualities and for the valuable services rendered by the Regiment during the eleven years that he commanded it. New York. 1859"

Museum of the City of New York, Bequest of Emily Frances Whitney Biggs

Colonel A. Duryee (1815–1890) was a New York merchant who made a fortune in the importation and sale of mahogany. His retirement from his volunteer post as a colonel in the National Guard was recognized by the presentation of a pair of pitchers and four goblets in December 1859.[127] While the pitcher and goblet or pair of pitchers and goblets were among the most common forms of presentation silver by the middle of the nineteenth century, this example varies from the norm, with its rich military iconography of banners, shields, and elaborate cast trophy at the base of the handle. These details suggest that the gift was specially designed by Moore for this specific presentation.

158. Tea service, 1861 *(cat. no. 108)*

Gorham Manufacturing Company (1831 to the present), Providence, Rhode Island. Marked with a lion passant, anchor, and Gothic "G". Silver, h. of urn 18 in. (45.7 cm.)

National Museum of American History, Smithsonian Institution, Washington, D.C.

After Abraham and Mary Todd Lincoln entered the White House in 1861, Congress appropriated $20,000 to renovate the executive mansion. Mrs. Lincoln immediately embarked on a lavish refurnishing campaign to make the president's house up-to-date and presentable. She took frequent trips to Philadelphia and New York, and her purchases, which far exceeded the budget, did not sit well with a nation on the verge of a war. She was sharply criticized by the press. It was perhaps to avert such criticism that Mrs. Lincoln described this large tea service as "a gift from New York

friends." It has been so characterized ever since, even though it has no presentation inscription or any other indication that it was a gift. In all likelihood, the First Lady purchased the service herself from Haughwout and Company, a New York retailer, from whom she also purchased a set of Haviland china embellished with the presidential seal.[128] It is possible that Mrs. Lincoln conceived the idea of calling the service a gift after a covered pitcher was presented to her husband on 4 March 1861 by his Washington friends.[129] After Lincoln's assassination, Mrs. Lincoln's behavior became increasingly eccentric, and in 1875 her son Robert Todd Lincoln was forced to send her to a private sanitarium in Batavia, Illinois. Upon her release the following year, Mrs. Lincoln wrote an angry and demanding letter to her hapless son, outlining the household goods and personal possessions he was to forward to her immediately. Among the items listed was "my silver set with large silver waiter presented to me by New York friends."[130] Mrs. Lincoln's seven-piece tea and coffee service is typical of the multiple specialized forms made for the tea ceremony at the middle of the last century. While clearly special to Mrs. Lincoln, the service was not a special order but rather a collection of stock items personalized with her initials and family coat of arms.

160

161

159–61. Urn, 1859 *(cat. no. 107)*

Gorham Manufacturing Company (1831 to the present), Providence, Rhode Island. Marked with a lion passant, anchor, "G", "sterling" and "Canfield Bro. & Co" stamped on bottom of the body. Silver, h. 19 1/2 in. (49.5 cm.)

Inscribed "Presented by the Officers & employees of the B.&O. R.R. Co. to Wendel Bollman late master of Road as a testimonial of their regard & esteem 1859"

The Maryland Historical Society, Baltimore, Gift of Miss Hermes Bollman

In 1829 Wendel Bollman, trained as a carpenter, took a job with the Baltimore and Ohio Railroad building permanent track near the Mount Clare Terminus at Baltimore. He eventually became an outstanding engineer and bridge builder. This urn is part of a service given him as a retirement present. In 1827 the Baltimore and Ohio Railroad was founded as a westward link by a group of Baltimore merchants who were responding to the commercial threat of New York's Erie Canal. By 1830 it had become the first railroad in America to generate revenue. Bollman's career paralleled the westward growth of the railroad. His particular genius lay in the design and construction of bridges, at first of wood and later of cast iron, utilizing a truss system designed by him and bearing his name.[131] Bollman's innovative bridge at Harpers Ferry, West Virginia, is depicted in the engraved scene on the front of this presentation urn rich in railroad iconography and detail. It was ordered from the Baltimore jewelers Ira and William Canfield, who sent the order on to Gorham in Providence.[132]

162

162. Butter dish, 1870 *(cat. no. 109)*

C. H. Zimmerman (active 1866–1870), New Orleans. Marked on the bottom of the bowl "C. H. ZIMMERMAN" and with a crescent moon with incised face above "NEW ORLEANS". Silver, h. 4 3/4 in. (12.1 cm.)

Inscribed "Helen Dec. 1st, 1870 from TLB"

Anglo-American Art Museum, Louisiana State University, Baton Rouge, Gift of the Friends of the Museum

In the second half of the nineteenth century, as silver became more readily available, an enormous variety of small items were presented from one individual to another to commemorate birthdays, anniversaries, holidays, and other occasions, as well as to honor friendship. This butter dish is not typical of the forms that were usually chosen for such gifts, which ranged from flatware to small cups of every description. The classical medallions in the Renaissance-revival style recall the portraits on Cyrus West Fields's service (fig. 106), and the cast recumbent figure on top recalls finials on English ceramic butter dishes of the eighteenth century.

FROM THE GILDED AGE TO MODERN DESIGN

KATHERINE S. HOWE

When the United States celebrated its centennial in Philadelphia in 1876, it celebrated not only its one hundredth birthday but also a milestone in its development. The country had entered the ranks of self-supporting industrial nations. Rich in natural resources, innovative, growing, and aggressive, it was embarking upon almost fifty years of domestic peace and prosperity. Its railroads, mills, mines, factories, ships, and inventions funded a wealthy new elite who were America's first conspicuous consumers, the ideal clientele for presentation silver and gold. The years 1876 to 1910 were truly the golden years of American presentation silver. Silver and gold objects continued to be familial gifts of love and continued to honor heroic deeds and to mark rites of passage, but they also took on a different dimension, one of conscious display—and the bigger the better.

It was during these years, in 1899 to be exact, that Thorstein Veblen, a widely read turn-of-the-century economist, published *The Theory of the Leisure Class*, a wordy treatise relating the role of conspicuous consumption (a term that he used) to the upper classes. His observations help put presentation silver of this period in context. Veblen wrote that "wealth confers honour" upon its owner, and that as men moved away from their roles as predators, accumulated property replaced hunters' trophies as measures of their success and prowess. The more wealth one had and the more one displayed it, he argued, the more successful one was in society. Indeed, Veblen decided that conspicuous consumption and the desire to emulate those more successful than ourselves were the driving forces of a property-owning society.[1]

Even religion, according to Veblen, practiced a form of conspicuous consumption: "devout consumption," as he called it. He believed that extravagant buildings and gifts to houses of worship provided the donor with a tangible link with God. As an added benefit, since God could not make personal use of the gifts, the worshiper had the pleasure of using them for Him.[2] Just as the three Wise Men offered gold to the infant Jesus, citizens of Boston, Chicago, and countless other nineteenth- and twentieth-century communities also made offerings of gold and silver to their houses of worship. The practice continues today, although on a less ostentatious scale.

Silver and gold presentation objects are uniquely compatible with Veblen's interpretation of wealth. These universally valuable metals can be shaped and molded into glittering, monumental, symbolic objects which can be (and were) presented to recipients with all the extravagant pomp and ceremony that a group could muster. Presentation ceremonies played a key role in turn-of-the-century American society. During presentations, donors, especially committees and communities, paid homage to the recipient, while the recipient, confident in his elevated status, assumed his role with a studied sense of noblesse oblige. Admiral George Dewey, fresh from his 1898 victory at the battle of Manila Bay, was a master of this role. In addition to the monumental Dewey Loving Cup (figs. 164, 205), made from more than seventy thousand melted dimes, Dewey also received a house in Washington, D.C., purchased with contributions to the Dewey Home Fund; a 22-carat-gold Tiffany and Company sword presented to him by President William McKinley; an 18-carat-gold vase, also by Tiffany, from the City of New York; and a seventy-piece silver tea service from the City of Chicago. Dewey, of course, had to visit each of these cities to receive these gifts as well as attend all of the parades, speeches, and banquets associated with them. Dewey's every movement was scrupulously recorded in the newspapers, as were the speeches, decorations, gifts, and banquets which were part of the pageant.[3]

Indeed, the enthusiasm surrounding Dewey's triumphant return to the United States is typical of silver presentations in the period. There seems to have been a human need on the part of donors to ritualize their relationship formally and publicly with personalized gifts made of precious metals. In other words, whether it was the loving cup Anton Seidl received from his admirers (fig. 220), President Benjamin Harrison's silver model of Boatswain's Mate Riggin (fig. 203), also made from melted dimes, or William Cullen Bryant's testimonial

163. Water jug and stand, 1879. Samuel Kirk and Son. *See pages 173–74*

164. "Vast Throng in Broadway Admiring the Journal's Dewey Loving Cup." *New York Journal*, 28 September 1899. According to the article, two thousand people per hour saw the Dewey Cup when it was displayed at the Gorham shop on Broadway at Nineteenth Street

vase (fig. 217), silver and gold were both acknowledgments of success and offerings made by lesser individuals to greater ones.

Although social factors and prosperity were important, developments in the mining industry also played a key role in the manufacture of turn-of-the-century presentation silver. In 1849 gold was discovered in California. California, Colorado, Nevada, Mexico, and Alaska all took their turns developing gold and/or silver reserves. These precious metals, especially silver, became much more accessible than in the past.

Another coincidence directly affected presentation-silver manufacture. For decades the United States had had a bimetallic standard for its currency, with sixteen ounces of silver equal to one ounce of gold. By the middle of the nineteenth century, however, the demand for silver so far exceeded its supply that producers chose to sell the metal to businesses for more than the Treasury's fixed price. As a result (and following the practice of most European governments), the United States abandoned the bimetallic standard in 1873. Without government price supports, the cost of silver plummeted. In spite of the Bland-Allison Act (1878) and the Sherman Silver Purchase Act (1890), silver's price remained low

through the end of the century.[4] Silver's reasonable price and ready availability encouraged the manufacture of some truly gargantuan objects. Little earlier silver approached them in size or opulence.

It was during these years that America's great silver manufacturers, such as Tiffany, Gorham, Whiting, and Kirk, completed the transition from silver makers to silver manufacturing companies. It was also during these years that these companies greatly expanded their markets. For example, Gorham's presentation-silver designs were frequently sold under local silver-shop names. The silver presented in 1903 to the USS *Pennsylvania* (fig. 210) was ordered from J. E. Caldwell and Company of Philadelphia, who competed against Strawbridge and Clothier; Bailey, Banks and Biddle; the International Silver Company; and Reed and Barton for the $25,000 contract. Although J. E. Caldwell took credit for its manufacture, this service was actually made by Gorham.[5] Tiffany and Gorham were the leaders in the field of magnificent turn-of-the-century presentation silver.

The vast majority of presentation-silver objects were vessels that, at least nominally, served domestic or church functions. Traditional forms such as tea sets, goblets, bowls, boxes, pitchers, and other household goods continued to be presentation-silver staples. However, silversmiths also served a large special-order clientele. Virtually anything that could be was made or copied in silver or gold, including bicycles, ship models, a Bessemer converter, a curling stone on a broomstick pedestal, and Babe Ruth's crown.[6] Clients could be quite specific about their special orders, leaving the maker little license. A 1905 letter from John Strother of Consolidation Coal Company to Gorham illustrates this point:

I am sending you to-day via U.S. Express the following articles to be used as models.

   1 Mining Pick not a clay pick as your design shows
   1 Canteen—handle shown on your design should be a cord.
   1 Shovel—note change of form from blue print.
   1 Dinner Bucket
   1 Cup
   1 Lamp
   1 Oil Flask

Please follow models as near as possible as these forms are typical of the Cumberland Coak [sic] *Field.*[7]

In spite of all the special orders and traditional objects, one form did emerge during this period as the standard presentation silver object, the loving cup. The term "loving cup" seems to have first appeared in the English language in the early 1800s with reference to large drinking vessels with two or more handles that could be passed from hand to hand. The cup's function

      GILDED AGE TO MODERN DESIGN

evokes a sense of camaraderie and well-being. Its vertical shape makes it easy to display, while its usually conservative, neoclassical form makes it acceptable to any recipient. The form is best known, of course, as a long tapering cylinder flanked by two handles and standing on a circular foot (an example is the cup presented to Captain Rostron of the RMS *Carpathia*, see fig. 185). It is clearly inspired by the Greek amphora, but probably also evolved out of the caudle cup. It sometimes takes on eccentric forms, as, for example, when antlers are substituted for silver handles. The first fully developed American presentation loving cup seems to be the three-handled repoussé prize presented to Anton Seidl in 1887 (fig. 220). It is also one of the most spectacular. It should be noted here that the term "cup" is sometimes loosely defined. The New York Yacht Club's Buck and Goelet cups are, in reality, two punch bowls, one ewer, and one model of a seventeenth-century yacht (figs. 188, 193, 190, 189).

Gorham Company records contain some revealing information regarding "love cups," as the factory initially called them. In 1881, the first year for which records are available, Gorham introduced into their product line eight loving cups, which they sold to retailers for between $19 and $100, exclusive of gilding, chasing, engraving, and etching. Their product line steadily increased, peaking in 1900 with seventy-seven new stock models; it continued strong through 1914. Gorham's loving cups cost from $2.55 for a small example introduced in 1901 to a special order fabricated in 1923 for $1,850.[8] With this wide price range, virtually any group or individual who wanted to present a silver loving cup could do so. Gorham's records also show an important shift in taste. By the end of World War I their loving-cup production had dropped dramatically, so much so that they filled only thirty-four special orders between 1920 and 1941. A new presentation category appeared in their records: trophies. Like the Borg-Warner Trophy, which is presented annually at the Indianapolis 500 automobile race (fig. 165), these objects were more obviously sculptural and specifically symbolic. The Curtiss Marine Flying Trophy (fig. 186) is an early example of this transition. It is intended exclusively for display and its form directly relates to the occasion at hand.

Except for a few notable bright spots, the years since 1929 have not been kind to presentation silver. No sooner did the United States start to recover from the Depression than it plunged into World War II. Silversmiths' ranks, already thinned in the 1930s by America's depressed economy, grew thinner still as workers went to war. Factory output was drastically reduced and raw materials were rationed.[9] Not enough American-trained master silversmiths survived these hard years and few apprentices have followed them. In short, there are fewer great craftsmen than there used to be. Because of high

165. The original presentation of the Borg-Warner Trophy (1936). Left to right: Fred Lockwood of Borg-Warner; drivers Tony Gulotta, Louis Meyer, Ted Horn, and Harry Hartz; flagman Seth Klein; and driver Wilbur Shaw. Courtesy Indianapolis Motor Speedway Corporation

labor and material costs, not to mention changing buyers' tastes, postwar silver companies have not been too daring. They cannot afford to be, nor can the majority of their clients afford the thousands of dollars in labor and materials that go into a truly great piece of silver.

There has been another subtle but important shift in presentation silver: the client has changed. Although rites of passage—births, marriages, and anniversaries—continue to be extremely important occasions for presenting silver among individuals, corporate America is the new major client, and the barons of industry no longer operate their companies as fiefdoms. Rather, corporate officers, accountable to their shareholders, are uncomfortable with ostentatious presentation silver and would just as soon present glass, steel, aluminum, brass, or granite awards as silver ones. Because these materials are not as expensive as silver, the awards can be much more monumental. As a result, postwar presentation silver tends to be smaller, more utilitarian, more conservative, and less eccentric, and it frequently imitates eighteenth-century prototypes.[10] Modern presentation silver seems to come from the jeweler's tradition in which greater emphasis is placed on unusual arrangements of sheet metal rather than on more traditional methods of raising silver through stamping, spinning, or pounding.[11] Not only is it a question of contemporary style but it is, perhaps, because many modern designs tend to come from independent silversmiths who do not have the machinery necessary for these more complex techniques. The days of magnificent chasing, engraving, and repoussé work seem past.

Nineteenth- and twentieth-century presentation occasions run the gamut from the most elevated circumstances to the questionable. Among the most touching objects, of course, are those given within families to mark special events. Certainly the gold anniversary cup (fig. 225) given to Marcus and Bertha Goldman by their children and grandchildren is among the most thoughtful and sophisticated in this genre. By giving gifts of silver, Americans celebrate anniversaries in all aspects of their lives: work, club and church affiliations, and volunteer activities. Such presentations are formal declarations of long, fruitful relationships shared by people with a common bond.

Awards for heroism are also on this same high plane. Among the most poignant in this group are the cup and medals presented to the captain and crew of the RMS *Carpathia* from the survivors of the *Titanic* disaster. Within six weeks of their rescue, led by Mrs. J. J. Brown (the Unsinkable Molly Brown), the survivors presented the specially commissioned medals in a "quiet, personal tribute by those of us who realize what it is meant to be saved." The six senior officers received gold medals, the junior officers silver ones, and the remaining crew bronze (fig. 183).[12]

Created for less altruistic reasons is presentation silver given either to enhance the status of the donor or to obligate the recipient. While such manipulations are not unique to silver, they are a recurrent and unsavory aspect. Whether it is a silver baby's rattle sent to an infant by a parent's would-be business associate, the autographed flask given by Alexander R. Shepherd to promote his mine (fig. 223), or the silver and lapis sphere (fig. 214) sent to Franklin Delano Roosevelt by the jeweler Pierre Cartier and accompanied by a request for an appointment with the president, the intent is the same.

RELIGION AND EDUCATION

Religious silver continues to be a vibrant part of our American presentation tradition, perhaps because religion seems to encourage formal, precious gifts. Unlike eighteenth-century ecclesiastical plate, which was often adapted for church use, nineteenth- and twentieth-century religious silver is usually quite specialized. Monstrances (figs. 169, 172), crosses (fig. 171), chalices, christening basins (fig. 173), menorahs, and Torah pointers are generously represented in silver. Episcopalians and Jews seem to be the two religious groups that present on a regular basis silver that is original, of

unusually high quality, and in keeping with the times.

America's Jewish community has maintained a very active presentation-silver tradition. Not only are commissions made and given to synagogues, but they are also presented to individuals. Mezuzahs, nailed to the doorposts of Jewish homes, are frequent housewarming gifts. Hanukkah lamps and spice boxes (fig. 231) are also given to individuals for services in the home. Some Jewish silversmiths, such as Ilya Schor (1904–1961), made traditional Jewish forms, continuing a tradition begun in eastern Europe generations ago; others, such as Ludwig Wolpert (1900–1981), Kurt Matzdorf, and Janet Dash (b. 1944) adapt modern forms to traditional religious objects.[13]

Other denominations also endorse presentation silver (at the end of the nineteenth century, the demand for church silver was so strong that Gorham established its own ecclesiastical department in about 1885 to provide silver, gold, and bronze fittings for the country's growing number of churches),[14] but many churches and synagogues have lost the histories of these gifts or think of them as furnishings and not as objects of historical or design significance. Indeed, postcolonial church silver is unusually difficult to locate.

Although schools and universities continue to be great repositories for presentation silver, their priorities have shifted in this century. Faculty members and scholarly accomplishments continue to be honored, but silver associated with educational institutions now centers on athletic prowess and auxiliary groups. Virtually every school has its trophy case bursting with prizes and prominently positioned in its athletic department lobby. Rarely, alas, are the newer awards made of silver; rather they are silverplate, brass, wood, or, sadly, even plastic. These lesser materials seem to diminish the importance of the victory they celebrate. There is, however, an interesting corpus of alumni silver: silver given to devoted graduates for service to their alma maters (fig. 199), gifts given by fraternal groups to fellow members when they are married (fig. 226), and even, as in the case of Yale University, a birth gift given to the first male child born to a member of the class of 1888.[15]

INDUSTRY AND PROGRESS

If the early years of the Industrial Revolution are known for inventions that revolutionized American life, the later years should be known for America's insatiable desire to be better and faster. Americans fell in love with speed. It was a love nurtured by newspaper men and industrialists who grew up on wagons and sailing ships and matured with steamboats, locomotives, automobiles, and airplanes. The industrialists built railroads, subways, automobiles, and airplanes, while the newspaper men sponsored races that challenged these machines

166. Punch bowl, 1889. Tiffany and Company. *See pages 156–57*

to go faster and faster.[16] Although people continued to celebrate agricultural excellence as they had at least since 1808,[17] Americans were preoccupied with the ability to move more people and to move them farther, faster, and in greater comfort. There was more than idle recreation at work here, for westward expansion, a growing population, and greater industrialization meant that more people and goods had to be moved over greater distances than ever before. The race was not unrewarded. The trip from New York to Chicago, which had taken several weeks in the early nineteenth century, took fourteen and one-half days by water and six and one-half days by rail in 1850.[18] Today, of course, it takes two and one-half hours by jet.

Seen within this context, the tremendous impact that rapid transportation had on America and why much of our great late-nineteenth- and twentieth-century silver is related to it is easy to understand. The Hill plaque (fig. 175), the Belmont tray (fig. 182), the vase given to the director of the Transportation Building at the 1893 World's Columbian Exposition in Chicago (fig. 179), and the Curtiss Marine Flying Trophy (fig. 186) are all part of our quest for speed. The Borg-Warner Trophy, awarded to the winner of the Indianapolis 500 automobile race, is a direct descendant of this tradition, as is the Igor I. Sikorsky International Trophy for outstanding achievement in the advancement of the helicopter art, made in 1961 by Cartier.[19]

PURSUITS OF LEISURE AND AVOCATION

More leisure time, increased incomes, and a profusion of tradition-bound universities and clubs had profound effects upon nineteenth- and twentieth-century presentation silver. Although horse racing remained a popular sport, it was equaled and occasionally eclipsed by another sport of kings—yachting. The New York Yacht Club, long known as the club that defended the London-made America's Cup,[20] has been a bastion of American yachting since it was founded in 1844. Its members were New York's old guard and merchant princes, whose many activities, including their races, were chronicled in great detail in New York newspapers. These wealthy yachtsmen owned schooners, sloops, and other large sailing craft, manned by professional crews. They raced for prizes, cash, or subscription stakes, often placing hefty bets on the side. They ordered silver prizes that were commensurate with both their incomes and their extravagant hobbies. As a result, Tiffany, Gorham, and Whiting produced some of their most original and outstanding examples of American presentation silver for them. In some races, such as the competition for the America's Cup, the same prize cup is awarded repeatedly, but for others, such as the Goelet cups for schooners and sloops (1882–97), new prizes were commissioned by Ogden Goelet and awarded annually.[21]

More leisure time also meant that more Americans had time to observe and play many different sports. Indeed, it was during the nineteenth century that our favorite team sports—baseball, basketball, and football—were born. The passionate devotion to a team, the hero worship, local pride, and zeal elicited by teams are not unlike the admiration enjoyed by the military heroes Washington, Lafayette, and Dewey in earlier centuries. In an age when actual warfare is so devastating, these athletes provide safe, spectator combat and are honored for it with symbolic prizes made of silver. The Vince Lombardi Trophy, presented annually by the National Football League to the winner of the Super Bowl

(fig. 202), is probably America's best-known symbol of team-sport prowess.

Additional time also means that men and women can enjoy at leisure the camaraderie of private clubs and pursue avocations such as volunteering for their temples, churches, colleges, and other philanthropic organizations. Beginning in the mid-nineteenth century, one sees a national proliferation of private clubs. Some, closely allied with sports such as tennis and golf, abound with presentation silver;[22] others, such as the Cliff Dwellers and Lotos clubs, follow more artistic pursuits. Invariably, clubs ended up honoring members for their loyalty or accomplishments (figs. 201, 217, 227). Americans have also continued their long tradition of volunteering their time and talents. Both Lewis May, president of Temple Emanu-El for twenty-five years, and Edwin Hale Abbot, secretary of his Harvard class for fifty years, were honored for their service (figs. 191, 199). Under these circumstances, presentation silver is a public, nonremunerative way of saying thank you.

POLITICS AND THE MILITARY

While building our fleet into a world-class naval power, the U.S. Navy also encouraged the creation of some of America's greatest presentation silver. By custom, United States battleships are named for states, and cruisers are named for cities. Also by custom, the states and cities present to their namesake ships silver services to be used at receptions and on other formal occasions. Battleship silver is extraordinary. Individual pieces are

167. The Armored Cruiser USS *California* silver service (1908) in the wardroom of the USS *Forrestal*, 14 July 1960. Silver with gold bears. Courtesy United States Navy, Naval Supply Systems Command

large (the USS *Pennsylvania*'s punch bowl holds fifteen gallons) and the services are extensive—even a modest service such as the USS *California*'s 1908 service made by Shreve and Company in San Francisco includes thirty-two service pieces (fig. 167).[23] Each service is personalized with iconography inspired by the donor's history: the *Florida*'s service has cast pelican handles on its punch bowl and alligator handles on its punch cups. All are profusely engraved. Most states and cities ordered their services from local silver shops, which, unbeknown to the purchasers, subcontracted the work to Gorham. Although Tiffany and Company and Shreve and Company each made presentation silver services, Gorham was the undisputed leader in this field, producing sixty services between 1891 and 1961.[24]

National pride also plays a role in military presentation silver. When the United States perceived itself as a glorious victor, it celebrated with silver. It is significant that America's most monumental example of presentation silver, the Dewey Cup, came from that "splendid little" Spanish-American War.[25] The war was clean, quick, and well publicized, and was fought on foreign soil with minimal loss of American life. Twentieth-century wars have not been so genteel. Perhaps because presentation silver was already in decline, or perhaps because the tremendous cost of the two world wars precluded the extravagance of silver, very little memorable military silver has been made in this century. None has surfaced from the Korean and Vietnam wars.

Silver also has played a diminished role in politics. Whereas President William McKinley presented a Tiffany and Company loving cup with eagles and exquisite reticulated handles to French ambassador Jules M. Cambon in 1898 (fig. 168),[26] modern presidents tend to give engraved glass. It, too, is American-made. It is also, in the eyes of government watchdogs, not as extravagant as silver.

RITES OF PASSAGE AND FRIENDSHIP

The underlying theme of this essay and book has been the continuity of presentation silver in a changing nation. It is reassuring to conclude with a topic that transcends politics or industry or other temporal matters and addresses two central concerns of the human condition: rites of passage and friendship. Births and marriages, always occasions for celebration, continue to be marked with silver. Silver, because of its value and shining perfection, also symbolizes all the optimism and hope that loving family and friends can bestow upon a special, newborn child. Marriages, too, celebrate a beginning, the creation of a new family and a new household. In this

168

168. Cup, 1899. "Presented by the President of the United States to his Excellency M. Jules Cambon Ambassador of France in Token of his Friendly Services in the Negotiation of the Protocol of the Peace Between the United States and Spain August 12, 1898." The cup was made by Tiffany and Company. Silver, h. 13³/4 in. (35.05 cm.). Courtesy The White House

century brides frequently receive silver. Often given as tableware, it reinforces the formalism and ritual associated with marriage and the value of the commitment made by two people to each other. In addition, brides frequently receive silver from their parents, perhaps in part as a vestige of the dowry tradition. Certainly, silver helps declare a daughter's place in society (fig. 224).

Anniversaries celebrate milestones of accomplishment, recognizing that people or organizations have persevered with affection and grace. Modern Americans celebrate birthdays (fig. 217), wedding anniversaries (fig. 225), years of service (fig. 199), and institutional birthdays (fig. 230). Each provides an occasion for presentation silver.

Last to be mentioned here is the silver given by one person to another affirming an affectionate relationship between them (fig. 231). Silver tokens, by their personalized nature and value declare a bond; they are peace offerings between individuals or groups of individuals who look together to the future.

170

169, 170. Monstrance, 1909 *(cat. no. 110)*

Designed by Frank E. Cleveland for Cram, Goodhue and Ferguson, Boston. Modeled by Johannes Kirchmayer (d. 1930). Cast
by Thomas Murray for Frank W. Smith Silver Company,
Gardner, Massachusetts. Made by Arthur J. Stone (1847–
1938), Gardner, Massachusetts. Marked "Stone" crossed by a
silversmith's chasing hammer. Gold, 9 amethysts, 87 diamonds, 2 pearls, 1 garnet, crystal, h. 15⅝ in. (39 cm.)

Inscribed on the base "To the glory of God and in loving remembrance of Catherine E. Tarbell and John D. Tarbell, given by
their daughter, Easter, 1909"

Private collection

Although Boston's Church of the Advent, one of the first churches
in the United States to subscribe to the tenets of England's Oxford
movement, was organized in 1844, the present edifice, a handsome high-Victorian Gothic structure designed by John Hubbard
Sturgis, was not completed until 1892. Sturgis died before its

completion. Soon thereafter, the church turned to the Boston firm
noted for its American medieval architecture, Cram, Goodhue
and Ferguson. The firm did a succession of interior projects for
this Anglo-Catholic parish. It fell to Frank E. Cleveland, a member of the firm, to design this exquisite monstrance, which
Catherine Tarbell presented to the church in memory of her
parents.

Cleveland worked with Arthur J. Stone, the Boston silversmith
with whom Cram, Goodhue and Ferguson frequently collaborated
on ecclesiastical silver (see fig. 171), and Johannes Kirchmayer, a
highly regarded ecclesiastical wood carver. Their effort is one of
America's most outstanding examples of twentieth-century presentation silver and gold. Although used primarily as a monstrance, in which is revealed the consecrated host, this object has
a hexagonal box that can serve as a pyx, a container reserved for
carrying the host. The vaulted canopy above the monstrance is a
ciborium.[27]

171. Altar cross, 1913 *(cat. no. 111)*

Designed by Cram, Goodhue and Ferguson, Boston. Crafted by
Herbert A. Taylor (active 1908–1937), Gardner, Massachusetts. Made by Arthur J. Stone (1847–1938), Gardner, Massachusetts. Marked on the bottom "Stone" crossed by a
silversmith's chasing hammer, and the letter "T". Silver, gilt,
ebony, ivory, h. 18½ in. (47 cm.)

Inscribed on the base "IN MEMORIAM IACOBI LAURANTII
HOUGHTELING OBIIT XXVIII IULII AD MDCCCCX" and:

IC	XC	[28]
NI	KA

Cathedral Church of St. James–St. Andrew's Chapel, Chicago

From its founding in 1834 to the present, the Church of St. James
has been an important and affluent center for Episcopalianism in
Chicago. Parts of the present church, including a side altar
designed by Calvert Vaux and Frederick Law Olmsted survived
the 1871 Chicago fire, as did a small undercroft meeting room,
whose Gothic arches support the church above. In this room in
1883, lay member James L. Houghteling (1855–1910) organized
an Episcopal men's evangelical organization, the Brotherhood of
St. Andrew.[29] Upon Houghteling's death, his family gave the St.
Andrew's Chapel in his memory. It is located in the very room
where the Brotherhood was founded. St. James's turned to Cram,
Goodhue and Ferguson to execute the project. As they had at the
Church of the Advent in Boston (see fig. 169), the architects commissioned Arthur J. Stone to make the altar plate.

The chapel is wonderfully complete. Scottish iconography,
such as the St. Andrew's cross and thistles, appear in the tiles,
woodwork, gilt frame for the altar triptych, and communion service, which includes the altar cross, chalice, paten, and basin, all
executed in an intricate pattern of cast, pierced, and chased ornament by Herbert A. Taylor for Arthur J. Stone. Although surviving
drawings of the cross call for semiprecious stones, they were omit-
ted from the final version.[30]

172. Monstrance, 1941 *(cat. no. 112)*

Tiffany and Company (1837 to the present), New York City.
Marked "TIFFANY & CO MAKERS STERLING SILVER
23419" on the underside at the rim. Silver, gilt, amethyst, h.
39½ in. (100.3 cm.)

St. Patrick's Cathedral, New York City

171

In 1853 noted American architect James Renwick initiated the design for a new Roman Catholic church in the Gothic-revival style to be located uptown in booming, affluent Manhattan, on Fifth Avenue between Fiftieth and Fifty-first streets. Although the church was opened in 1859, as with its European prototypes, construction continued well into the next century.

In 1930 the church fathers decided to replace the high altar, largely because it obscured the new Lady Chapel behind it, completed in 1906. They turned to Charles D. Maginnis, of the firm Maginnis and Walsh, to execute the design. Because of the Depression, the design was not completed until 1939. Maginnis designed an airy fifty-seven-foot-high bronze baldachin that soared above the altar. This monstrance, a tall, majestic, yet restrained receptacle for the consecrated host was made to stand on the altar beneath the baldachin. Its Celtic-inspired ornament, reminiscent of ancient Irish manuscripts and stone carvings, clearly alludes to Saint Patrick, for whom the cathedral was named. The baldachin and high altar, including the monstrance, were anonymous gifts to the church. They are extraordinary private gifts to the glory of God. The high altar was consecrated on 9 May 1942, five months after the United States entered World War II.[31] The monstrance is one of the last great examples of American factory-made presentation silver.

173. Christening basin, 1980 *(cat. no. 113)*

Joseph Parker (b. 1940), Medfield, Massachusetts. Marked "Joseph Parker Sterling". Silver, diam. 12 in. (30.5 cm.)

Inscribed in the well "Given in memory of Sarah Lothrop Ames 30 October 31 1967 by her family" and on the bottom "Presented to the First Church in Boston on the occasion of its 350th Anniversary 1980"

Silver Collection, First and Second Church in Boston

It is proper to conclude this section with a christening basin shaped by a modern Boston silversmith. For all its newness, it brings our story full circle. The basin, handwrought in a tradition begun in Boston more than three centuries ago, is the touching gift to a church from a family in memory of their infant daughter. The hope and joy of each new christening recalls the memory of another loved infant who was part of this church circle. The church that has embraced the bowl is the First and Second Church in Boston, whose John Hull beaker (fig. 15) is the earliest piece of American silver in this book. Here in one church the presentation silver tradition has flourished since the mid-seventeenth century, honoring the past and looking to the future.

174. Centerpiece, 1882 *(cat. no. 114)*

Whiting Manufacturing Company (active 1866–1905), North Attleboro, Massachusetts. Marked with a griffin passant holding a shield and with "W/sterling/1001". Silver, gilt, h. 15⅝ in. (39 cm.)

Inscribed "Presented to Franklin B. Gowen, as a token of our grateful remembrance of his services in suppressing lawless violence and re-establishing security for life and property in the anthracite coal regions of Pennsylvania."

Historical Society of Pennsylvania, Philadelphia, Gift of James E. Gowen

Coal mines, immigrant gangs, and murder are part of the history of this majestic oval centerpiece. The most imaginative playwright might have been hard-pressed to create such a scenario. Franklin Benjamin Gowen (1836–1889) was president of the Philadelphia and Reading Railroad, which did a large business transporting anthracite coal from the Schuylkill area to Philadelphia. Whenever there was trouble in the mines, the Reading lost money;

therefore, Gowen became increasingly active in the coal industry. The mines and the communities that worked them were frequently terrorized by a secret society of Irish immigrant miners known as the Molly Maguires. Since the early 1860s, the Molly Maguires had preyed upon foremen, superintendents, and others who crossed them. In 1873 Gowen hired a Pinkerton detective, James McParlan, to infiltrate the Maguires and report their activities to him. McParlan assumed a new identity and remained undercover until 1876. Through his testimony and Gowen's tenaciousness, twenty men were hung for Molly Maguire crimes. The group was disbanded, and calm returned to the coal fields.[32]

It is no wonder that eighteen grateful coal barons, whose names appear on the bowl, gave Gowen this handsome centerpiece with its hammered surface and silver-gilt medallions, anthemia, and miners' tools (the inside of the bowl was also gilt). At the time of the presentation, the Philadelphia *Inquirer* reported that this was the largest bowl that Bailey, Banks and Biddle had ever made.[33] However, like other retailers, this firm had turned to a major manufacturer for help—in this instance, the Whiting Company of North Attleboro, Massachusetts, which ultimately was purchased by the Gorham Company of Providence, Rhode Island, in 1905.

175. Plaque, 1884 *(cat. no. 115)*

Tiffany and Company (1837 to the present), New York City. Marked on the bottom "TIFFANY & CO/7913 MAKERS 3600/ STERLING SILVER/925–1000/M". Silver, l. 33⁷/₈ in. (85.7 cm.)

The Minneapolis Institute of Arts, Gift of Mr. and Mrs. G. Richard Slade

In the 1870s and 1880s, Minneapolis enjoyed a period of unusual growth and prosperity. Surrounded by rich farm and ranch land, located at the northernmost navigable point on the Mississippi River, linked to East and West by railroads, and blessed with St. Anthony's Falls, which provided waterpower for its flour mills, Minneapolis was emerging as an important midwestern city. Two momentous things happened in 1884 that were worthy of special celebration in the Minneapolis business community: a great stone railroad bridge was built over the Mississippi River and the new West Hotel (see page 146) was opened.

Businessman George A. Brackett led a committee that raised $8,145 to honor James J. Hill and Charles W. West for their roles in these important projects. Eighteen men subscribed, and Charles A. Pillsbury was the chief donor, contributing $1,500 to the cause. On 2 September 1884, Tiffany and Company billed Brackett for "Sil Vase. Sil Plaque & 2 Oak Cases" in the amount of $7,805.[34]

On 10 September 1884, Brackett and his committee presented the plaque, which we would call a tray, to James J. Hill during a small dinner party at the home of William D. Washburn. Hill, president of the predecessor of the Great Northern Railroad, developed this 2,100-foot-long curving stone bridge and its new depot, which linked St. Paul and Minneapolis below the falls. It was a considerable political, engineering, and financial accomplishment. According to newspaper accounts, Hill was surprised to receive the plaque, which was presented "upon a slightly inclined easel which is part of its case, imbedded in a retaining cushion of crimson plush, and occupying a place under a dozen brilliant gas jets in Gen. Washburn's library,"[35] in spite of the fact that George A. Brackett had hired photographer A. H. Beal to photograph both the bridge and the cattle at the Hill farm.[36] Beal's photographs were sent to Tiffany and Company to be copied on the tray. The vignettes bordering the tray are biographical and include a buffalo chase; a dog sled; Hill assisting the injured driver of a broken cart; shipping on the Minnesota River; the steamboat *Selkirk*, in which Hill once owned an interest; a farm; and Angus, Shorthorn, and Jersey cattle, which he had introduced to the Midwest.[37]

176. Vase, 1884 *(cat. no. 116)*

Tiffany and Company (1837 to the present) New York City. Marked "TIFFANY AND CO./7912 MAKERS 3600/Sterling Silver/925–1000/M". Silver, h. 33 in. (83.8 cm.)

Hennepin County Historical Society Museum, Minneapolis

The West Hotel was an eight-story structure that stood at Fifth and Hennepin streets in downtown Minneapolis. When it was dedicated, on 19 November 1884, it was considered one of the best in America. Its opulent design, electric lighting, electrical generating plant, speaking tubes, two hundred private bathrooms, and hot and cold running water in every room were state-of-the-art. Minneapolis citizens were justifiably proud. For this reason, George A. Brackett and other Minneapolis businessmen wanted to mark the hotel's grand opening by presenting a great vase to Charles W. West, a Cincinnati investor and the hotel's owner. Brackett raised funds for the urn and ordered it at the same time as the Hill plaque (fig. 175). On 11 September 1884, Charles W. West died. His nephew, John T. West, accepted it in his stead.[38] The cup is certainly less personal than the Hill tray, probably because West was less well known to the subscribers. The midsection is decorated with an exterior view of the hotel on one side and a portrait of West on the other. Buffalo heads, symbols of the American West, serve as handle terminals. Streetcars, reminders of the source of Charles West's fortune, decorate the base. The West Hotel vase is a typical late-nineteenth-century presentation-silver form. Its bulbous body, small neck, and small, unstable base are variations on the classic Greek amphora shape.

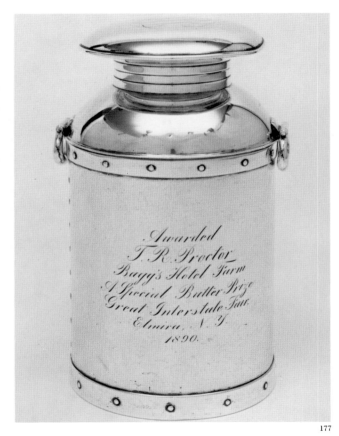

177.

177. Cigar humidor and lighter, 1890 *(cat. no. 117)*

Tiffany and Company (1837 to the present), New York City. Marked on the bottom "TIFFANY & CO./11132 T 7214/STERLING". Silver, gilt, h. 7 in. (17.8 cm.)

Inscribed "Awarded T.R. Proctor Baggs Hotel Farm A Special Butter Prize Great Interstate Fair. Elmira, N.Y. 1890."

Munson-Williams-Proctor Institute Museum of Art, Utica, New York

Thomas Redfield Proctor (1844–1920) was a wealthy hotel owner who prided himself on providing excellent dairy products for his guests. To do so, his Baggs Hotel, located in downtown Utica, maintained a dairy farm on the outskirts of town.[39] Proctor ran a successful dairy, as this prize attests. It is part of the ongoing American tradition of honoring excellence in agriculture (see figs. 100, 101). The form—a handsomely scaled, meticulously crafted version of a milk can—is typical of the eccentric, highly specialized silver executed at the turn of the century. The lighter is hidden in the cap; the domed section lifts to reveal a gilt humidor. A repoussé cow on the reverse completes the composition.

178. Adams Vase, 1893–95 *(cat. no. 118)*

Designed by Paulding Farnham (active 1889–c. 1904) for Tiffany and Company (1837 to the present), New York City. Marked on the underside "TIFFANY & CO./MAKERS/SOLID GOLD" and on the tube inside "TIFFANY & CO./STERLING SILVER/T". Gold, quartz, rock crystal, pearls, spessartites (garnets), tourmalines, amethysts, enamel, h. 19 1/2 in. (49.5 cm.)

The Metropolitan Museum of Art, New York, Gift of Edward D. Adams, 1904

In 1893 Edward Dean Adams (1846–1931) was given the ultimate presentation gift, a gold, enamel, and jeweled vase inspired by the Renaissance and fit for royalty. Adams, a prominent financier, received it with the gratitude of the American Cotton Oil Company. The company's creditors and stockholders had called upon Adams for help, for he had a reputation for rescuing financially distressed companies, including the New Jersey Central Railroad. Adams served as chairman of the American Cotton Oil Company without compensation, provided funds and credit, and quickly restored it to solvency.[40] The grateful stockholders and directors commissioned Tiffany and Company to make a suitable award. Paulding Farnham, Tiffany's head jewelry designer at the time, designed and modeled the vase, which was supposed to be as uniquely American in form and materials as the American Cotton Company. Its gold came from Forest City, California, and its precious stones and pearls are also American. Even the base upon which it originally stood was made of American woods. Farnham used cotton blossoms, stems, and balls as design motifs. The figures of Atlas and Husbandry (holding a cotton branch) rest on the foot. Modesty and Genius, flanked by Agriculture and Commerce, decorate the vase, while four falcons fly above.[41] In its opulence the Adams Vase has yet to be equaled by any other object of American presentation silver or gold.

179. Vase, 1893 *(cat. no. 119)*

Tiffany and Company (1837 to the present), New York City. Marked "TIFFANY & CO./11839 MAKERS 5600/STERLING SILVER /925–1000/T". Silver, h. 24 in. (61 cm.)

Inscribed "From American exhibitors, Department of Transportation Exhibits, World's Columbian Exposition, Chicago, U.S.A., 1893, To Willard A. Smith, Chief. In commemoration

180

of the conception, perfection and administration of the first distinctive Transportation Department in the history of international expositions. . . ."

National Museum of American History, Smithsonian Institution, Washington, D.C.

180. Entrance to the Transportation Building, Chicago. World's Columbian Exposition, 1893. Louis Sullivan, architect. Photograph Collection of the Chicago History Society

In the great White City erected for Chicago's 1893 World's Columbian Exposition stood an anachronism, the 256-by-960-foot Transportation Building designed by Louis Sullivan (fig. 180). Its long, polychrome, rectilinear facade of repeating Romanesque arches faced the lagoon designed by Frederick Law Olmsted. Its most spectacular feature, however, was its huge portal, a dramatic arrangement of five receding arches richly carved and overlaid with gold leaf. It was without question the most memorable facade at the exposition. A nine-acre annex lay west of the building.[42]

Willard Adelbert Smith was chief of the Department of Transportation exhibits. A lawyer by training and owner of *Railway Review*, an important trade publication in its day, he was thoroughly familiar with America's most advanced mode of transportation—the train. Smith must have been an exceptionally good chief, for he later assumed leadership positions at the 1900 Paris Exposition and the 1904 Louisiana Purchase Exposition.[43] In appreciation, the American exhibitors in Chicago gave him this ponderous vase. Like the building itself, the vase reflects an uneasy truce between a classical form in a beaux-arts idiom and Sullivan's golden Romanesque door. The remaining ornament has to do with the history of transportation: maritime vignettes encircle the neck and the history of land transportation is depicted below. The figures at either side of the door also pay homage to land and sea transportation. An 1893 photograph shows the vase with its original ebony base decorated with at least one plaque, an ocean liner, mounted on it.[44]

182 (overleaf). Tray, 1904 *(cat. no. 120)*

Tiffany and Company (1837 to the present), New York City. Marked on the bottom "TIFFANY & CO./16015 MAKERS 6070/925–100/C". Silver, l. 37⅞ in. (96 cm.)

Museum of the City of New York, Gift of August Belmont, grandson of August Belmont

181. Map of the Interborough Rapid Transit Line, New York City. *New York Times*, 28 October 1904. Collection of Fondren Library, Rice University, Houston, Texas

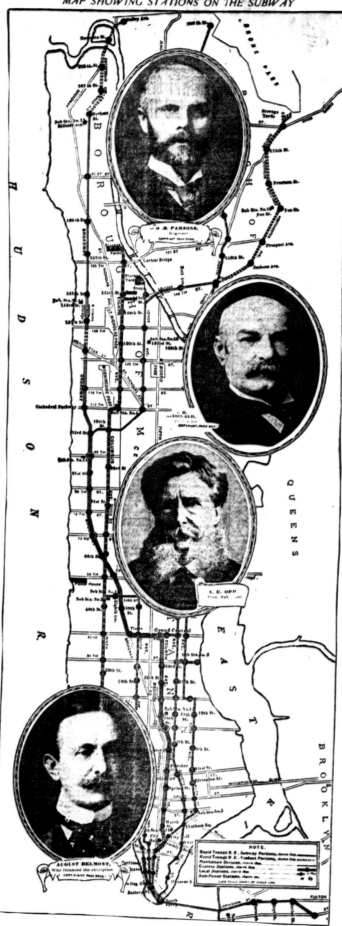

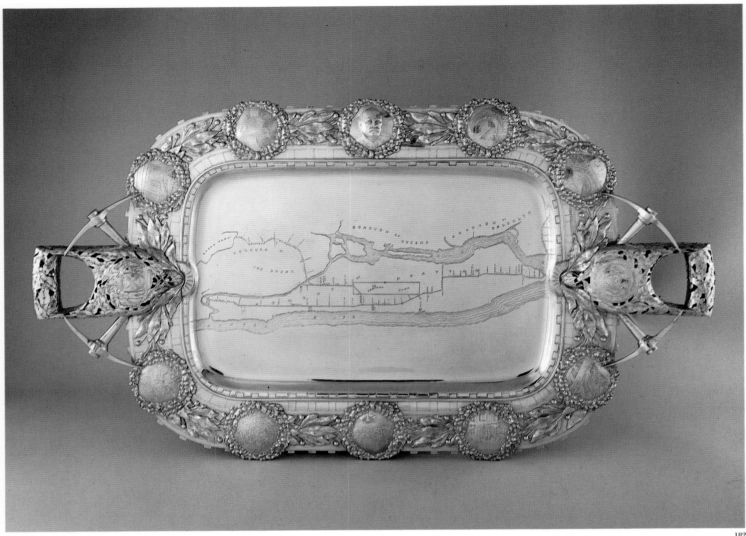

182

During the nineteenth century, New York was the largest city in the United States. It was also one of its most congested. It had trolley lines that moved at grade level and it had noisy elevated trains; desperately needed was an underground rail system to move people about. Between 1868 and 1900 at least seven different companies tried to build a subway system in New York, but each was overwhelmed by the herculean task of building a railroad under functioning streets; negotiating private easements and public rights-of-way; issuing public bonds for funding; and ironing out the problems of city ownership, private construction, private management, and indemnification that would guarantee the city against loss. So stringent were the city indemnification and funding requirements that no investors would underwrite the project until August Belmont, Jr., took it on. As president of the Rapid Transit Subway Construction Company and its successor, the Interborough Rapid Transit Company, Belmont supplied the leadership and put together the financing that made possible the $37.7-million subway.[45]

This tray, which is almost as monumental as the undertaking itself, remained in the Belmont family until it was given to the Museum of the City of New York. The map of Manhattan clearly shows the new subway route, while the roundels depict vignettes of its construction. A portrait of the contractor, John B. McDonald, is prominent in a center roundel. Why would Belmont own a tray with McDonald's portrait on it? Perhaps Belmont had originally intended to present the tray to McDonald, but decided against it after the men had had an argument that was significant enough to make headlines just four days before the subway's

opening.[46] The tray immediately calls to mind the Hill plaque (fig. 175), which also marked a major transportation accomplishment. Equally impressive, the Belmont tray, perhaps like America itself in 1904, is more formal than its antecedent.[47]

183, 184. Medal, 1912 *(cat. no. 121)*

Dieges and Clust Mint (active 1898 to the present; purchased in 1980 by Herff Jones, Providence, Rhode Island), New York. Marked "Sterling/DIEGES & CLUST/N.Y." Silver, l. 1³⁄₈ in. (3.6 cm.)

Inscribed "Presented to the Captain, Officers & Crew of R.M.S. "Carpathia" in recognition of gallant & heroic services from the survivors of the S.S. "Titanic" April 15th 1912."

The American Numismatic Society, New York City

185. Captain Rostron of the RMS *Carpathia* holding the *Titanic* Cup, with Mrs. J. J. Brown beside him. Captain Rostron is wearing his *Titanic* medal for heroism. Collection of The Denver Public Library, Western History Department.

The story of the steamship *Titanic*'s hitting an iceberg and sinking on her maiden voyage in the spring of 1912 is one of the best-known and most tragic tales in modern maritime history. Had the Cunard Line's RMS *Carpathia* not responded to the emergency so

183

184

quickly, even more lives would have been lost. On 17 April the survivors assembled on the *Carpathia*, some still wearing the nightclothes they had worn when they were rescued, and formed a committee to raise funds for destitute steerage passengers and to present a loving cup to Captain Rostron of the *Carpathia* and medals to his officers and crew. Any remaining funds were to be given to the crew of the *Titanic*.[48] Within six short weeks the committee, led by Mrs. J. J. Brown (the Unsinkable Molly Brown), was back on board the *Carpathia* for the presentation. In an affecting ceremony in the first-class dining salon, the committee presented the loving cup, gold medals to the six senior officers, silver medals to the junior officers, and bronze medals to the crew[49] (fig. 185). Showing Neptune and dolphins encircling the *Carpathia* as it speeds through ice floes to the rescue, the medals are part of a continuing tradition of honoring unusually brave or accomplished people with a presentation.

186

186. Curtiss Marine Flying Trophy, 1915 *(cat. no. 122)*

Gorham Company (1831 to the present), Providence, Rhode Island. Marked on the airplane an anchor/"Sterling/IHA" and on the cloud "IHA". Silver, onyx, h. 45³/₄ in. (113.7 cm.)

National Air and Space Museum, Smithsonian Institution, Washington, D.C.

185

151

In 1903 Wilbur and Orville Wright made their first successful airplane flight. From that moment on, men and women began the difficult task of making airplanes into viable transportation machines. Seaplanes and flying boats were two of the earliest innovations. First developed by Glenn H. Curtiss in 1911, seaplanes were large enough to carry passengers and cargo. They could land wherever there was a large body of water, including at the piers of such cities as New York and Chicago. In those days of limited fuel supplies, inefficient engines that had to refuel frequently, and a dearth of runways, water landings were very advantageous.

In 1915 Glenn H. Curtiss (1878–1930) presented this trophy to the Aero Club of America so that the organization could hold an annual airboat race open to all American aero-club members with the victory awarded on the basis of speed and performance. The trophy was conceived by Henry Woodhouse to symbolize the triumph of aviation over both the sea and the air. The gods of those elements, Neptune and Boreas, symbolically reach for a flying boat, which eludes them.[50] The boat portrayed happens to be Curtiss's own *America*, designed by him in 1914. Oscar A. Brindley was the first man to win the trophy, after flying 526 miles in ten hours, at an average speed of sixty-five miles per hour.[51]

The Curtiss trophy was one of several air-race trophies made by Gorham during these years. They invariably show spheres, balloons, globes, clouds and/or a figure reaching to the heavens.[52]

187. Centerpiece, 1931 *(cat. no. 123)*

Tiffany and Company (1837 to the present), New York City. Marked on the base, "TIFFANY & CO./MAKERS/47023/ STERLING SILVER/925–1000 M". Silver, diam. 11⅞ in. (30.2 cm.)

Inscribed on the bowl "Matt C. Brush February 19, 1931"; under the tusks "J.E. King, C.M. Curry, J.M. Davis, E.P. Thomas"; and on the rim of the foot "In appreciation of the elephantine effort of the arch-alchemist in transmuting a debacle of July 1929 into a Godsend of October 1930."

Museum of the City of New York, Bequest of Elizabeth H. Brush

Matthew Chauncey Brush (1877–1940) was a railroad and shipping executive who was prominent in New York social and business circles in the 1920s and 1930s. Although the specific circumstances associated with this gift are unknown, Brush evidently saved the investments of associates J. E. King, Chester M. Curry, John M. Davis, and Eugene Peeples Thomas during the volatile months before and after the stock-market crash of October 1929. Brush's appreciative friends ordered this "elephantine" centerpiece from Tiffany and Company. Tiffany made the centerpiece for $561 and probably sold it to the men for $1,125, a not inconsiderable sum during the Depression.[53]

188. Punch bowl (Buck Cup for Schooners), 1881 *(cat. no. 124)*

Tiffany and Company (1837 to the present), New York City.
Marked on the underside "TIFFANY & CO./6175 MAKERS
2977/STERLING-SILVER/925–1000/M/29 P'TS". Silver,
gilt, h. 12 in. (30.5 cm.)

Inscribed on the bowl "'Buck' Cup for all Schooners of N.Y.Y.C.
& E.Y.C. New Bedford Aug. 5, 1881 won by Halcyon Chas. J.
Paine, owner."

New York Yacht Club, New York City

The New York Yacht Club participated in many interclub races,
among them the Buck Cup race, named for Elisha A. Buck, a club
member who underwrote the two $500 prizes—one of which is
this punch bowl—awarded in 1881. Charles J. Paine (see page
154), a railroad magnate and former Union Army general,
belonged to the Eastern Yacht Club when he won this New
Bedford, Massachusetts, race with *Halcyon* at a foggy, contested
finish. When competitors protested, the race was rerun, this time
off New York City. The *Gracie* won the rematch, although the trophy still bears the *Halcyon*'s name.[54] The Buck Cup is a superb
example of Tiffany and Company's Japanesque style, which the
company introduced in 1878. Its hammered surface is enlivened
by a serenely rolling school of fish, possibly sturgeon, which form

a series of repeated cyma curves at the rim of the bowl. Beneath
them, a waterbug and a crab crawl on the base much as they might
on the ocean floor. The Buck Cup is a particularly happy marriage
of art, nature, and symbolism in one presentation piece.[55]

189. "Yaght" (Goelet Cup for Schooners), 1884 *(cat. no. 125)*

Tiffany and Company (1837 to the present), New York City.
Marked on the base "TIFFANY & CO/7891 M 4766/
STERLING SILVER". Silver, gilt, h. 18³/4 in. (47.6 cm.)

Inscribed in a cartouche on the stern "The Goelet Cup for Schooners 1884" and on the open book on the stern "Won by Grayling"

New York Yacht Club, New York City

In 1882 New York Yacht Club member Ogden Goelet (1846–
1898) instituted a custom that he would honor until his death: he
donated a Goelet Cup valued at $1,000 for schooners and a Goelet
Cup valued at $500 for sloops, to be awarded at annual races off
Newport, Rhode Island.[56] Although they are known as Goelet
cups, the prizes took many forms. The unusual form of this particular example is inspired by yachting lore. The first sailors to

design a ship for pleasure cruising were the seventeenth-century Dutch. They called it "yaght" (now "jaght"), a term that evolved into the English word "yacht." The basic shape, reticulated stern lights, cartouche, and balustrade are inspired by the elaborately carved seventeenth-century yaght. Neptune and dolphins complete the theme.[57] *Grayling*, a yacht owned by Latham A. Fish, which measured 84 feet at the waterline, won the cup on 8 August 1884. In doing so, it proved itself an honorable successor in the Dutch sailing tradition and worthy of this grand award.

190. Ewer (Goelet Cup for Sloops), 1886 *(cat. no. 126)*

Whiting Manufacturing Company (active 1866–1905), North Attleboro, Massachusetts. Marked "WHITING MF'G CO/ New-York"/ griffin passant/"STERLING 2071". Silver, h. 18¹/₂ in. (47 cm.)

Inscribed "Goelet Cup won by Mayflower, Aug. 7th, 1886."

New York Yacht Club, New York City.

In 1886 the *Mayflower*, owned by Charles J. Paine (see page 153), defeated fourteen other sloops in the annual New York Yacht Club Goelet Cup race.[58] Its prize, a matte-finished, cast, and repoussé ewer, is among the most original New York Yacht Club trophies (figures 189 and 193 are also Goelet cups). Its sensuous rhythmic form and asymmetrical ornament evoke the romance of the sea. The virgin Andromeda, daughter of the Ethiopian king Cepheus and his vain queen Cassiopeia, is shown chained to a rock near the water while the sea monster to whom she is about to be sacrificed to appease him and protect Ethiopia's shores undulates around her and conveniently allows its long body to be grasped as a handle.[59]

191

191. Vase, 1888 *(cat. no. 127)*

Tiffany and Company (1837 to the present), New York City. Marked on the base "TIFFANY & CO/9757 M 1382/ STERLING SILVER". Silver, h. 19 in. (48.1 cm.)

Inscribed "Presented to Mr. Lewis May, President of the Congregation Temple Emanu El. New York. In grateful recognition of his twenty five years faithful and devoted service as leader and administrator of the affairs of the Congregation by a number of its members. May years of life and usefulness be added thereto; blessing and peace be with him, his beloved wife and children."

Congregation Emanu-El of the City of New York

192. Temple Emanu-El, northeast corner of Fifth Avenue and Forty-third Street, New York City, c. 1890. Courtesy of The New York Historical Society, New York City.

Lewis May (1823–1897), a beloved member of Congregation Emanu-El, was a highly regarded businessman and philanthropist who served for many years as volunteer president of his synagogue. Under May's leadership the congregation moved in 1868 to a new home designed by Leopold Eidlitz and Henry Fernbach at Fifth Avenue and Forty-third Street (fig. 192). This large, elaborate repoussé vase, given to May upon his twenty-fifth anniversary as the congregation's president, is an excellent measure of the donors' affection for him. It is covered with Middle Eastern and Jewish-inspired decoration. Of special note are the two stars of David set in the handles, the tablets symbolizing the Ten Commandments, and the engraved view of the congregation's new synagogue.

192

193

193. Punch bowl (Goelet Cup for Sloops), 1889 *(cat. no. 128)*

Tiffany and Company (1837 to the present), New York City. Marked "TIFFANY & CO/10221 M 0510/STERLING SILVER". Silver, gilt, h. 12 in. (30.5 cm.)

Inscribed "The Goelet Prize for Sloops 1889 won by Titania from Bedouin, Gracie and Katrina."

Museum of the City of New York, Gift of Mrs. C. Oliver Iselin

194. Working drawing for Tiffany and Company's Prize Cup Number 10221 (Goelet Cup for Sloops), 1889. Collection of the Museum of the City of New York

In 1889 Ogden Goelet offered the Goelet Cup for Sloops to the victorious sloop in a New York Yacht Club race off Newport,

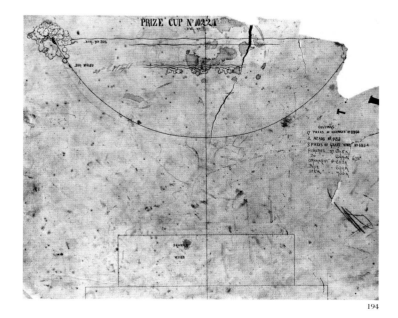

194

195. Punch bowl, 1894 (cat. no. 129)

Tiffany and Company (1837 to the present), New York City. Marked under the base "TIFFANY & COMPANY/12063 Makers 7650/Sterling Silver/925–1000/50 QTS". Silver, h. 19 in. (48.3 cm.)

Mr. and Mrs. John W. Mecom, Jr.

196. Captain Tom Jay, of Rowhedge, aboard the cutter *Ailsa*, 1894. The owners at right. Collection of John Leather

196

Rhode Island, as he had since 1882. The 1889 prize went to the *Titania*, a new 70-foot steel centerboarder designed by Edward Burgess for club member C. Oliver Iselin.[60] Although this punch bowl is inscribed with stylish Art Nouveau lettering, it is in a traditional shape that is not as eccentric as some of the earlier Goelet cups (see figs. 189, 190). A surviving drawing for the bowl (fig. 194) shows that it was a combination of stock and special-order castings (the border, seventeen pieces of seaweed, bacchanalian handles, and grapevine were stock castings; the base, including its voluptuous mermaids, was made for this particular bowl).[61] The combined ornament is symbolic of a sailor's two great loves: the sea and the wine that soothes and cheers him.

In the 1890s international yacht racing was dominated by English, American, and German vessels. James Gordon Bennett,

195

Jr., the rambunctious heir to the *New York Herald* and commodore of the New York Yacht Club in 1871–74 and 1884–85 was one of the principal figures in this cosmopolitan group.[62] Bennett, who in 1894 was living in France, continued a tradition he had begun in New York, commissioning major presentation-silver objects as yachting prizes. The *Ailsa*, a new 283-ton English cutter, won this Bennett prize, possibly during the winter racing season in the Mediterranean. Its English owners, Mr. and Mrs. A. D. Walker, became the improbable possessors of this gargantuan trophy decorated with American Indian and river iconography: Indian maidens, canoes, and Indian regalia, and sail-assisted steamships.[63] The cup was ordered by Bennett from Tiffany and Company at a cost of $2,500 for its labor and its considerable silver (753 ounces). Tiffany completed the drawings on 30 July 1894 and entered the pattern into their files on 10 January 1895.[64]

197. Punch bowl, 1896 *(cat. no. 130)*

Gorham Company (1831 to the present), Providence, Rhode Island. Marked under the base with a lion passant, anchor, and Gothic "G/STERLING/M" and shell. Silver, h. 8⅝ in. (22 cm.)

Inscribed "Presented by the New York Yacht Club to Edward M. Brown, Commodore of the Club 1895 and 1896; in recognition of his services and as a token of the esteem and affection of his fellow members."

New York Yacht Club, New York City

Not all New York Yacht Club presentation silver is related to racing, nor do all of its commodores receive punch bowls as handsome as the one Edward M. Brown received in 1896. Like many recipients of presentation silver, Brown was honored for a job well done. He had served during a particularly trying time in the club's history. In 1895 the New York Yacht Club again defended the America's Cup. Not only were the American trials unusually contentious, but the international competition between the earl of Dunraven's *Valkyrie III* and the *Defender*, owned by a syndicate headed by William K. Vanderbilt, was tainted by Dunraven's complaints, protests, and charges of foul play, which made international headlines. Brown appointed a blue-ribbon committee, which investigated the complaints and exonerated the *Defender* and the New York Yacht Club.[65] The club chose Gorham to design Brown's stately award. The bowl is a basin suspended from four Corinthian columns, each anchored to a base. A delicate frieze of dolphins and shells encircles the bowl beneath its dedication.[66]

197

198. Belmont Memorial Challenge Cup, 1897 *(cat. no. 131)*

Tiffany and Company (1837 to the present), New York City. Marked under the base "TIFFANY & CO./MAKERS/STERLING SILVER". Silver, h. 17½ in. (44.5 cm.)

Inscribed on the cover "August Belmont Memorial Cup 1926" and on the bowl "Fenian winner of the Belmont Stakes supported by the three great sires Eclipse, Herod and Matchem"

New York Racing Association, Inc.

The 5 June 1869 issue of the *New York Times* reported that the spring meeting of the American Jockey Club was to commence that day. The races were to be held in Jerome Park, and the third race was to be the Belmont Stakes for three-year-olds. The stakes had been established in 1867 by August Belmont (1818–1890), the noted New York financier and sportsman. The day was glorious—the newspaper related—the crowd brilliant, and the Belmont Stakes were won by Belmont's own Fenian against a field of eight. Belmont's Glenclq (*sic*) came in second.

The stunning victory of Belmont's stable at the third annual running of the Belmont Stakes is commemorated by this monu-

mental vase made almost thirty years later, which is still one of the most highly prized trophies in thoroughbred racing. An entry in Tiffany and Company's pattern books lists order number 12763 entered on 19 April 1897 "Prize Cup Horse Mr. Belmont."[67] In 1926 the cup was donated by Mrs. Eleanor Belmont as a permanent trophy to be held by the winning owner for one year.[68] As in 1869, the race is traditionally held in the first week of June. In design, the trophy symbolizes the development of the thoroughbred horse in America and the establishment of bloodlines from the eighteenth century onward. The names of three great sires imported into America, Matchem (1748), Herod (1758), and Eclipse (1764), are inscribed on the side of the bowl, and depictions of them stand below. All registered thoroughbred racehorses trace their ancestry to this trio.[69] A sculpture of Fenian, the winner of the trophy and their descendant, stands on the lid. The bowl is in the form of a giant acorn, and the imagery of the oak, suggesting a family tree, appears in the trunklike stem of the bowl and the leaf-and-acorn ornament on the base, rim, and lid. This commissioned trophy, with its vivid symbolism, extraordinary design, and monumental scale, represents a culmination of developments that began in silver made for racing trophies at the opening of the nineteenth century.

199. Cup, 1906 *(cat. no. 132)*

Designed by H. Langford Warren (1857–1917). Made by Arthur J. Stone (1847–1937), Gardner, Massachusetts. Marked on the bottom "STONE STERLING HLW". Silver, gold, enamel, h. 5³/4 in. (14.6 cm.)

Inscribed on the rim "Edwin Hale Abbot from his Harvard class-mates in loving recognition of his fifty years service as their sec-retary" and at the waist "1855:1905"

Harvard University Art Museums, Fogg Art Museum, Cambridge, Massachusetts, Bequest of Edwin Hale Abbot

Founded in 1897, the Boston Society of Arts and Crafts was one of the principal advocates of the Arts and Crafts movement in America. Its twenty-four founders included some of Boston's leading thinkers, architects, and artists. Both Arthur J. Stone and H. Langford Warren were charter members of this society. Warren was a professor of architecture at Harvard, and Stone owned one of the last great independent American silversmith shops. A number of Stone's secular presentation-silver commissions came from nearby Harvard University, including this loving cup presented to Edwin Hale Abbot (1834–1927) in honor of his fifty years as class secretary.[70] Abbot's loving cup is a variation of the Greek *kantharos* form. Decorated with the seal of Harvard University, it is a reminder of the strong bond that exists between alumni and their colleges, one that is frequently acknowledged in ceremony and marked with presentation silver.

200. Punch bowl, 1910 *(cat. no. 133)*

Robert Jarvie (1865–1941), Chicago. Marked on the base "Jarvie 1910 Chicago". Silver, h. 10 in. (25.4 cm.)

Inscribed on the bottom "The-Cliff-Dwellers Jarvie 1910 Chicago Presented. by. Charles. L. Hutchinson"

The Cliff Dwellers, Chicago, Illinois

The two decades between 1890 and 1910 were extraordinary years in Chicago's cultural history. Louis Sullivan and Frank Lloyd Wright were architects there, the 1893 World's Columbian Exposition (see page 149) changed the face of the city forever, and the American Arts and Crafts movement flourished. A key person in Chicago's civic life at this time was Charles L. Hutchinson (1854–1924), a philanthropist who served as president of the Art Institute of Chicago for forty-two years. Hutchinson, like Wright and Sullivan, was a member of the Cliff Dwellers, a social club founded in 1907 to bring artists and patrons of the arts together. How appropriate, then, for Hutchinson to give the club a hand-crafted bowl made by a fellow club member who was one of Chicago's best Arts and Crafts silversmiths, Robert Jarvie. Unlike contemporaneous factory-made silver, which relied heavily on cast ornament, Jarvie's beautiful bowl is entirely handwrought. With characteristic thoroughness, Jarvie studied bowls made by the cliff-dweller Indians of the American Southwest that were in the collection of Chicago's Field Museum of Natural History and used them as design sources.[71]

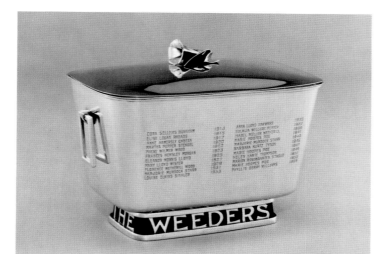

Philadelphia Museum of Art, Gift of The Weeders Garden Club, Philadelphia

The Weeders is a women's garden club that has been active in the Philadelphia area since at least 1913. It is representative of the multitude of genteel women's garden, literary, and music clubs organized at the turn of the century, when many women had servants working in the home and time for leisure pursuits. This casket honors past presidents of the garden club. It was given to the club by Louise Elkins Sinkler in memory of her good friend Isabel Müller Wetherill (d. 1958), whose name appears on one side of the bowl with those of all the presidents from 1913 to 1956.[72] More recent presidents are listed on the other side. The Weeders commissioned Olaf Skoogfors, a Swedish-American craftsman, to make their box, whose form and ornament come from a Scandinavian silver tradition.[73]

201. Casket, 1958 *(cat. no. 134)*

Olaf Skoogfors (1930–1975), Philadelphia. Marked on the bottom "HANDWROUGHT/STERLING/OLAF SKOOGFORS". Silver, l. 9³/₄ in. (24.8 cm.)

Inscribed on the body with the names of thirty-three presidents (through 1978) and "Presidents Cup in memory of Isabel Müller Wetherill 1888 1958"; and twice on the foot "The Weeders"

202. Vince Lombardi Trophy, 1972 *(cat. no. 135)*

Designed by Oscar Riedener for Tiffany and Company (1837 to the present), New York City. Marked "TIFFANY & CO. MAKERS STERLING SILVER 65194". Silver, h. 20¹/₄ in. (51.4 cm.)

Inscribed on the front of the base "Vince Lombardi Trophy NFL Super Bowl VI AFC vs NFC"

Dallas Cowboys Football Club, Irving, Texas

202

Football, baseball, and basketball are, without question, the most popular spectator sports in the United States today. Of the three, only professional football honors its national-championship team with silver. The first Vince Lombardi Trophy, popularly known as the Super Bowl trophy, was designed by Oscar Riedener for Tiffany and Company in 1966 and presented to the Green Bay Packers in 1967. (Vince Lombardi was the coach who led the Packers to five NFL Championships and two Super Bowl victories.)

Each year the company fabricates a new prize for that year's winner. The Dallas Cowboys own two Vince Lombardi trophies, the first one won in 1972 in a twenty-four-to-three victory over the Miami Dolphins; the second one was won in 1978. Each is a gleaming reminder of the team's history, years it earned the right to be called the best in the nation. Each Vince Lombardi Trophy presented to a team publicly affirms that that particular team has been admitted to the select fraternity of football greats.

203. Statuette (Boatswain's Mate Charles Riggin), 1892 (cat. no. 136)

Alexander J. Doyle (1857–1922), New York City. Silver, h. 31¼ in. (79.4 cm.)

Inscribed "Charles William Riggin in memoriam"

President Benjamin Harrison Memorial Home, Indianapolis, Indiana

204. "Rough Sketch for the Proposed Statue to Riggin by George Wharton Edwards," New York Recorder, 13 March 1892. Collection of the State Historical Society of Wisconsin.

Boatswain's Mate Charles Riggin, a young sailor assigned to the USS Baltimore, was killed by a mob while on shore in Valparaiso, Chile, on 19 October 1891. This statuette and two others like it are the only presentation-silver statues known to date. They cast light on international diplomacy, American nationalism, the press, and marketing at the end of the nineteenth century.

What began as a small incident quickly escalated as the United States government, pressured by inflammatory newspaper articles and a growing, aggressive navy, demanded an apology from Chile. When Chile did apologize, in January 1892, a scrappy new newspaper, the New York Recorder, announced a subscription to honor President Benjamin Harrison, Secretary of State James G. Blaine, and Secretary of the Navy Benjamin F. Trace for bringing about a peaceful resolution of the Riggin affair. Americans were asked to send in dimes, which would be melted and cast into statuettes to be presented to the three dignitaries. The Recorder listed the names of the donors in the newspaper and in a presentation book,

offered Waltham watches for the most contributions, and, on the Recorder's first birthday, even sent a free color picture of Riggin to each contributor. The dimes flooded in—26,382 in all—and readership undoubtedly increased at the same time. The Recorder periodically published designs proposed for the Riggin statuettes (fig. 204). All of them were patriotic versions of an enlisted man in uniform.[74] From the beginning, the newspaper referred to the figures as statuettes and planned to engage a sculptor rather than a silver manufacturer to make them. The ultimate choice was Alexander Doyle, a New Yorker trained in Italy, who had done numerous public bronze and marble sculptures.

The Riggin statuettes are yet another example of the public need to identify with and participate in patriotic occasions. Perhaps the New York Journal in 1898 remembered the Recorder's march of dimes when it organized the subscription for the Dewey Loving Cup (fig. 205).[75]

205, 207.   Dewey Loving Cup, 1898 *(cat. no. 137)*

Designed by William C. Codman (active 1891–1914) for Gorham Company (1831 to the present), Providence, Rhode Island. Marked on the base with a lion passant / Gothic "G" / anchor / and "Sterling". Silver, gilt, h. 102 in. (259.1 cm.)

Inscribed "The Dewey Loving Cup presented to the Conquering Admiral by seventy thousand American citizens as a tribute of their gratitude"

Chicago Historical Society, Gift of George G. Dewey

206.   Preliminary drawing for the Dewey Loving Cup, 1898. Pencil and watercolor on paper, 84 x 38 in. (213.4 x 96.5 cm.). Collection of Gorham Textron

In 1898 the United States was flexing its naval muscle. Its growing fleet of ships (many outfitted with presentation silver donated by the states and cities for which they were named (figs. 167, 210, 212) gave America an expanded international presence that it had not previously enjoyed. When the USS *Maine* was sunk in Havana harbor, the United States declared war against Spain and dispatched Commodore George Dewey from China to Manila, the port for the Spanish fleet in the Pacific. Dewey defeated the Spanish without loss of life, thereby becoming a national hero and symbol of America's new confidence and might. (That he censored all journalists' communiqués from Manila and that he was the darling of William Randolph Hearst's *New York Journal* may have had some bearing on his rapid rise.)[76]

The *Journal* began its Dewey Cup campaign on 11 May 1899, as Dewey, promoted to the rank of admiral, set sail for his first visit to the United States since his victory. From the very beginning, the *Journal* wanted the cup to be donated by Everyman: "The idea is to have something that will represent the great mass of the people and not a few wealthy men." Americans from every walk of life sent in their dimes to be melted down for the loving cup. The *Journal* made special appeals to parents, offering them, their children, and all subscribers a taste of immortality: each donor's name would be entered in a memorial book to be presented to Dewey. Lucky children holding dimes even had their pictures printed in the newspaper.[77]

The *Journal* turned to William Christmas Codman, chief designer at Gorham, to design the Dewey cup. Codman proposed a large, classical vase, surmounted by Victory holding Dewey's portrait. The three reserves on the body illustrate the battle of Manila Bay, Dewey's home in Montpelier, Vermont, and the New York City Dewey celebration at Grant's Tomb. In a nice touch, Codman even soldered dimes as scales on the fish supporting its plinth.

So successful was the drive that the *Journal* found itself with more dimes than anticipated. The subscription deadline was extended while Gorham hurriedly designed a comparatively simple cylindrical base. At the end of the drive the newspaper proudly reported that 70,000 dimes had been contributed to the cause. Gorham factory records show that the company charged its New York retail store $5,700 for the cup.[78]

Compared with Dewey's welcome to New York, the cup's presentation was subdued, chaired by Senator Chauncey M. Depew. At the conclusion of the festivities Dewey told the *Journal*, "Tell the people who contributed, and tell Mr. Hearst who thought of it and brought it to such a splended perfection, it's a tribute to me, yes, and it's a tribute to Mr. Hearst's enterprise and loyalty."[79] So much for Everyman.

208–10.   Punch bowl, waiter, cups, and ladle (from USS *Pennsylvania* service), 1905 *(cat. no. 138)*

Designed by Gilbert Crowell, for the Gorham Company (1831 to the present), Providence, Rhode Island. Marked "J.E. Caldwell & Co./Philadelphia/Sterling/1904". Silver, h. of punch bowl 19½ in. (49.5 cm.)

The State Museum of Pennsylvania–Pennsylvania Historical and Museum Commission, Harrisburg

211.   Preliminary drawing for the USS *Pennsylvania* punch bowl and ladle, c. 1905. Pencil and watercolor on paper, 42 x 61 in. (106.7 x 154.9 cm). Collection of Gorham Textron

Even in an age of opulence and monumentality, the silver service presented by the State of Pennsylvania to the armored cruiser USS *Pennsylvania* in 1905 would rank among the greatest services made. It is grand and extensive. (State records indicate that Pennsylvania allocated $25,000 for the 162 pieces, which required 12,000 ounces of silver.) The fifteen-gallon punch bowl and the elaborate two-tiered centerpiece (not shown), outfitted with ten shaded electric lights, are the most dramatic objects in the service. The punch set is an ornate combination of cast and engraved sea and state motifs. The body is decorated with four delicate cartouches that celebrate Pennsylvania's role in the coal, steel, and oil industries. Because many of the pieces bear J. E. Caldwell and Company marks, the service has always been credited to that firm. However, photographs and records at Gorham prove it was Gorham that made the service (fig. 211).

In 1916 the silver service was transferred to the new battleship USS *Pennsylvania*, where it remained in the wardroom, except during the two world wars, until the ship was decommissioned in 1946. The service was turned over to the State of Pennsylvania in 1970, with the exception of a few pieces that since 1986 have been aboard the new cruiser USS *Valley Forge*.[80]

210

POLITICS AND MILITARY

212

213

POLITICS AND MILITARY

214

212. Centerpiece (from USS *Delaware* service), 1910 *(cat. no. 139)*

Designed by William C. Codman (active 1891–1914) for the Gorham Company (1831 to the present), Providence, Rhode Island. Marked on the bottom of the centerpiece with a lion passant/anchor/and Gothic "G"/"STERLING/SBF/MADE BY/THE/GORHAM CO./FOR/MILLARD F. DAVIS/WILMINGTON, DEL." and on the candles "TIFFANY & CO./Pat. Apr. 29, 1902/Gorham SBF". Silver, h. 23³/₈ in. (59.4 cm.)

Delaware Division of Historical and Cultural Affairs, Dover

213. Preliminary drawing for the USS *Delaware* centerpiece, 1910. Pencil and watercolor on paper, 31¹/₂ x 50¹/₂ in. (80 x 128.3 cm.). Collection of Gorham Textron

Like the USS *Pennsylvania* (see fig. 210) the battleship USS *Delaware* needed a silver service early in the twentieth century. The Delaware Battleship Committee of the Wilmington Board of Trade

raised $9,592 and placed an order with Gorham through Millard F. Davis, a Wilmington jeweler. The pieces are fairly typical of presentation battleship services: a punch bowl and ladle, a plateau (or tray), a centerpiece, two candelabra, a waiter, a pitcher, four compotes, meat, fish, fruit, and entree dishes, a sauce boat and tray, a coffee urn, and cream, sugar, and coffee pots. Like the punch bowl, the basin of the centerpiece is supported by eagles. Four cornucopias spring from its base, each supporting a small dish for fruit. Illuminating the centerpiece are four electrified candlesticks, originally covered by fragile fringed silk shades with pierced silver frames.[81]

214. Silver sphere, 1944 *(cat. no. 140)*

Cartier (1847 to the present, Paris; 1909 to the present, New York). Marked on the silver band on the base with a pentagon and "CARTIER" and "MADE IN FRANCE". Silver, gilt, lapis lazuli, precious stones, h. 10 in. (25.4 cm.)

Inscribed "To The President of the United States Franklin Delano Roosevelt Christmas 1944 from Pierre C. Cartier"

Franklin D. Roosevelt Library and Museum, Hyde Park, New York

I hope the President will like the Silver Sphere, on a silver and lapis-lazuli base which I have made to mark his conferences. . . .

I know how busy the President is but I should very greatly appreciate it if, when it is convenient for him, he would grant me an appointment."[82]

Pierre Cartier (1878–1965) of the House of Cartier was understandably concerned about France during World War II. Born in that country and an owner of the leading French jewelry company, he doubtless had many reasons to speak with Franklin Delano Roosevelt in 1944.[83] Evidently, Cartier thought that a little Christmas gift might open the president's door, for he gave Roosevelt this sphere, which marks the four major Allied conferences that had been held to date. Roosevelt, who appreciated the gift but was not to be swayed, responded: "I have been just a little busy lately . . . and that is the reason why I have not had a chance to arrange to see you. However, I am asking General [Edwin Martin] Watson to get in touch with you to set a date at the first opportunity."[84]

Spheres, or globes as we would call them, were fairly common presentation forms between 1915 and 1945. They were especially popular at Gorham, where they were often recommended for air-race trophies (fig. 186). The Cartier sphere, like the air-race globes, are indicative of the revolution in transportation that had taken place in the twentieth century. For the first time in our history man was thinking globally, not just of regions or countries or continents.

Since Paris was not liberated until 25 August 1944, and this sphere was designed, fabricated, and delivered to President Roosevelt from Cartier in New York between 11 September (the date of the Quebec Conference), and 22 December 1944, everyone assumed it was American-made until its "Made in France" mark was noted. The firm did maintain limited production in France during the Occupation,[85] yet it is remarkable that Roosevelt's sphere could have been fashioned so quickly and shipped or carried across the Atlantic in time for Christmas.

215

215. Teapot, sugar bowl, cream pot (from USS *Long Beach* service), 1961 *(cat. no. 141)*

Designed by Richard L. Huggins for Gorham Company (1831 to the present), Providence, Rhode Island. Marked on the teapot with a lion passant, anchor, Gothic "G" and "JNA/M" and on the sugar bowl with a lion passant, anchor, Gothic "G" and "JNA". Silver, h. of teapot 12 in. (30.5 cm.)

The United States Navy and the City of Long Beach

The U.S. Navy's first nuclear-powered cruiser was the USS *Long Beach*, a ship that is still on active duty. Also on active duty is the silver service presented to the ship at its commissioning by the City of Long Beach. The service originated in a time-honored way (see page 169): the navy solicited the gift from the city, and the city placed the order through a local store, in this instance the C. C. Lewis Jewelry Company, which worked with Gorham to execute the order.[86]

Richard L. Huggins recalls that his design was controversial. The commission began as a private project for Gorham's head designer, but it was soon opened to his entire staff. Gorham submitted six or seven largely traditional designs plus this one to the Long Beach City Council. In selecting this design, the council recognized the progressive role that their cruiser would have in the nuclear navy. Theirs was a new world of Sputniks, the race to the moon, and nuclear power. Clearly this silver is part of that world.[87] The *Long Beach* service was very avant-garde in its day. Certainly the finials based on a model of an atom with circling electrons, the teardrop bodies, and the elongated legs give it a futuristic quality that is unique in silver design.

216, 217. Bryant Vase, 1875 *(cat. no. 142)*

Designed by James Horton Whitehouse (1833–1902) for Tiffany and Company (1837 to the present), New York City. Marked on the foot ring "TIFFANY & CO. UNION SQUARE New York. DESIGN PAT. MAY 1875" and on the back of the square plinth "TIFFANY & CO. MAKERS". Silver, gilt, h. 33⅜ in. (97.5 cm.)

Inscribed on the neck "Truth, crushed to earth" and on the open book on the back of the vase: "Matthew Chap VI Verse 28, 29 ['And why are you so anxious about clothing? Consider the lilies of the field, how they grow; they neither toil nor spin; yet I tell you, even Solomon in all his glory was not arrayed like one of these']"

The Metropolitan Museum of Art, New York, Gift of William Cullen Bryant, 1877

When William Cullen Bryant celebrated his eightieth birthday, on 3 November 1874, members of the Century Club wondered how to honor this beloved journalist, editor, poet, and translator of the *Iliad* and the *Odyssey*. Led by the committee chairman, the Reverend Dr. Samuel Osgood, a group of men called on Bryant at his home and stated their intent:

> *We give you our heartiest wishes for your continued health and happiness, and we inform you respectfully of the intention to embody in a commemorative vase, of original design and choice workmanship, the lessons of your literary and civic career in its relations with our country, whose nature, history, liberty, law, and conscience you have so illustrated. We believe that such a work will be an expressive fact of our coming National Centennial, and a permanent treasure of our Metropolitan Museum of Art.[88]*

216

These fine men not only honored Bryant, but in effect issued a challenge to the American silver industry to design the ultimate presentation piece, one that would be given to a great man, displayed at the Centennial celebration, and then permanently enshrined in a museum. The Gorham and Whiting companies, Starr and Marcus, and Black Starr and Frost all competed against Tiffany and Company for the contract. Each company except for Starr and Marcus submitted a vasiform design on a square plinth bursting with classical allegories and ornamented with Bryant's portrait.[89] Tiffany and Company won the $5,000 contract with James H. Whitehouse's design, a beautifully scaled vase covered with a portrait of Bryant, a fretwork of apple blossoms and branches, a medallion of Poetry contemplating Nature, and four biographical medallions.[90] It communicated Bryant's feelings about nature and nature's importance in God's hierarchy, as Bryant perceived it. Also gracing the vase are a printing press, a waterfowl, broken shackles (symbolic of Bryant's stand on emancipation), Indian corn, and water lilies.[91]

The Bryant Vase evidently cost Tiffany approximately $10,000 to produce—twice what the committee would pay for it. The company obviously recognized the importance of the vase in the eyes of the American public as a harbinger of the Centennial and measure of artistic accomplishment. Their effort did not go unnoticed, for Bryant referred to its makers as "the worthy successors of Benvenuto Cellini," the great Italian Renaissance goldsmith. He went on:

> *Hereafter someone may say, "This beautiful vase is made in honor of a certain American poet, whose name it bears, but whose writings are forgotten. It is remarkable that so much pains should have been taken to illustrate the life and writings of one whose works are so completely unknown at the present day." Thus, gentlemen artists, I shall be indebted to you for causing the memory of my name to outlast my writings.[92]*

218

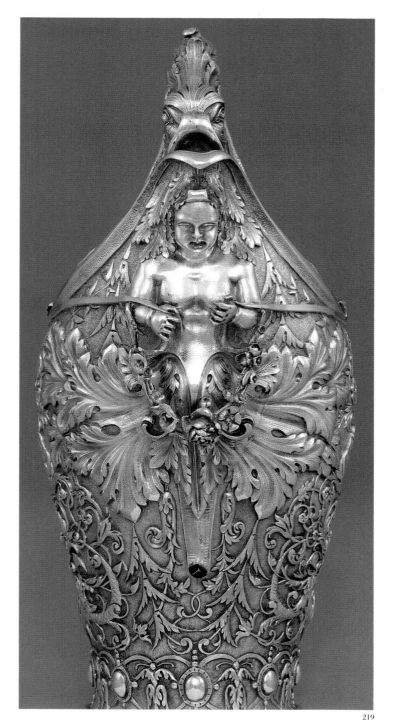

219

218, 219. Water jug and stand, 1879 *(cat. no. 143)*

Samuel Kirk and Son (1815 to the present), Baltimore, Maryland. Marked on the underside of the stand and the jug "S. Kirk & Son 11 oz". Silver, h. of jug 13 1/4 in (33.7 cm.)

Inscribed on the bottom of the jug and the stand "To Alexander Biddle from the children of his brother J. Williams Biddle as a token of their grateful recognition of his continuous services and devotion to their interests. Nov. 1879."

The Maryland Historical Society, Baltimore, Gift of the Samuel Kirk Museum Foundation, Inc.

Alexander Biddle (1819–1899) and Jonathan Williams Biddle (1821–1856) were the fourth and fifth sons of Thomas Biddle and Christina Williams. J. Williams Biddle married Emily S. Meigs (1824–1905) and had children before his untimely death. Of their

six children, only three lived beyond childhood: Christine Williams Biddle (b. 1847), Thomas Biddle (b. 1853), and Emily Williams Biddle (b. 1855). These were the children who probably honored their uncle in his sixtieth year with this water jug and stand.[93] Just as in 1815 Lady Houstoun honored James Johnston for his counsel with the gift of a pitcher (fig. 147), J. Williams Biddle's children honored their uncle Alexander, who was a prominent Philadelphia businessman and a director of the Pennsylvania Railroad.

The Biddle water jug was made by Samuel Kirk and Son in the ornate repoussé style for which the firm had been known since the 1820s.[94] Although classically inspired, this handsome object is much more original in its shape than most water jugs of the day.

220–22. Prize cup, 1887 *(cat. no. 144)*

Gorham Company (1831 to the present), Providence, Rhode Island. Marked with a lion passant, anchor, and Gothic "G/ STERLING"/and a fleur-de-lis. Silver, h. 11½ in. (29.2 cm.)

Inscribed "Anton Seidl from his New York admirers Feb 25th 1887."

Museum of the City of New York, Gift of Mrs. Anton Seidl

Anton Seidl (1850–1898) seems to have been one of those rare men who combine professional excellence with warm human qualities that make them truly admired by their contemporaries. Seidl, who was born in Budapest and was one of Richard Wagner's closest disciples, came to New York in 1885 to direct the young Metropolitan Opera Company. Seidl soon introduced *Die Meistersinger* (4 January 1886), *Die Walküre* (10 November 1886), and *Tristan and Isolde* (1 December 1886) into the repertory. Seidl and his German operas were so well received that he was given this extraordinary prize cup just two years after his arrival at the Metropolitan. The presentation celebrated the end of his second suc-

cessful season and his forthcoming departure for Europe. Henry Marquand, president of the Metropolitan Museum of Art, William Steinway, the piano maker, and Joseph Pulitzer, the journalist, were among its donors.

The cup, which cost $1,000 to make, is one of the earliest loving cups found in American presentation silver. It is a virtuoso example of repoussé and chasing in the silversmith's medium. The designer used the handles to imitate the trees of naturalistic theater sets, while the greenery framing each vignette like a stage flat gracefully and uniformly unites three scenes from three operas that Seidl introduced to America.[95] Illustrated here are views of the three sides of the cup. At left is the scene from act 2 of *Die Meistersinger*. At right, in two nineteenth-century Gorham factory photographs, are the scenes from act 2 of *Tristan and Isolde* (above) and from act 3 of *Siegfried* (below).

223

223. Whiskey flask, 1888 *(cat. no. 145)*

Gorham Company (1831 to the present), Providence, Rhode
 Island. Marked on the bottom with a lion passant, anchor, and
 Gothic "G/STERLING/167 [in a rectangle] /GORHAM. MFG.
 CO." and a star in a circle. Silver, h. 7³/4 in. (19.7 cm.)

Inscribed on the back "Alex R. Shepherd to Dr. C. R. Bissell
 1888" and on the cap "Batopilas"

The Museum of Fine Arts, Houston, museum purchase with funds
 provided by Dr. and Mrs. John R. Kelsey, Jr.

Alexander Robey Shepherd (1835–1902), the man who ordered
this flask and at least nine others like it from Gorham, was a color-
ful plumbing contractor known as "Boss Shepherd" during his
days as governor of Washington, D.C., under President Ulysses S.

Grant. He left Washington in 1880, bankrupt and disgraced, to
run the Batopilas silver mine high in Mexico's remote Sierra
Madre Mountains. When Shepherd returned to the United States
in 1887, he did so in a flurry of parades and publicity. While on
this trip, Shepherd also commissioned these flasks. Each cost $80
wholesale, although Gorham charged Shepherd only $75, proba-
bly because he supplied his own silver from the Batopilas mine.[96]
Engraved with the name of the mine and the recipient, a view of
Batopilas, and Shepherd's portrait and autograph, the flasks were
an effective tool to promote Shepherd and the mine and to sell its
stock. Shepherd gave his flasks to both Americans and Mexicans;
one of the latter thanked him in Spanish, "Even though for my part
I do not have the honor of knowing you personally. . . ."[97] The
Batopilas flask is representative of the darker side of presentation
silver, given to curry favor, to promote the donor, or to establish a
sense of obligation on the part of the recipient.

224

224. Candelabrum, 1890 *(cat. no. 146)*

Tiffany and Company (1837 to the present), New York City.
    Marked: "TIFFANY & CO./5727 MAKERS 3128/STERLING
    SILVER/925–1000/M". Silver, h. 27½ in. (69.9 cm.)

Inscribed "CCS"

Museum of the City of New York, given in memory of Daisy Beard
    Brown by her daughters, Bertha Shults Dougherty, and Isabel
    Shults

When Charles J. Grosjean (1841–1888) created the Chrysanthemum flatware pattern, in 1880, he introduced a style that brides
would favor well into the next century. Tiffany and Company soon
translated it into tea and coffee services, serving dishes, candelabra, and a variety of other forms.[98] Caroline C. Shults (née Daisy
Beard Brown) was representative of many wealthy young brides in
her day. She was given a pair of candelabra, one of which is shown
in the above illustration, and 163 other pieces of hollowware and
flatware in the Chrysanthemum pattern when she was married in
1890.[99]

Sixteen years later, Bessie May Kirby, only daughter of the wealthy Houston lumberman John Henry Kirby, received the same silver pattern when she married John Schuyler Stewart of Amsterdam, New York. The bride's gift was a model of conspicuous consumption that has seldom been equaled in the annals of presentation silver:

The popularity of the groom in his Eastern home, and that his bride is well-beloved in all parts of the Southland, was evidenced in a wealth of tokens—in silver, glass, bronze, porcelain, paintings, embroideries, priceless Turkish and Persian rugs. Notable, among others, is a rosewood chest of silver, containing eleven hundred pieces, in the chrysanthemum pattern, each piece engraved with the monogram of the bride and groom. This is the loving offering of Mr. and Mrs. Kirby. An ornate full silver service, matching in pattern the chest of silver, was the gift of Mr. and Mrs. Stewart, father and mother of the groom.[100]

226

225. Cup, 1900 *(cat. no. 148)*

Designed by Karl Bitter (1867–1915). Made by William B. Durgin Company (1853–1905), Concord, New Hampshire. Marked "WM. B. DURGIN CO."/"18" in a triangle; "K" in a circle; "D" in a triangle/"CONCORD. N. H." Gold, h. 14⁷/₁₆ in. (36.7 cm.)

Inscribed "Dem Yubelpaare Im Yubeljahre Von Kind und Kindeskind geweiht, an Becher's Schwelle Aus edler Quelle Trinkt Glück und Kraft auf ferne Zeit [Dedicated to the jubilee couple in the jubilee year by children and grandchildren, at the rim of the cup drink from the noble source good fortune and strength for a long time]"; "1850 21ten Juli 1900." "ARBEITSLUST [love of industry]"; "WOLTHAETIGKEIT [charity]"; "VATERLANDSLIEBE [patriotism]"; and "In Liebe erdacht In Liebe vollbracht Aus Goldener Tiefe Die Liebe Euch lacht [Conceived in love, completed in love, from golden depths love smiles at you]"

The Metropolitan Museum of Art, New York, Gift of Marcus I. Goldman

The Goldman children and grandchildren presented a gold cup to their parents, Marcus and Bertha Goldman, on their golden wedding anniversary, in July 1900. Goldman was a founder of the Goldman, Sachs investment house. As magnificent as this cup is, surely it was the completeness of the thought, the caring, and the love it symbolizes that made it the ultimate gift to these honored grandparents. The Goldman children engaged Karl Bitter and the William B. Durgin Company, a firm best known for its beautifully detailed Art Nouveau flatware, to execute this commission. Bitter brought his extensive experience as a sculptor to the project (he had collaborated with Richard Morris Hunt on both the Fifth Avenue facade of the Metropolitan Museum of Art in New York and the beaux-arts Administration Building of the 1893 Chicago World's Columbian Exposition). In Bitter's design, two separate trees grow on either side of a figure of Eros, god of love. Eros gently brings the trees together above his head, where they intertwine, leaf, and flower. Three medallions on the bowl depict three phases in the couple's life together: they are shown embracing, holding a child, and surrounded by their children and grandchildren.[101]

The cup is a symbol that encourages us to follow the Goldmans' example: that we may love so well and live so long, that we may be so honored in our families in our old age, and that our children may be prosperous enough to commission such a special gift.

226. Punch bowl, 1925 *(cat. no. 149)*

Tiffany and Company (1837 to the present), New York City. Marked "TIFFANY & CO./18457 MAKERS 9032 / STERLING SILVER/M". Silver, diam. at top 10¹/₂ in. (26.7 cm.)

Inscribed "Annetta Joanna Nicoll Philip Skinner Platt April 29, 1925"

Yale University Art Gallery, Gift of Philip Skinner Platt

*Hear the clumping of their feet
As they go marching down the street!
Perhaps some day if I am good,
I may be of that brotherhood....
For, tho I know not what they do,
I greatly want to do it, too.[102]*

Beginning in the 1880s, Yale College juniors assembled near Battell Chapel each May for Tap Day, a day of reckoning when select juniors were stoutly tapped on the back and were thereby invited to join senior societies. These small social clubs, some of which still exist, are bathed in secrecy and go by such names as Skull and Bones (established in 1833) and Scroll and Key (established in 1842).[103]

In 1913, Scroll and Key members of the class of 1912 asked Tiffany and Company to design a bowl for them to be given to each member by the others when he married. Philip Skinner Platt (Yale '12) and Annetta Joanna Nicoll received their wedding gift in 1925, twelve years after the pattern was listed in the company's records.[104]

227 (opposite). Loving cup, 1897 *(cat. no. 147)*

Wilcox and Evertsen (1892–1898), New York City. Marked on the base "Sterling"/an Indian head looking left/"SX212/13 Pts." Silver, h. 11¹¹/₁₆ in. (28.1 cm.)

Inscribed "To Anton Seidl from fellow members of the Lotos Club as a token of friendship and admiration. 1897." and

*In the afternoon they came unto a land
In which it seemed always afternoon.*

Museum of the City of New York, Gift of Charles M. Eckman

"IN THE AFTERNOON." · "IN THE AFTERNOON."

To
ANTON SEIDL
FROM
FELLOW MEMBERS OF
THE LOTOS CLUB
AS A TOKEN OF
FRIENDSHIP AND
MARCH 6th ADMIRATION.
1897

228

In 1897 Anton Seidl (see page 174) received yet another loving cup, this one from fellow members of the Lotos Club, given to thank him for arranging Wagner's "Siegfried Idyll" for a quartet and conducting it at a club concert. Like the Cliff Dwellers in Chicago (see page 160), the Lotos Club in New York drew its members from art and literary circles. Its very name, an alternate spelling of the lotus flower, and its motto, lines from Tennyson's 1832 poem "The Lotos-Eaters," reflect the Aestheticism of its members and their interest in Japanese culture. Samuel L. Clemens and John La Farge were Lotos Club members.[105] In honoring Seidl, the Lotos Club turned to a small but well-regarded factory, Wilcox and Evertsen, which the following year was incorporated into the International Silver Company. The firm produced this loving cup in the mature American Art Nouveau style. Lotus leaves, stems, and pads ornament this cup with graceful, upcurving handles and allude both to the name of the club and to its motto, which is quoted on the rim.

228. Madeira serving set, 1931 *(cat. no. 150)*

Samuel Kirk and Son, Inc. (1815 to the present), Baltimore, Maryland. Marked on the bottom of the punch bowl and cups and on the back of ladle "KIRK AND SON INC. STERLING". Silver, gilt, h. of punch bowl 11½ in. (29.2 cm.)

Inscribed "Harry Norman Baetjer January 12, 1932, Howard Baetjer December 20, 1929, Laurence Robert Carton November 19, 1935, Lewis Warrington Cottman* September 23, 1922, Robert Bell Deford February 8, 1935, Donald Newcomer Gilpin August 1, 1937, Douglas Gorman May 13, 1932, Thomas Edward Hambleton*, Richard Curzon Hoffman September 27, 1931, Francis Nash Iglehart August 1, 1931, Iredell Waddell Iglehart*, Richard Newton Jackson August 25, 1933, William Wallace Lanahan June 24, 1934, Gustavus Ober, Jr. July 4, 1931, Edwin Wingate Poe August 13, 1926, William Frank Roberts January 25, 1927, John Fife Symington January 20, 1927, Donald Symington October 28, 1931, John Gregg Thomas October 3, 1934, James Simpson Whedbee June 29, 1926, John Sawyer Wilson, Jr.* December 9, 1927"

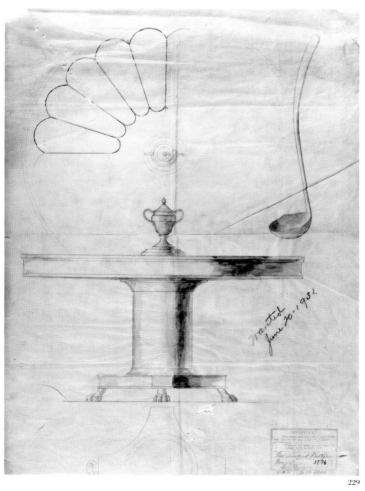

229

The Maryland Historical Society, Baltimore, Gift of Mr. Howard Baetjer, II

229. Working drawing for Madeira serving set. 1931. Samuel Kirk and Son. Pencil on paper, 27³/₄ x 20 in. (68.6 x 50.8 cm). Kirk Papers, Collection of The Maryland Historical Society, Baltimore

A handsome, round Empire-style dining table stood in Baltimore's Merchants Club. Between 1910 and 1950 it became the meeting place for a group of luncheon regulars who were friends of the textile manufacturer Howard Baetjer. Baetjer commissioned Kirk and Company to reproduce the table in silver as a Madeira server. Kirk did so with great style. The delicate urn centerpiece is actually the knob with which one lifts the table's top. Inside, the central column is a deep well from which Madeira is dispensed with a perfectly designed ladle. Twenty-one names radiate from the urn on the vessel's lid. Most are followed by the date of the man's fiftieth birthday. The name of each man is also inscribed on a gilt cup, perhaps symbolizing his golden birthday anniversary. The nineteen cups remaining with the serving set are tokens of the camaraderie that was enjoyed around the club's convivial table.[106]

230. Tea and coffee service, 1983–84 (cat. no. 151)

Ubaldo Vitali (b. 1944, Rome, Italy), Glen Ridge, New Jersey. Marked on the bottom of each piece "U. VITALI STERLING". Silver, ebony, ivory, plexiglass, h. of coffeepot 11 in. (27.9 cm.)

230

Inscribed on the bottom of the coffeepot "The Anniversary Service commissioned by The Newark Museum in celebration of its 75th Anniversary 1909–1984."

The Newark Museum, Newark, New Jersey.

When the Newark Museum wanted to celebrate its seventy-fifth anniversary in a special way, it presented itself with a beautiful tea and coffee service commissioned especially for the occasion. The museum turned to Ubaldo Vitali, a silversmith trained in Italy who has a small concern in nearby Glen Ridge. This museum, which has long been known for its progressive collecting policy, chose a traditional presentation form—a tea set—made of a material that has historically been associated with anniversaries, yet it saluted the 1980s and New Jersey craftsmen by commissioning one of America's most accomplished silversmiths to create a unique design.

231. Spice box, 1985 *(cat. no. 152)*

Janet Dash (b. 1939), New York City. Marked on the base "Janet Dash". Silver, ebony, brass, copper, gold, glass, l. 2³/₄ in. (7 cm.)

David and Alice Greenwald Ward (Presented to Alice M. Greenwald by the staff of the National Museum of American Jewish History, January 1986)

Shabbat is a weekly Jewish holiday. It begins at home on Friday evening, when candles are lit to mark the beginning of the Sabbath and ends on Saturday evening, when fragrant spices symbolizing the sweetness of this holiday are inhaled from *besamin*

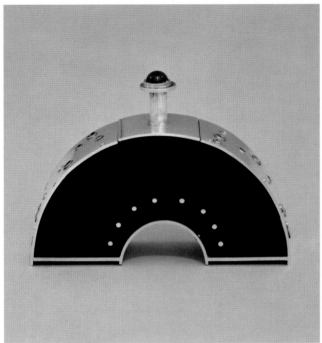

231

boxes to mark Sabbath's end.[107] Janet Dash has used a variety of precious materials to make this diminutive box that is as special as the spices it will hold. It was a fitting birthday gift to Alice Greenwald from her staff at the National Museum of American Jewish History.

NOTES

INTRODUCTION

I would like to thank Katherine S. Howe, David B. Warren, Michael K. Brown, and Ann Wood for their many contributions to this essay. I also am indebted to Barbara McLean Ward for her close reading of the text and for many helpful suggestions.

1. The opening quotation is taken from *The Iliad of Homer*, translated and with an introduction by Richard Lattimore (Chicago and London: University of Chicago Press, 1951), p. 470. My attention was drawn to the passage by D. E. Strong, *Greek and Roman Gold and Silver Plate* (London: Methuen, 1966). p. xxv.

2. In preparing these remarks, I have relied most heavily on the following publications: H. Maxson Holloway, "American Presentation Silver," *The New-York Historical Society Quarterly*, vol. 30, no. 4 (October 1946), pp. 215–33; *"Upon This Occasion": A Loan Exhibition of Important Presentation Silver from Colonial Times to Today* (Newburyport, Mass.: Towle Silversmiths, 1955); Margaret Brown Klapthor, *Presentation Pieces in the Museum of History and Technology*, Contributions from the Museum of History and Technology, Paper 47 (Washington, D.C.: Smithsonian Institution, 1965), pp. 81–108; Katharine Morrison McClinton, "American Presentation Silver of the Seventeenth and Eighteenth Centuries," *Connoisseur*, vol. 166, no. 670 (December 1967), pp. 256–60, and vol. 167, no. 671 (January 1968), pp. 58–63; Katharine Morrison McClinton, *Collecting American 19th-Century Silver* (New York: Charles Scribner's Sons, 1968), chapters 5–7; Martha Gandy Fales, *Early American Silver* (New York: E. P. Dutton, 1973), chapter 8; Barbara McLean Ward and Gerald W. R. Ward, eds., *Silver in American Life: Selections from the Mabel Brady Garvan and Other Collections at Yale University* (New York: American Federation of Arts; Boston: David R. Godine, 1979), pp. 35, 90–101; and Ross Fox, *Presentation Pieces and Trophies from the Henry Birks Collection of Canadian Silver* (Ottawa: National Gallery of Canada, 1985.)

3. Maureen O'Brien Quimby and Jean Woollens Fernald, "A Matter of Taste and Elegance: Admiral Samuel Francis Du Pont and the Decorative Arts," *Winterthur Portfolio*, vol. 21, nos. 2–3 (Summer–Autumn 1986), p. 108, fig. 6.

4. For many years the Winterthur Museum has awarded reproduction Paul Revere bowls to employees on their retirement. Made by Reed and Barton, these 5½-inch stock bowls are engraved locally with the name of the recipient, the name of the museum, the year the recipient joined the museum, and the year of his or her retirement. A photograph of eighteen Colonial Williamsburg employees who were honored for their twenty-five years of service by the gift of an even larger Revere bowl is included in Colonial Williamsburg's *Annual Report* for 1985 (p. 14).

5. Charles H. Carpenter, Jr., with Mary Grace Carpenter, *Tiffany Silver* (New York: Dodd, Mead, 1978), pp. 36–37. See also chapters 7–9, in which are discussed presentation silver, presentation swords and guns, and yachting and other sporting trophies. For other surveys of nineteenth-century presentation objects, see Charles H. Carpenter, Jr., *Gorham Silver, 1831–1981* (New York: Dodd, Mead, 1982), chapter 9; and McClinton, *Collecting American 19th-Century Silver*, chapters 5–7.

6. A copy of the Reed and Barton catalogue is in the Yale University Art Gallery; a copy of the C. F. Monroe catalogue is in the collection of the Harpers Ferry Center, National Park Service, Harpers Ferry, West Virginia; and a copy of the Bailey, Banks and Biddle catalogue is in the Winterthur Museum Library, Winterthur, Delaware.

7. See Eric Hobsbawm, "Introduction: Inventing Traditions," in Eric Hobsbawm and Terence Ranger, eds., *The Invention of Tradition* (Cambridge: Cambridge University Press, 1983), pp. 1–14. For Decatur and his silver, see *A Silver Tribute to Valor* (Washington, D.C.: Preservation Press, 1981), with essays by Jennifer Faulds Goldsborough, Kathleen Curran, and Vicki E. Sopher. Also see Eliza-

beth Ingerman Wood, "Thomas Fletcher: A Philadelphia Entrepreneur of Presentation Silver," in *Winterthur Portfolio III*, ed. Milo M. Naeve (Winterthur, Del.: Henry Francis du Pont Winterthur Museum, 1967), pp. 136–71, for other examples of early nineteenth-century presentation silver that reflect a desire to invent tradition for the heroes of the early Republic.

8. For the uses and qualities of gold, see Kenneth Blakemore, *The Book of Gold* (London: November Books, 1971); for silver, see William A. Lanford, "'A Mineral of that Excellent Nature': The Qualities of Silver as a Metal," in Ward and Ward, *Silver in American Life*, pp. 3–9; and Allison Butts and Charles D. Coxe, eds., *Silver: Economics, Metallurgy, and Use* (Princeton, N.J.: Van Nostrand, 1967).

9. The discussion that follows is based primarily on the concept of manifest and latent functions presented in Robert K. Merton, *On Theoretical Sociology: Essays Old and New* (New York: Free Press, 1967), pp. 73–138, which includes the relevant portions of Merton's *Social Theory and Social Structure*, published in 1949; on the distinction between technomic (normal, practical, utilitarian use), sociotechnic (how an object is used in a context of social interaction), and ideotechnic (how an object is used in religious or psychological contexts) functions put forth in Lewis R. Binford, "Archaeology as Anthropology," *American Antiquity*, vol. 28, no. 2 (October 1962), pp. 217–55; and on the application of these ideas to American decorative arts suggested by James Deetz, *In Small Things Forgotten: The Archaeology of American Life* (Garden City, N.Y.: Anchor Books, 1977), p. 51, and Kenneth L. Ames, "Material Culture as Non-Verbal Communication: A Historical Case Study," *Journal of American Culture*, vol. 3, no. 4 (Winter 1980), pp. 619–41, especially p. 620. See also Gerald W. R. Ward, "Silver and Society in Salem, Massachusetts, 1630–1820: A Case Study of the Consumer and the Craft" (Ph.D. diss., Boston University, 1984), chapter 3.

10. Alan Gowans, *Learning to See: Historical Perspectives on Modern Popular/Commercial Arts* (Bowling Green, Ohio: Bowling Green University Popular Press, 1981), p. 17.

11. Quoted in Maury Allen, *Where Have You Gone, Joe DiMaggio?*, reprinted in Anthony J. Conner, ed., *Voices from Cooperstown* (New York: Collier Books, 1984), p. 277.

12. Mihaly Csikszentmihalyi and Eugene Rochberg-Halton, *The Meaning of Things: Domestic Symbols and the Self* (Cambridge: Cambridge University Press, 1981).

13. McClinton, *Collecting American 19th-Century Silver*, pp. 270–72; also see M. E. Grimshaw, *Silver Medals, Badges, and Trophies from Schools in the British Isles, 1550–1850* (Cambridge: privately printed, 1985).

14. "Your Treasured Silver Awards" (1986), a pamphlet published by The Silver Institute, Washington, D.C.

15. For an illustration of the Metcalf cup, see *Bostonia*, vol. 58, no. 3 (March 1984), p. 53. A photograph of the presentation ceremony appears in the university's *Fulcrum* (September 1984), p. 10. The writer would like to thank Michaeline Fall of Boston University and Gail R. Shapiro of Shreve, Crump, and Low, Inc., for their assistance.

16. Roger M. Berkowitz, "The Patriotic Fund Vases," *Apollo*, vol. 113, no. 228 (February 1981), pp. 104–5.

17. On the Tyng cup, see Kevin L. Stayton, "Captain Tyng's Trophy," *Portfolio*, vol. 3, no. 2 (March–April 1981), pp. 44–45. On the value of silver in Boston, see John J. McCusker, *Money and Exchange in Europe and America, 1600–1775: A Handbook* (Chapel Hill: Univer-

sity of North Carolina Press for the Institute of Early American History and Culture, 1978), p. 152. The value of the silver in the Tyng cup was calculated as follows: The weight of the cup (96.25 ounces) was multiplied by the price of silver in Boston in 1744 (33 shillings per ounce); to compensate for inflation, the resulting sum (approximately £159) in Massachusetts currency was converted by a multiplier of 0.16, to arrive at a value of approximately £25 in pounds sterling. Estate values in Boston in the 1736–45 period are given in Gary B. Nash, *The Urban Crucible: Social Change, Political Consciousness, and the Origins of the American Revolution* (Cambridge, Mass.: Harvard University Press, 1979), p. 400, table 7. The cost of Hurd's workmanship probably equaled or exceeded the value of the metal, although this cost could not be recovered if the object was melted down.

18. The ideas about gift theory that follow are derived primarily from Marcel Mauss, *The Gift: Forms and Functions of Exchange in Archaic Societies*, trans. Ian Cunnison (Glencoe, Ill.: Free Press, 1954); and Lewis Hyde, *The Gift: Imagination and the Erotic Life of Property* (New York: Vintage Books, 1983).

19. Bauman L. Belden, *Indian Peace Medals Issued in the United States* (1927; reprint, New Milford, Conn.: N. Flayderman, 1966); Francis P. Prucha, *Indian Peace Medals in American History* (Madison, Wis.: State Historical Society of Wisconsin, 1971); and Francis P. Prucha, *Peace and Friendship: Indian Peace Medals in the United States* (Washington, D.C.: National Portrait Gallery, Smithsonian Institution, 1985).

20. See Gerald W. R. Ward, "Icons of Continuity and Change: Some Thoughts on Silver in the California Experience," in *Silver in the Golden State: Images and Essays Celebrating the History and Art of Silver in California*, ed. Edgar W. Morse (Oakland, Calif.: Oakland Museum History Department, 1986), pp. 96–97; also see plate 4. For the Phillips service, see Edmund P. Hogan, *An American Heritage: A Book About the International Silver Company* (n.p.: International Silver Company, 1977), p. 106.

21. Andy Rooney, *And More by Andy Rooney* (New York: Warner Books, 1983), pp. 221–23.

22. Quoted in John Culme, *Nineteenth-Century Silver* (London: Hamlyn Publishing Group for Country Life Books, 1977), p. 150.

23. See Wood, "Thomas Fletcher," figs. 4, 5; and Carpenter, *Tiffany Silver*, pp. 140–41, 32–36, 14–15. Some early glassmakers, such as John Frederick Amelung, sent pieces of presentation glass to various dignitaries in an even more overt form of self-promotion; see George S. McKearin and Helen McKearin, *American Glass* (New York: Crown Publishers, 1941), pp. 104–8.

24. Karl Marx, *Contribution to the Critique of Political Economy*, quoted in Eugenia W. Herbert, *Red Gold of Africa: Copper in Precolonial History and Culture* (Madison: University of Wisconsin Press, 1984), p. 301.

25. Herbert, *Red Gold of Africa*, p. 242.

26. Brian Greenberg, *Worker and Community: Response to Industrialization in a Nineteenth-Century American City, Albany, New York, 1850–1884* (Albany: State University of New York Press, 1985), pp. 25–31, 168, notes 17, 18.

27. For a specific instance, see Robert B. St. George, "Artifacts of Regional Consciousness in the Connecticut River Valley, 1700–1780," in *The Great River: Art and Society of the Connecticut Valley, 1635–1820* (Hartford, Conn.: Wadsworth Atheneum, 1985), p. 35.

28. Grahame Clark, *Symbols of Excellence: Precious Metals as Expressions of Status* (Cambridge: Cambridge University Press, 1986), pp. 86–87.

29. On the Liberty Bowl, see *The Glorious Ninety-Two Members of the House of Representatives: Selections from Journals of the Honourable House of Representatives . . .* (Boston, 1949), published to commemorate the return of the object to Massachusetts.

THE COLONIAL PERIOD

I would like to express my sincere appreciation to my colleagues at other institutions and the lenders to this exhibition for their ongoing interest in this undertaking. While I cannot name them all, they have my sincere thanks. I must, however, take this opportunity to recognize Martha Gandy Fales and the late Kathryn C. Buhler, not only for their support of this project but for the rich and remarkable contributions that they have made to our understanding of American silver.

1. Samuel Sewall, *The Diary of Samuel Sewall, 1674–1729*, ed. M. Halsey Thomas, 2 vols. (New York: Farrar, Straus & Giroux, 1973).

2. Ibid., vol. 1, p. 453. See also Samuel Green, "Sewall's Gift to the Artillery," *Proceedings of the Massachusetts Historical Society*, vol. 43 (Boston: Massachusetts Historical Society, 1910), pp. 491–92. The halberd's ferrule is in the Ancient and Honorable Artillery Company's collection.

3. Sewall, *Diary*, vol. 1, p. 564.

4. Ibid., p. 443.

5. Ibid., vol. 2, p. 871.

6. Alexander Brown, *The Genesis of the United States* (New York: Russell and Russell, 1964), vol. 2, p. 570.

7. Donald L. Fennimore, "Religion in America: Metal Objects in Service of the Ritual," *The American Art Journal*, vol. 10 (November 1978), p. 21.

8. John Marshall Phillips, *American Silver* (New York: Chanticleer Press, 1949), p. 24.

9. *Collections of the New York Genealogical and Biographical Society*, vol. 2, *Baptisms from 1639 to 1730 in the Reformed Dutch Church, New York* (New York: privately printed, 1901), p. 15. I am indebted to Margaret Stearns, Curator Emeritus, Museum of the City of New York, for bringing this corrected information to my attention.

10. *Church Silver of Colonial Virginia* (Richmond: Virginia Museum of Fine Arts, 1970), p. 21.

11. E. Alfred Jones, *The Old Silver of American Churches* (Letchworth, England: privately printed for the National Society of Colonial Dames of America at the Arden Press, 1913), p. 399.

12. Ibid., p. 237.

13. Ibid., p. 311.

14. Ibid., pp. 42–43.

15. "Harvard College Records, Part 1: Corporation Records, 1636–1750," *Publications of The Colonial Society of Massachusetts*, vol. 15: *Collections* (Boston: privately printed, 1925), p. 207.

16. John Samuel Ezell, *Fortune's Merry Wheel: The Lottery in America* (Cambridge, Harvard University Press, 1960), p. 14.

17. *Virginia Gazette* (Williamsburg), no. 52, 22–29, July 1737.

18. Rita Susswein Gottesman, *The Arts and Crafts in New York, 1726–1776* (New York: New-York Historical Society, 1938), p. 61.

19. Sewall, *Diary*, vol. 1, p. 467.

20. Gottesman, *Arts and Crafts in New York*, p. 78.

21. B. Fernow et al., *Documents Relating to the History of the Early Colonial Settlements, Principally on Long Island*, vol. 14 (Albany: Weed, Parsons and Company, 1883), p. 620.

22. John Hervey, *Racing in America* (New York: Jockey Club, c. 1944), vol. 1, p. 6.

23. Kathryn C. Buhler and Graham Hood, *American Silver: Garvan and Other Collections in the Yale University Art Gallery* (New Haven, Conn.: Yale University Press, 1970), vol. 2, pp. 67–68.

24. Thomas Jefferson, *The Writings of Thomas Jefferson*, ed. Paul Leicester Ford, (New York: G. P. Putnam's Sons, 1904), vol. 7, pp. 432–33.

25. E. B. O'Callaghan, ed., *Documents Relative to the Colonial History of the State of New-York* (Albany: Weed, Parsons and Company, 1855), vol. 5, p.222.

26. Burton W. F. Trafton, Jr., "Louisburg and the Pepperrell Silver," *The Magazine Antiques*, vol. 89, no. 3 (March 1966), pp. 364, 366–67. See also E. Alfred Jones, *Old Silver of Europe and America, from Early Times to the Nineteenth Century* (Philadelphia: J. B. Lippincott, 1928), pp. 87, 145; and Donald Blake Webster et al., *Georgian Canada: Conflict and Culture 1745–1820* (Toronto: Royal Ontario Museum, 1984), p. 55.

27. *Minutes of the Common Council of the City of New York 1675–1776* (New York: Dodd, Mead, 1905), vol. 1, pp. 326–28. A printed broadside announcing the gold cup's presentation is in the collection of the New-York Historical Society.

28. Ibid., vol. 4, p. 277. See also Martha Gandy Fales, *Early American Silver* (New York: Funk & Wagnalls, 1970), pp. 179–80.

29. Sewall, *Diary*, vol. 2, p. 1063.

30. A.J.F. Van Laer, ed., *Van Rensselaer Bowier Manuscripts* (Albany: University of the State of New York, 1908), p. 624.

31. Richard Walden Hale, *Catalogue of Silver Owned by Nicholas Sever, A.B. 1701, in 1728* (Boston: Tudor Press, 1931).

32. *A Collection of College Words and Customs* (Cambridge, Mass.: John Bartlett, 1851), pp. 207–8.

33. Kathryn C. Buhler, *American Silver 1655–1825 in the Museum of Fine Arts Boston* (Boston: Museum of Fine Arts, 1972), vol. 1, pp. 365–68. See also Buhler and Hood, *American Silver* vol. 1, pp. 179, 181.

34. *The Lyons Collection, Publication of the American Jewish Historical Society*, no. 21 (Waltham, Mass: American Jewish Historical Society, 1913) vol. 1, p. 79.

35. Sewall, *Diary*, vol. 2, pp. 914, 939, 971, 989, 1026, 1042.

36. Ibid., p. 1042.

37. Will of Bethiah Shrimpton 27 June 1713, in Suffolk County Probate Court Records (Boston), vol. 18, p. 137. This silver survives. See Buhler, *American Silver . . . Museum of Fine Arts Boston*, vol. 1, p. 33; and Buhler and Hood, *American Silver*, vol. 1, pp. 314–17.

38. Buhler, *American Silver . . . Museum of Fine Arts Boston*, vol. 1, p. 246.

39. Kathryn C. Buhler, *Colonial Silversmiths, Masters and Apprentices* (Boston: Museum of Fine Arts, 1956), p. 59.

40. Kathryn C. Buhler, *American Silver: From the Colonial Period through the Early Republic in the Worcester Art Museum* (Worcester, Mass.: Worcester Art Museum, 1979), pp. 42–47.

41. Sewall, *Diary*, vol. 1, p. 114.

42. Buhler, *American Silver . . . Museum of Fine Arts Boston*, vol. 2, p. 415.

43. Martha Gandy Fales, "The Early American Way of Death," in *Essex Institute Historical Collections*, vol. 100 (April 1964), p. 75.

44. Kathryn C. Buhler, *Massachusetts Silver in the Frank L. and Louise C. Harrington Collection* (Worcester, Mass.: Barre Publishers, 1965), p. 40. See also Will of Thomas Cheever, 13 October 1748, in Suffolk County Probate Court Records (Boston), vol. 43, pp. 315–18.

45. "The Diaries of John Hull, Mint-Master and Treasurer of the Colony of Massachusetts Bay," in *Transactions and Collections of the American Antiquarian Society*, vol. 3 (Boston: privately printed, 1857), p. 142. I am particularly indebted to Patricia E. Kane, Curator of American Decorative Arts, Yale University Art Gallery, for her comments regarding the work of Hull and Sanderson.

46. Will of John Cotton, 27 January 1652, in Suffolk County Probate Court Records (Boston), vol. 1, pp. 84–87. See also Robert W. Haney, ed., *The Historic Silver of the First and Second Church in Boston* (Boston: Museum of Fine Arts, 1980), p. 5.

47. *Diaries of John Hull*, pp. 144–45.

48. Ibid., p. 173.

49. Haney, *Historic Silver*, p. 1; Jones, *Old Silver of American Churches*, p. 28.

50. Jones, *Old Silver of American Churches*, p. 149. See also Jonathan L. Fairbanks and Robert F. Trent, *New England Begins: The Seventeenth Century* (Boston: Museum of Fine Arts, 1982), pp. 409, 416.

51. Frances Gruber Safford, "Colonial Silver in the American Wing," *The Metropolitan Museum of Art Bulletin* 41 (Summer 1983), pp. 6–7.

52. *The Manifesto Church: Records of the Church in Brattle Square Boston with lists of communicants, baptisms, marriages, and funerals 1699–1872* (Boston: Benevolent Fraternity of Churches, 1902), p. 7.

53. Ibid. See also Buhler, *American Silver . . . Museum of Fine Arts Boston*, vol. 1, pp. 112–13. The tankard illustrated on page 112 may be the one made for Deacon Barnard.

54. *The Manifesto Church*, p. 12.

55. Ibid., p. 90.

56. Jones, *Old Silver of American Churches* pp. 70–71. This tankard was later given by Lothrop's daughter to All Saints' Church, Dorchester, and is now on loan to the Museum of Fine Arts, Boston.

57. Sewall, *Diary*, vol. 2, p. 1023.

58. Bruce Cooper Gill, "Christ Church in Philadelphia: Furnishings, the Early Years," *1981 Antiques Show: A Benefit for the Hospital of the University of Pennsylvania* (Philadelphia: privately printed, 1981), p. 129.

59. Ibid., p. 130.

60. Will of Robert Quary, no. 268-A, 1713, in Register of Wills, City Hall (Philadelphia).

61. Jones, *Old Silver of American Churches*, pp. 366–67. See also *Philadelphia: Three Centuries of American Art* (Philadelphia: Philadelphia Museum of Art, 1976), pp. 19–20.

62. Jones, *Old Silver of American Churches*, pp. 166–167. See also George Barton Cutten, *The Silversmiths of Virginia (Together with Watchmakers and Jewelers) from 1694 to 1850* (Richmond, Va.: Dietz Press, 1952), pp. 199–202.

63. Anne Allston Porcher, ed., "Minutes of the Vestry of St. Stephen's Parish, South Carolina, 1754–1873," *The South Carolina Historical and Genealogical Magazine*, vol. 45, no. 3 (July 1944), p. 160. This silver remains in the possession of St. Stephen's Church, St. Stephen's, South Carolina.

64. Vestry Minutes, St. Paul's Church, 1703/4–1727/8, Edenton, North Carolina. I am indebted to Miss Elizabeth Vann Moore for her thorough research of the church's records.

65. William L. Saunders, *The Colonial Records of North Carolina* (Raleigh: R. M. Hale, 1886), vol. 2, p. 134.

66. Barbara McLean Ward, "The Craftsman in a Changing Society: Boston Goldsmiths, 1690–1730" (Ph.D. diss., Boston University, 1983), p. 94.

67. *Philadelphia: Three Centuries*, pp. 5–6.

68. Jones, *Old Silver of American Churches*, pp. 367–68.

69. Ibid., pp. 96–98, 317–18, 385–86, 495–96.

70. Henry N. Flynt and Martha Gandy Fales, *The Heritage Foundation Collection of Silver, with Biographical Sketches of New England Silversmiths 1625–1825* (Old Deerfield, Mass. Heritage Foundation, 1968), pp. 164–65. See also Ralph E. Carpenter, Jr., *The Arts and*

Crafts of Newport, Rhode Island 1640–1820 (Newport, R.I.: Preservation Society of Newport County, 1954), p. 157.

71. Henry C. Wilkinson, *Bermuda in the Old Empire* (New York: Oxford University Press, 1950), pp. 439, 441.

72. Martha Gandy Fales, *Joseph Richardson and Family: Philadelphia Silversmiths* (Middletown, Conn.: Wesleyan University Press, 1974), pp. 104–5. See also *Old Devonshire Church Bermuda* (1973) pp. 28, 31; and Bryden Bordley Hyde, *Bermuda's Antique Furniture & Silver* (Hamilton, Bermuda: Bermuda National Trust, 1971), p. 174. I am indebted to Mr. Henry D. W. Laing for his assistance in researching Samuel Sherlock.

73. Gottesman, *Arts and Crafts in New York*, p. 59.

74. Jones, *Old Silver of American Churches*, pp. 334–35. See also Arthur Edward Lowndes, *An Inventory of the Church Plate and Altar Ornaments belonging to the Parish of Trinity Church in the City of New York*. (New York: Knickerbocker Press, 1905), pp. 33, 35, 59.

75. Buhler, *Colonial Silversmiths*, p. 92, fig. 118.

76. *Philadelphia: Three Centuries*, pp. 70–71.

77. Jones, *Old Silver of American Churches*, pp. 438–39. See also Samuel Sympson, *A New Book of Cyphers More Compleat and Regular Than Any Yet Extant* (London, 1726), p. 25.

78. Will of Reverend Jenkin Jones, no. 306, 1760, in Register of Wills, City Hall (Philadelphia).

79. Minutes of the First Baptist Church of Philadelphia, 3 July 1762.

80. Alfred Coxe Prime, ed., *The Arts and Crafts in Philadelphia, Maryland and South Carolina, 1721–1785: Gleaning from Newspapers* (New York: Da Capo Press, 1969), vol. 1, p. 44.

81. Minutes of the First Baptist Church of Philadelphia, 4 December 1762.

82. Jones, *Old Silver of American Churches*, pp. 163–64.

83. Buhler and Hood, *American Silver*, vol. 1, pp. 135, 137–38, 286–87.

84. Jones, *Old Silver of American Churches*, pp. 118–19. See also E. Milby Burton, *South Carolina Silversmiths 1690–1860* (Charleston, S.C.: Charleston Museum, 1942), pp. 146–49.

85. *South Carolina and American General Gazette*, Charleston, 18 March 1768.

86. A French "jatte" reminiscent of Petrie's dish is illustrated in the catalogue of an auction at Christie, Manson & Woods International, Inc., New York, 24 January 1987: *Fine American Furniture, Silver, Folk Art and Decorative Arts*. It bears French hallmarks and a discharge mark and is also marked by Myer Myers.

87. Jones, *Old Silver of American Churches*, pp. 119, 466.

88. "Boyle's Journal of Occurences in Boston 1759–1778," *New England Historical and Genealogical Register*, vol. 84, no. 2 (1930), p. 166.

89. Suffolk County Probate Court Records (Boston), vol. 63, pp. 283–84.

90. Nathaniel Hurd to Thomas Hancock, 17 September 1763, Massachusetts Historical Society, Hancock Family Miscellaneous Papers, 1728–1815.

91. Jones, *Old Silver of American Churches*, pp. 68, 70–71. See also Buhler, *American Silver . . . Museum of Fine Arts Boston*, vol. 1, pp. 86–87.

92. Buhler, *American Silver . . . Museum of Fine Arts Boston*, vol. 1, pp. 316, 364–65. See also Buhler, *American Silver . . . Worcester Art Museum*, pp. 40–41; Safford, "Colonial Silver," p. 46; and *American Decorative Arts: From the Pilgrims to the Revolution* (Detroit: Detroit Institute of Arts, 1967), p. 39.

93. This unpublished teapot is presently on loan to the Museum of Fine Arts, Boston.

94. Paul Revere's daybooks (in the collection of the Massachusetts Historical Society, Boston) record several occasions in 1766 when Coburn employed Revere to engrave silver for him, suggesting that Coburn was not a skillful engraver.

95. An account of the consistory's search for a minister and their gift may be found in the Records of the Collegiate Reformed Protestant Dutch Church of the City of New York, Liber B, 1700–1775 (1870 translation), pp. 224–27, 229–37, 241, 260, 267–68. See also Flynt and Fales, *Heritage Foundation Collection*, pp. 63–65.

96. Jeanette W. Rosenbaum, *Myer Myers, Goldsmith, 1723–1795* (Philadelphia: Jewish Publication Society of America, 1954), pp. 32–34.

97. Edwin Wolf II and Maxwell Whiteman, *The History of the Jews of Philadelphia from Colonial Times to the Age of Jackson* (Philadelphia: Jewish Publication Society of America, 1957), pp. 59, 397.

98. Rosenbaum, *Myer Myers*, pp. 68, 100. See also Guido Schoenberger, "The Ritual Silver Made by Myer Myers," *Publication of the American Jewish Historical Society*, vol. 43, no. 1 (1953) pp. 1–9.

99. Jones, *Old Silver of American Churches*, pp. 242–43. See also Jessie Harrington, *Silversmiths of Delaware 1700–1850 and Old Church Silver in Delaware* (Wilmington, Del.: National Society of Colonial Dames of America in the State of Delaware, 1939), pp. 119–20.

100. Robert W. Lovett, ed., "Documents from the Harvard University Archives 1638–1750," in *Publications of The Colonial Society of Massachusetts*, vol. 49: *Collections* (Boston: privately printed, 1975), p. 73.

101. Hermann Frederick Clarke and Henry Wilder Foote, *Jeremiah Dummer, Colonial Craftsman and Merchant, 1645–1718* (New York: Da Capo Press, 1970), p. 88.

102. Jones, *Old Silver of American Churches*, p. 109. See also Fairbanks and Trent, *New England Begins*, pp. 144–45.

103. William C. Lane, "Early Silver Belonging to Harvard College," in *Publications of The Colonial Society of Massachusetts*, vol. 24: *Transactions 1920–1922* (Boston: privately printed, 1923), p. 171.

104. Sewall, *Diary*, vol. 1, pp. 449–50.

105. Jones, *Old Silver of American Churches*, pp. 146–47, 289–90.

106. Flynt and Fales, *Heritage Foundation Collection*, pp. 56–58.

107. *American Silver and Pressed Glass: A Collection in The R. W. Norton Art Gallery* (Shreveport, La.: R. W. Norton Art Foundation, 1967), p. 15. See also Buhler, *American Silver . . . Museum of Fine Arts Boston*, vol. 1, pp 220–21.

108. Walter M. Whitehill, "Tutor Flynt's Silver Chamber-pot," in *Publications of The Colonial Society of Massachusetts*, vol. 38 (Boston, Mass.: privately printed, 1951), pp. 360–63.

109. Richard Walden Hale, *Catalogue of Silver Owned by Nicholas Sever*. See also Lane, "Early Silver Belonging to Harvard College," p. 172; and Philip H. Hammerslough, *American Silver Collected by Philip H. Hammerslough* (Hartford, Conn.: privately printed, 1960), vol. 2, p. 86a.

110. The candlesticks and the one known cann are now in the collection of the Fogg Art Museum, Harvard University, and the chafing dishes are now in the collection of Eric M. Wunsch. The present location of the two salvers is not known.

111. Buhler and Hood, *American Silver*, pp. 96, 98–99. See also Buhler, *Colonial Silversmiths*, p. 52; fig. 40.

112. Jones, *Old Silver of American Churches*, pp. 420–21.

113. "Harvard College Records, Part 1: Corporation Records, 1636–1750," p. 282.

114. Lane, "Early Silver Belonging to Harvard College," pp. 172–73.

115. Buhler and Hood, *American Silver*, vol. 1, pp. 230–31, 289–91.

116. Two other teapots by Hurd are also inscribed for presentation, one the gift of Theophilus Burrill to the Reverend Nathaniel Henchman of Lynn in 1737, and a second, dated 1738, presented to tutor Henry Flynt by his Harvard students. See Hollis French, *Jacob Hurd and His Sons Nathaniel and Benjamin, Silversmiths, 1702–1781* (Cambridge, Mass.: Riverside Press for the Walpole Society, 1939), p. 47; and Buhler, *American Silver . . . Museum of Fine Arts Boston*, vol. 1, pp. 218–21.

117. On the Franklin medal, see Edward Potts Cheyney, *History of the University of Pennsylvania 1740–1940* (Philadelphia: University of Pennsylvania Press, 1940), pp. 114–15; Benjamin Franklin, *The Papers of Benjamin Franklin*, ed. Leonard W. Labaree, vol. 10 (New Haven: Yale University Press, 1966), pp. 143–45. On the medals given by Lord Botetourt, see Raymond H. Williamson, "The Botetourt Scholastic Medals Awarded by the College of William and Mary, 1772–1775, *The Virginia Numismatist*, vol. 19, no. 5 (1983), pp. 20–32.

118. David C. Humphrey, *From Kings College to Columbia 1746–1800* (New York: Columbia University Press, 1976), pp. 180–81, 188.

119. Minutes of the Literary Society in New York, 1766–1772, NYC-Misc. Box 8, No. 95, New-York Historical Society, New York. Further information on Gallaudet may be found in Rev. Alfred V. Wittmeyer, *Registers of the Births, Marriages, and Deaths, of the Eglise Française à la Nouvelle York* . . . (Baltimore: Genealogical Publishing Company, 1968), pp. 241–42, 246, 250; and Gottesman, *Arts and Crafts in New York*, p. 12. I am indebted to Deborah D. Waters, Curator of Decorative Arts, Museum of the City of New York, for her assistance in researching Gallaudet.

120. Howard I. Chapelle, *American Small Sailing Craft* (New York: Norton, 1951), p. 9.

121. Hermann Frederick Clarke, *John Coney, Silversmith, 1655–1722* (Boston: Houghton Mifflin, 1932). An appraisers' inventory is reproduced between pages 12 and 13.

122. James Biddle, *American Art from American Collections* (New York: Metropolitan Museum of Art, 1963), p. 54.

123. *Minutes of the Common Council of the City of New York 1675–1776*, vol. 5, p. 225.

124. "The Memorial of Col. Morris Concerning the State of Religion in the Jerseys, 1700," in *Proceedings of the New Jersey Historical Society*, vol. 4: 1849–50 (Newark, N.J.: 1850), p. 119.

125. John E. Stillwell, *Historical and Genealogical Miscellany: Data Relating to the Settlement of New York and New Jersey* (New York, 1906), vol. 2, p. 355.

126. John N. Pearce, "New York's Two-handled Paneled Silver Bowls," *The Magazine Antiques*, vol. 80 (October 1961), pp. 341–45; and John N. Pearce, "Further Comments on the Lobate Bowl Form," *The Magazine Antiques*, vol. 90 (October 1966), pp. 524–25.

127. J. Hall Pleasants and Howard Sill, *Maryland Silversmiths, 1715–1830* (Baltimore: Lord Baltimore Press, 1930), pp. 6, 55–58. See also R. J. McKinney, "A Rare Silver Bowl," *Museum-Quarterly of The Baltimore Museum of Art*, vol. 1, no. 2 (1936), pp. 1–3. The bowl is also discussed in the following: Jennifer Faulds Goldsborough, *Eighteenth and Nineteenth Century Maryland Silver in the Collection of The Baltimore Museum of Art* (Baltimore: Baltimore Museum of Art, 1975), p. 33; Jennifer Faulds Goldsborough et al., *Silver in Maryland* (Baltimore: Maryland Historical Society, 1983), p. 131.

128. Annapolis Records, Mayor's Court Proceedings, Liber B, 1720–1722, Maryland State Archives No. 7833, pp. 49–50.

129. Pearce, "New York's Two-handled Paneled Silver Bowls," p. 343.

130. Prime, *Arts and Crafts in Philadelphia, Maryland and South Carolina*, vol. 1, p. 75.

131. Hervey, *Racing in America*, vol. 1, pp. 86–87.

132. Vincent D. Andrus, "Andrew Gautier's Silver Bowl," *The Metropolitan Museum of Art Bulletin*, vol. 9 (December 1950), pp. 118–19.

133. Hervey, *Racing in America*, vol. 1, pp. 33–35.

134. *New-York Gazette Revived in the Weekly Post-Bay*, no. 454 (30 September 1751).

135. Safford, "Colonial Silver," pp. 43–45. See also the catalogue of an auction on 14 March 1984 at Christie, Manson & Woods International, Inc., New York, *Fine English and Continental Silver, Objects of Vertu and Russian Works of Art*, p. 48. A similar design appears on a gold cup of 1725. See Michael Clayton, *The Collector's Dictionary of the Silver and Gold of Great Britain and North America* (New York: World Publishing, 1971), p. 100, which suggests a common British source for this design.

136. Biographical Records of Members, Grand [Masonic] Lodge of Massachusetts, Boston.

137. Paul Revere's daybook for 1761–83, Massachusetts Historical Society, Boston. See also Minutes of the Lodge of Saint Andrew, 30 November 1762 (microfilm), Grand Lodge of Massachusetts, Boston.

138. On the Rhode Island–Massachusetts dispute, the settlement, and the presentation, see John Russell Barlett, ed., *Records of the Colony of Rhode Island and Providence Plantations, in New England* (Providence: Knowles, Anthony & Co., 1859), vol. 4, pp. 464, 470–71, 474, 477–78, 482, 484–86, 488–89. On the tankard, see Buhler and Hood, *American Silver*, vol. 1, pp. 273–75.

139. *The Boston Weekly News-Letter*, 27 December 1744, quoted in George Francis Dow, *The Arts and Crafts in New England, 1704–1775* (Topsfield, Mass.: Wayside Press, 1927), p. 61.

140. Buhler and Hood, *American Silver*, vol. 1, pp. 133–35. One other cup, by William Swan of Boston, is similar in appearance to the Hurd cups and commemorates a related event. It was presented to Colonel Benjamin Pickman by the Massachusetts Bay Colony in honor of his valuable contributions to the Louisburg expedition during the French and Indian War. See Martha Gandy Fales, *Silver at the Essex Institute* (Salem, Mass.: Essex Institute, 1983), pp. 18–19. All these monumental vessels are similar to a cup owned by Thomas Hancock that he ordered from George Wickes, the London goldsmith, about 1740. See Jonathan L. Fairbanks et al., *Paul Revere's Boston: 1735–1818* (Boston: Museum of Fine Arts, 1975), pp. 52–53.

141. Buhler, *Massachusetts Silver*, pp. 57–60.

142. John Marshall Phillips, "Mr. Tyng's Bishop," *Bulletin of the Associates in Fine Arts at Yale University*, vol. 4, no. 3 (1932), pp. 148–49.

143. Harrold E. Gillingham, *Indian Ornaments Made by Philadelphia Silversmiths* (New York: Museum of the American Indian–Heye Foundation, 1936), p. 25.

144. Fales, *Joseph Richardson and Family*, pp. 140–42, 297–98.

145. Ibid., pp. 140–41, 297–98.

146. On the Johnson medals, see Buhler and Hood, *American Silver*, vol. 2, pp. 135–36.

147. William Johnson, *The Papers of Sir William Johnson*, Alexander C. Flick, ed. (Albany: University of the State of New York, 1931), vol. 7, pp. 494–95.

148. *Philadelphia: Three Centuries*, pp. 129–30.

149. Prime, *Arts and Crafts in Philadelphia, Maryland and South Carolina*, vol. 1, pp. 72–73.

150. *Philadelphia: Three Centuries*, pp. 128–29.

151. Kathryn C. Buhler, *Mount Vernon Silver* (Mount Vernon, Va.: Mount Vernon Ladies' Association of the Union, 1957), pp. 24–26.

152. Prime, *Arts and Crafts in Philadelphia, Maryland and South Carolina*, vol. 1, pp. 27–28.

153. William Dunlap, *History of the Rise and Progress of the Arts of Design in the United States* (New York: George P. Scott and Co., 1834), vol. 1, p. 156.

154. Fales, *Joseph Richardson and Family*, p. 306. See also Kenneth Scott, *Counterfeiting in Colonial America* (New York: Oxford University Press, 1957), p. 256.

155. Buhler, *American Silver . . . Museum of Fine Arts Boston*, pp. 31–32. See also Kathryn C. Buhler, "The Pickman Silver," in *The Ellis Memorial Antiques Show* (privately printed, 1961), pp. 19–29.

156. Kathryn C. Buhler, *Masterpieces of American Silver* (Richmond: Virginia Museum of Fine Arts, 1960), p. 36.

157. The work done by Coney for Mary Willoughby is discussed in detail in Buhler, *American Silver . . . Museum of Fine Arts Boston*, pp. 48–49, 56–57, 61–62, 64, 67.

158. Samuel Eliot Morison, "Mistress Glover's Household Furnishings at Cambridge, Massachusetts, 1638–1641 ," *Old-Time New England*, vol. 25, no. 1 (1934), p. 32.

159. Buhler, *American Silver . . . Museum of Fine Arts Boston*, pp. 41–42. The Nortons are known to have patronized Coney on at least one other occasion: they commissioned a handsome early-Baroque-style tankard with a gadrooned lid and the Norton arms and crest engraved on the body. See Buhler, *American Silver . . . Worcester Art Museum*, pp. 12–13.

160. Edward J. Nygren, "Edward Winslow's Sugar Boxes: Colonial Echoes of Courtly Love," *Yale University Art Gallery Bulletin*, vol. 33 (Autumn 1971), pp. 38–52.

161. *History of the Town of Hingham*, (Hingham, Mass., 1893), vol. 3, p. 93.

162. Buhler and Hood, *American Silver*, vol. 2, pp. 7–8. See also Norman S. Rice, *Albany Silver, 1652–1825* (Albany, N.Y.: Albany Institute of History and Art, 1964), p. 54.

163. Carolyn Scoon, "Cornelia Duyckinck's Birthday Spoon Inscribed and Dated: August 25, 1686," *The New-York Historical Society Quarterly*, vol. 34 (October 1950), pp. 315–17.

164. Berenice Ball, "Whistles with Coral and Bells," *The Magazine Antiques*, vol. 80 (December 1961), pp. 552–55.

165. Albert Ten Eyck Gardner and Stuart P. Feld, *American Paintings: A Catalogue of the Collection of The Metropolitan Museum of Art* (New York: Metropolitan Museum of Art, 1965), vol. 1, pp. 52–53. More recently, these portraits have been ascribed to William Johnston.

166. Peter J. Bohan, *American Gold, 1700–1860* (New Haven, Conn.: Yale University Art Gallery, 1963), pp. 10–11, 29–30.

167. Florence Van Rensselaer, *The Livingston Family in America and Its Scottish Origins* (New York: privately printed, 1949), pp. 84, 92, 112.

168. Buhler and Hood, *American Silver*, vol. 2, pp. 134–35.

169. Martha Gandy Fales, *American Silver in the Henry Francis du Pont Winterthur Museum* (Winterthur, Del.: Henry Francis du Pont Winterthur Museum, 1958), no. 101. See also Charles F. Montgomery and Patricia E. Kane, eds., *American Art: 1750–1800, Towards Independence* (Boston: New York Graphic Society, 1976), pp. 196–97.

170. The information presented here on Moses and Anna Brown's silver is taken from Robert P. Emlen, "Wedding Silver for the Browns: A Rhode Island Family Patronizes a Boston Goldsmith," *The American Art Journal*, vol. 16, no. 2 (1984), pp. 39–50.

171. Sarah Dennie estate administrator's account, 3 January 1753, in Suffolk County Probate Court Records (Boston), vol. 47, pp. 386–88.

172. *A Volume of Records Relating to the Early History of Boston, Containing Boston Marriages From 1752 to 1809* (Boston: Municipal Printing Office, 1903), p. 420. See also Andrew Oliver and James Bishop Peabody, eds., "The Records of Trinity Church, Boston 1728–1830, in *Publications of The Colonial Society of Massachusetts*, vol. 56: *Collections* (Boston: privately printed, 1982), p. 779.

173. Fales, "The Early American Way of Death," fig. 1; and Bohan, *American Gold*, p. 20. This symbol was one frequently employed, as evidenced by the 1740 inventory of George Hanners, a Boston silversmith, which listed a "Deaths head Stamp." See Suffolk County Probate Court Records (Boston), vol. 35, p. 90.

174. Buhler and Hood, *American Silver*, vol. 2, p. 100.

175. David Franks, *The New-York Directory* (New York: Shepard Kollock, 1786), p. 90; and Jones, *Old Silver of American Churches*, pp. 337–38.

176. Rosenbaum, *Myer Myers*, pp. 96, 119.

177. Joseph T. Butler, *Sleepy Hollow Restorations: A Cross Section of the Collection* (Tarrytown, N.Y.: Sleepy Hollow Press, 1983), p. 133.

178. Philip Van Wyck, "The Story of a Dutch Colonial Family," 1979, p. 97. Collection of the New-York Historical Society, New York City.

From the New Republic to the Centennial

1. Thomas Affleck, *Affleck's Southern Rural Almanac and Plantation and Garden Calendar for 1854* (Washington [Adams County], Miss., 1854), p. 88.

2. *New York Times*, 12 and 15 April 1868.

3. Anthony N. B. Garvan et al., "American Church Silver: A Statistical Study," in *Spanish, French, and English Traditions in the Colonial Silver of North America. 1968 Winterthur Conference Report* (Winterthur, Del.: Henry Francis du Pont Winterthur Museum, 1968), p. 83.

4. George Barton Cutten, *The Silversmiths of North Carolina 1696–1850* (Raleigh, N.C.: State Department of Archives and History, 1948), p. xix.

5. The cup remains in the collection of St. Paul's Church, Baltimore, Maryland.

6. South Church, Ipswich, Mass. See Kathryn C. Buhler and Graham Hood, *American Silver: Garvan and Other Collections in the Yale University Art Gallery* (New Haven, Conn.: Yale University Press, 1970), vol. 1, p. 218.

7. Morgan Dix, *A History of the Parish Church of Trinity Church in the City of New York* (New York: G. P. Putnam's Sons, 1905), vol. 3, p. 511.

8. William Barrow Floyd, "Kentucky Coin-Silver Pitchers," *The Magazine Antiques*, vol. 105 (March 1974), pp. 576–80.

9. Collection Old Salem, Inc. See *The Magazine Antiques*, vol. 111 (March 1977), p. 490.

10. Kathryn C. Buhler, *American Silver 1655–1825 in the Museum of Fine Arts Boston* (Boston: Museum of Fine Arts, 1972), vol. 2, p. 495.

11. The du Pont medal is number 63 in Martha Gandy Fales, *American Silver in the Henry Francis du Pont Winterthur Museum* (Winterthur, Del.: Henry Francis du Pont Winterthur Museum, 1958).

12. Elkanah Watson, *History of Agricultural Societies on the Modern Berkshire System* (Albany; N.Y.: D. Steere, 1820), p. 184.

13. The tea set is in the collection of the Society for the Preservation of New England Antiquities, Boston, Massachusetts. The pitcher and tray are owned by the United States Naval Academy Museum, Annapolis, Maryland.

14. Buhler and Hood, *American Silver*, vol. 2, p. 235.

15. Collection of the Cunard Line, presently exhibited on *Queen Elizabeth II*.

16. Collection of Stanford University Museum of Art, Stanford, California.

17. These objects are in the collections, respectively, of the Rhode Island School of Design, Providence; the Museum of the City of New York; and the Smithsonian Institution, Washington, D.C.

18. Rush's tray is in the collection of the Smithsonian Institution, Washington, D.C. Blackburn's pitcher is in the collection of the Kentucky Historical Society, Frankfort.

19. Barbara McLean Ward and Gerald W. R. Ward, eds., *Silver in American Life: Selections from the Mabel Brady Garvan and Other Collections at Yale University* (New York: American Federation of Arts, 1979), p. 98.

20. David B. Warren, *Southern Silver: An Exhibition of Silver Made in the South Prior to 1860* (Houston, Tex.: Museum of Fine Arts, Houston, 1968), no. A-2-A.

21. Collection of the Charleston Museum, Charleston, South Carolina.

22. These cups are in a private collection in Baltimore, Maryland.

23. The Woodlawn cup, now the Preakness Trophy, is on loan to the Baltimore Museum of Art, Baltimore, Maryland.

24. Anthony H. Clark, *The History of Yachting 1600–1815* (New York: G. P. Putnam's Sons, 1904), p. 198.

25. John Parkinson, Jr., *The History of the New York Yacht Club* (New York: New York Yacht Club, 1975), p. 6.

26. Collection of the Historic Mobile Preservation Society, Mobile, Alabama.

27. Collection of the Naval Historical Foundation, U.S. Navy; illustrated in Elizabeth Ingerman Wood, "Thomas Fletcher: A Philadelphia Entrepreneur of Presentation Silver," *Winterthur Portfolio III*, ed. Milo M. Naeve (Winterthur, Del.: Henry Francis du Pont Winterthur Museum, 1967), p. 145.

28. Collection of the Historical Commission of South Carolina; illustrated in Wood, "Thomas Fletcher," p. 153.

29. Cadwalader's urn is in a private collection, on loan to the Historical Society of Pennsylvania, Philadelphia. Perry's tea service is jointly owned by the New-York Historical Society, New York City, and the Newport, Rhode Island, Historical Society. Lafayette's map case is in the collection of the Metropolitan Museum of Art, New York, and his gold medal is in the collection of the Henry Francis du Pont Winterthur Museum, Winterthur, Delaware.

30. Collection of the Boston Public Library, Boston, Massachusetts.

31. Buhler and Hood, *American Silver*, vol. 2, p. 198.

32. Collection of the New-York Historical Society, New York City.

33. Buhler and Hood, *American Silver*, vol. 2, p. 129.

34. Collection of the Albany Institute, Albany, New York.

35. Jonathan L. Fairbanks et al., *Paul Revere's Boston: 1735–1818* (Boston: Museum of Fine Arts, 1975), p. 214.

36. Collection of the Yale University Art Gallery, New Haven, Connecticut.

37. The Adams cup is in the collection of the Smithsonian Institution, Washington, D.C. E. Pfohl's snuffbox is in the collection of Old Salem, Inc. The present location of Mary Phoenix Warren's porringer and spoon is unknown (ex. coll. Philip Hammerslough).

38. Warren, *Southern Silver*, no. F-5-L.

39. *New York Times*, 12 April 1869.

40. Ibid., 28 April 1869.

41. Kathryn C. Buhler, *Masterpieces of American Silver* (Richmond, Va.: Virginia Museum of Fine Arts, 1960), no. 323.

42. Private collection, Houston, Texas.

43. Two are in the Mabel Brady Garvan Collection at Yale University; the third is in the A. T. Clearwater Collection at the Metropolitan Museum of Art, New York City.

44. E. Alfred Jones, *The Old Silver of American Churches* (Letchworth, England: privately printed for the National Society of Colonial Dames of America at the Arden Press, 1913), pp. 15, 18.

45. Buhler, *American Silver . . . Museum of Fine Arts Boston*, vol. 1, p. 317; vol. 2, p. 521.

46. "Detroit: Ste. Anne, Founded in 1701, Sacramental Records from 1704." Typewritten manuscript in the archives of the Archdiocese of Detroit, p. 8

47. George Paré, *The Catholic Church in Detroit 1701–1888* (Detroit: Samuel Richard Press, 1951), p. 287.

48. John E. Langdon, "Silversmithing During the French Colonial Period," in *Spanish, French, and English Traditions in the Colonial Silver of North America, 1968 Winterthur Conference Report* (Winterthur, Del.: Henry Francis du Pont Winterthur Museum, 1969), p. 63.

49. Raymond B. Clark, Jr., and Sara Seth Clark, *Talbot County Maryland Marriage Licenses 1794–1864 with a History of Talbot County Churches and Biographical Sketches of the Ministers* (Washington, D.C.: privately printed, 1965), pp. 53, 54.

50. Edward Claves Chorley, *Quarter of a Millennium, Trinity Church in the City of New York 1697–1947* (Philadelphia: Church Historical Society, 1947), p. 72.

51. Morgan Dix, ed., *A History of the Parish of Trinity Church in the City of New York*, vol. 3, p. 511. *Trow's Directory* (New York, 1856) lists Cooper and Fisher as silversmiths at 131 Amity Street. Dix also mentions that the silver was engraved by H. P. [sic] Horlor and chased by Segal. *Trow's Directory* also locates Henry B. Horlor, engraver, at 67 Nassau Street and William J. Seely, chaser, at 102 Nassau.

52. *Massachusetts Soldiers and Sailors of the Revolutionary War, a Compilation from the Archives* (Boston: Wright Potter Printing Company, 1900), vol. 7, pp. 192, 311.

53. Justin Winsor, ed., *The Memorial History of Boston Including Suffolk County Massachusetts 1630–1880* (Boston: James R. Osgood & Company, 1881), vol. 3, pp. 553, 562.

54. For a contemporary description of the bridge and festivities see Buhler, *American Silver . . . Museum of Fine Arts Boston*, vol. 1, p. 378. A tankard by Benjamin Burt presented by the proprietors to Richard Devens and also engraved with the bridge scene is illustrated on p. 348.

55. Information about this presentation and Captain Seton came from the files of the Fine Arts Museums of San Francisco.

56. The letter was published in Claypoole's *American Daily Advertiser* on 4 October 1799. See *The Magazine Antiques*, vol. 81 (June 1962), p. 612.

57. *Philadelphia: Three Centuries of American Art* (Philadelphia: Philadelphia Museum of Art, 1976), p. 223.

58. The pitcher, made by Edward Lownes, is similarly ornamented with leaf decoration in the French style. It is also in the collection of the Historical Society of Pennsylvania.

59. The letter is quoted in full in the 2 October 1823 issue of the *Essex Register*.

60. Ibid., 18 December 1823.

61. Wood, "Thomas Fletcher," pp. 136–71.

62. The committee members were: Peter Crary, James Heard, Nathaniel Richards, John Haggerty, Arthur Tappan, Edward M. Grenway, Amos Palmer, Ralph Olmstead, Frederick Sheldon, and Isaac S. Hone.

63. *New York Commercial Advertiser*, 18 and 22 March 1825. The second vase is in a private collection in Houston.

64. For a full consideration of Oakes's cup, see Phyllis Kihn, *Bulletin* (Hartford: Connecticut Historical Society, January 1967), pp. 9ff.

65. The Philadelphia Society for Promoting Agriculture was founded in 1805.

66. Born John Powel Hare, Powel changed his name when adopted by his aunt, Elizabeth Willing Powel (see page 120).

67. *United States Gazette*, 3 December 1824.

68. Merrill Denison, *Canada's First Bank: A History of the Bank of Montreal* (Toronto-Montreal: McClelland & Stewart, 1966), p. 70.

69. Robert Luther Thompson, *Wiring a Continent* (Princeton, N.J.: Princeton University Press, 1947), p. 174.

70. Pieces survive in the collections of the Metropolitan Museum of Art, New York, and the Museum of the City of New York.

71. One is part of a service of gold plate presented by the citizens of New York to Edward K. Collins upon the successful establishment of an American line of transatlantic steamers in 1851. It was exhibited at the Crystal Palace in New York. See Benjamin Silliman, Jr., and Charles R. Goodrich, eds., *The World of Art, Science, and Industry Illustrated from the New York Exhibition 1853–1854* (New York: G. P. Putnam, 1854), p. 107. A second, presented to James E. Birch, has

the figure of a miner as a finial and repoussé ornament on the theme of mining. See Charles H. Carpenter, Jr., with Mary Grace Carpenter, *Tiffany Silver* (New York: Dodd Mead, 1978), p. 20. The third, presented in 1854 by railroad stockholders and ornamented with railroad iconography, is in the Virginia Carroll Crawford Collection, High Museum of Art, Atlanta, Georgia.

72. Margaret Brown Klapthor, *Presentation Pieces in the Museum of History and Technology*, Contributions from the Museum of History and Technology, Paper 47 (Washington, D.C.: Smithsonian Institution, 1965), p. 94.

73. West's first efforts were recognized by the City of New York with a gold box, New York's traditional mark of achievement (collection of the Metropolitan Museum of Art, New York). Tiffany and Company purchased a section of rescued cable and advertised for sale four-inch lengths mounted and bound with brass ferrules. See Carpenter, *Tiffany Silver*, p. 14.

74. Edward Hungerford, *Men and Iron: The History of the New York Central* (New York: Arno Press, 1976), p. 224.

75. Buhler, *American Silver . . . Museum of Fine Arts Boston*, vol. 2, p. 458. One of the four punch urns is number 406 in Buhler's catalogue.

76. On the history of Boston theater and theaters, and on the involvement of Bulfinch and Brown in the China trade, see Justin Winsor, ed., *The Memorial History of Boston* (Boston: James R. Osgood, 1881). vol. 4, pp. 208, 362.

77. *Washington Federalist*, 7 November 1803.

78. J. Hall Pleasants and Howard Sill, *Maryland Silversmiths 1715–1830* (Baltimore: Lord Baltimore Press, 1930), p. 89.

79. Robert B. Davidson, *History of the United Bowmen of Philadelphia* (Philadelphia: Allen, Lane & Scott's Printing House, 1888). See also *Constitution and Regulations of the United Bowmen of Philadelphia* (Philadelphia: Hogan & Thompson, 1844), p. 10, article X.

80. *Columbian Centinel* [Boston], 2 January 1811.

81. The records of the Old South Church list the gift and identify the maker as "Ebenr Moulton." See Buhler, *American Silver . . . Museum of Fine Arts Boston*, vol. 2. p. 519.

82. On the Brennan Stake and the prizes awarded, see Marquis Boultinghouse, *Silversmiths, Jewelers, Clock and Watch Makers of Kentucky 1785–1900* (Lexington, Ky.: Marquis Boultinghouse, 1980), pp. 16, 18; plate 17.

83. *New York Yacht Club 1844–1944* (New York: privately printed, 1944), pp. 9, 21.

84. The name of Voorhis's ship is incorrectly spelled in the inscription.

85. 17 August 1872, p. 664.

86. Buhler and Hood, *American Silver*, vol. 2, p. 107.

87. J. Thomas Scharf and Thompson Westcott, *History of Philadelphia, 1609–1884* (Philadelphia: L. H. Everts and Company, 1884, vol. 1, p. 435.

88. *Philadelphia: Three Centuries*, p. 152.

89. Francis Paul Prucha, *Indian Peace Medals in American History* (Madison, Wis.: State Historical Society of Wisconsin, 1971), pp. xiv, 9.

90. O'Bannon's given name is spelled incorrectly in the inscription.

91. Harold L. Peterson, *The American Sword 1775–1945* (Philadelphia: Ray Riling Arms Books, 1977), pp. 189, 192.

92. Howard I. Chapelle, *The History of American Sailing Ships* (New York: Bonanza Books, 1985), p. 153.

93. Fairbanks, *Paul Revere's Boston*, p. 200.

94. *Columbian Centinel* [Boston], 29 September 1813.

95. Ibid., 25 May 1814. The presentation consisted of salver, two ice pails, two pitchers, two wine-glass coolers, and a coffeepot, teapot, sugar basin, cream ewer, tea caddy, and slop bowl. The salver and coffee and tea service are in the collection of the Smithsonian Institution, Museum of American History, Washington, D.C. (acc. no.

1985.0121.1–7).

96. Prucha, *Indian Peace Medals*, p. 33.

97. Jeffrey Kimball, "The Battle of Chippewa: Infantry Tactics in the War of 1812," *Military Affairs* (American Military Institute), vol. 31, no. 9 (Winter 1967–68), p.186.

98. *Minutes of the Common Council of the City of New York 1784–1831* (City of New York, 1917), vol. 8, pp. 59, 124, 133.

99. *Baltimore Gazette and Daily Advertiser*, 5 September 1817.

100. Joan Sayers Brown, "Silver and Gold Owned by Stephen Decatur, Jr.," *The Magazine Antiques*, vol. 123 (February 1983), p. 400.

101. On the defense of Fort McHenry and the response of the people of Baltimore to Armistead's victory, see J. Thomas Scharf, *The Chronicles of Baltimore, Being a Complete History of "Baltimore Town" and Baltimore County from the Earliest Period to the Present Time* (Baltimore: Turnbull Brothers, 1874), pp. 379, 381, 392.

102. *Baltimore Gazette and Daily Advertiser*, 27 April 1818.

103. The lid of the punch bowl is missing its finial. Identical beakers made by Warner in 1816 are in the collection of the Maryland Historical Society, Baltimore.

104. On Lafayette's visit and medal, see Dorothy Welker, "The La Fayette Medal," *Journal of Early Southern Decorative Arts* (May 1976), pp. 27–37. The information in this entry is taken primarily from Welker's article.

105. Scharf, *Chronicles of Baltimore*, p. 414.

106. *United States Gazette* [Philadelphia], 1 December 1824.

107. Henry M. Brackenridge, *History of the Late War Between the United States and Great Britain Containing a Minute Account of the Various Military and Naval Operations*, 4th ed. (Baltimore, 1818), p. 255.

108. The matching pitcher and salver are in the collection of the Historical Society of Pennsylvania, Philadelphia, as is the letter dated February 1841 describing the presentation.

109. Joan Sayers Brown, "Henry Clay's Silver," *The Magazine Antiques*, vol. 120 (July 1981), pp. 172–77.

110. For further data on the connections between the Ames Company and John Quincy Adams Ward, see Lewis I. Sharp, *John Quincy Adams Ward, Dean of American Sculpture*, (Newark, Del.: University of Delaware Press, 1985), pp. 40–41.

111. The county is called Jo Dairess in various sources, but the correct name is Jo Daviess County. Inscribed on the blade of the sword in script is: "U.S.G. Jo Daviess County Illinois to Major General Ulysses S. Grant U.S.A., U.S.G. the hero of the Mississippi." On the price of the gift and the manufacturer, see John Hamilton, *The Ames Sword Company* (Providence, R.I.: Mobray, 1981), pp. 94, 169.

112. Peter Kemp, ed., *The Oxford Companion to Ships and the Sea* (London: Oxford University Press, 1976), p. 355.

113. Carpenter, *Tiffany Silver*, p. 143.

114. *New York Times*, 12 April 1869.

115. Collection of the Museum of the City of New York. See *The Magazine Antiques*, vol. 112 (July 1977), p. 68.

116. Buhler, *American Silver . . . Museum of Fine Arts Boston*, vol. 2, p. 514.

117. This information comes from the Winterthur Museum object file.

118. William Bentley, *The Diary of William Bentley, D. D. Pastor of the East Church Salem, Massachusetts* (Gloucester, Mass.: Peter Smith, 1962), vol. 4, p. 513.

119. *The Revolutionary Records of the State of Georgia* (Atlanta: Franklin Turner Company, 1908), vol. 3, p. 142.

120. Jessie Lee Yost, "Elizabeth Willing Powel of 18th Century Philadelphia as revealed through her correspondence and papers" (1984), typewritten manuscript in the collection of the Historical Society of Pennsylvania, Philadelphia.

121. George Gibbs, *The Gibbs Family of Rhode Island* (Providence: Derrydale Press, 1933).

122. Wendy A. Cooper, *In Praise of America: American Decorative Arts, 1650–1830* (New York: Alfred A. Knopf, 1980), p. 84.

123. *New York Commercial Advertiser*, 5 January 1825.

124. *Crescent City Silver: An Exhibition of Nineteenth-Century New Orleans Silver* (New Orleans: Historic New Orleans Collection, 1980), p. 86.

125. *The Magazine Antiques*, vol. 112 (September 1982), p. 446.

126. The information on De Grauw and his family presented here is taken from Augustine Costello, *Our Firemen: A History of The New York Fire Departments* (New York: privately printed, n.d.), pp. 451, 461.

127. The pitchers were left separately to the Museum of the City of New York, as were the goblets, which are similarly engraved but are unmarked.

128. Charles H. Carpenter, Jr., *Gorham Silver, 1831–1981* (New York: Dodd, Mead, 1982), p. 55

129. Collection of the Smithsonian Institution, Washington, D.C.

130. Carpenter, *Gorham Silver*, p. 59.

131. Edward Hungerfield, *The Story of the Baltimore and Ohio Railroad 1827–1927* (New York: G. P. Putnam's Sons, 1928), vol. 1, pp. 69, 151.

132. An identical urn, presented in 1860 by the merchants of San Francisco to encourage the construction of a transcontinental railroad, was ordered through John Tucker, a local jeweler, and made by Gorham. It is now in the Oakland Museum. See Edgar W. Morse, ed., *Silver in the Golden State: Images and Essays Celebrating the History and Art of Silver in California* (Oakland, Calif.: Oakland Museum History Department, 1986), plate 4.

FROM THE GILDED AGE TO MODERN DESIGN

1. Thorstein Veblen, *The Theory of the Leisure Class* (New York: Macmillan Co., 1917), pp. 26, 28, 68.

2. Ibid., p. 120.

3. For example, see *New York Times*, 29 July 1899; 10 January 1900; 4 October 1899; 1 October 1899; and 21 October 1899.

4. Phyllis Flanders Dorset, *The New Eldorado: The Story of Colorado's Gold and Silver Rushes* (New York: Macmillan Co., 1970), pp. 336–38.

5. John B. B. Trussell and James R. Mitchell, *The Silver Service of the U.S.S. Pennsylvania* (Harrisburg, Pa.: William Penn Memorial Museum, 1981), n.p.; Charles H. Carpenter, Jr., *Gorham Silver, 1831–1981* (New York: Dodd Mead, 1982), p. 178.

6. For example, the silver bicycle given to Lillian Russell by her admirers (see Charles H. Carpenter, Jr., with Mary Grace Carpenter, *Tiffany Silver* [New York: Dodd, Mead, 1978], p. 42); the Commodore's cup of the Larchmont Yacht Club, made by the Whiting Manufacturing Company in 1894 and belonging to the New-York Historical Society; the Carnegie Steel Company's 1929 Safety Trophy, made by Gorham (see "Garage Sale Bonanza—Christmas in July," *U.S. Steel News*, vol. 44 [December 1979], pp. 16–17); the John Johnston Trophy for curling, pictured in the Photograph Scrapbook No. 9 (c. 1892–94), p. 91, Archives, Gorham, Providence, Rhode Island; and the Babe Ruth Crown, designed by Franklin Hugh Ellison and presented to Ruth in 1921, in the National Baseball Hall of Fame, Cooperstown, New York.

7. John Strother to the Gorham Company, New York City, 14 January 1905, Archives, Gorham, Providence, Rhode Island.

8. "Silver Ware," vols. 5–11 (c. 1881–1902), vol. 5, p. 216; vol. 11, pp. 317, 327, 329–43; see also "G. M. Co.," special-order ledger (c. 1901–41), Archives, Gorham, Providence Rhode Island.

9. Carpenter, *Gorham Silver*, p. 265.

10. For example, see *Winterthur Point-to-Point Races: 1983 Program* (Winterthur, Del.: Henry Francis du Pont Winterthur Museum, 1983).

11. For example, see William Frederick's silver crucifix made for Grace Chapel, Chicago, in Sharon S. Darling, *Chicago Metalsmiths* (Chicago: Chicago Historical Society, 1977), p. 121.

12. "Capt. Rostron Here To-Day," *New York Times*, 29 and 30 May 1912.

13. Ilya Schor Papers, Archives of American Art; *Ludwig Yehuda Wolpert, A Retrospective* (New York: Jewish Museum, 1976); Collections of the Jewish Museum, New York City, and the National Museum of American Jewish History, Philadelphia.

14. Carpenter, *Gorham Silver*, p. 141.

15. Carpenter, *Tiffany Silver*, p. 147.

16. For example, James Gordon Bennett of the *International Herald* (see pages 157–58) commissioned two aircraft trophies from Tiffany and Company. See "Two Aviation Trophies," *Art and Decoration*, vol. 1 (December 1910), p. 86. The *Detroit News* commissioned a ballooning trophy from Gorham, see item EBJ, "Gorham Trophies and Bronzes," photograph album, Design Department Archives, Gorham, Providence, Rhode Island.

17. This early award is a goblet made by Adam Lynn (active 1796–1836) of Alexandria, Virginia, for the best one-year-old lamb at the 1808 Arlington Sheep Shearing. The goblet belongs to the Museum of Early Southern Decorative Arts, Winston-Salem, North Carolina.

18. Richard N. Current, T. Harry Williams, Frank Freidel, *American History: A Survey* (New York: Alfred A. Knopf, 1961), p. 285.

19. The Borg-Warner Trophy was designed by Gorham designer Robert Hill "to recognize the speed kings who have contributed so much to the progress of transportation," according to the 18 February 1936 press release issued at its unveiling, and preserved in an unpublished photograph album, p. 21, Design Department Archives, Gorham, Providence, Rhode Island. the trophy is in the collection of the Indianapolis Motor Speedway Corporation Hall of Fame Museum, Indianapolis, Indiana. The Sikorsky trophy belongs to the National Air and Space Museum, Smithsonian Institution, Washington, D.C.

20. Ironically, the America's Cup is not American-made; hence it was not a candidate for this book. It was made in 1848 in London by Robert Garrard, Jr. See Charles H. Carpenter, Jr., "Nineteenth-Century Silver in the New York Yacht Club," *The Magazine Antiques*, vol. 112 (September 1977), p. 496.

21. John Parkerson, Jr., *The History of the New York Yacht Club*, ed. Robert W. Carrick, 2 vols. (New York: privately printed, 1975).

22. The International Tennis Hall of Fame and Museum in Newport, Rhode Island, has an extensive collection of tennis trophies.

23. L. W. Hanagan, Assistant Deputy Commander, Naval Supply Systems Command, Washington, D.C., to Katherine S. Howe, 7 November 1985.

24. Carpenter, *Gorham Silver*, pp. 174–78.

25. Theodore Roosevelt's friend Secretary of State John Hay called the Spanish-American War "a splendid little war."

26. Cambon's cup is in the collection of The White House, Washington, D.C. See *The American Renaissance 1876–1917* (New York: Brooklyn Museum, 1979), p. 217, and Carpenter, *Tiffany Silver*, p. 148.

27. [Elenita C. Chickering], *Arthur J. Stone: Handwrought Silver, 1901–1937* (Boston: Boston Athenaeum, 1981), pp. 7, 10–11; Elenita C. Chickering, "Arthur J. Stone, Silversmith," *The Magazine Antiques*, vol. 129 (January 1986), p. 276; Mark A. Wuomola, *Church of the Advent, Boston: A Guidebook* (Boston: privately printed, 1975), pp. 1–2. I am grateful to Betty Morris, historian of the Church of the Advent, for sharing the results of her research with me.

28. The cross's transept is decorated with an ancient symbol of Christ the Conqueror: (IC = Ihucue, "Jesus," in Greek; XC = Xpictoc, "Christ"; NIKA = "Conqueror").

29. The organization was named for Andrew, the apostle who brought his brother, Simon, to Jesus (John 1:35–42). Andrew is the patron saint of Scotland.

30. [Chickering], *Arthur J. Stone*, p. 21; Rima Lunin Schultz, *The Church and the City, A Social History of 150 Years at Saint James, Chicago.* (Chicago: privately printed, 1986). The drawing for the cross belongs to the Cathedral Church of St. James, Chicago.

31. Leland A. Cook, *St. Patrick's Cathedral* (New York: Quick Fox, 1979), pp. 52, 56, 59, 129, 137; Margaret Carthy, *A Cathedral of Suitable Magnificence: St. Patrick's Cathedral, New York* (Wilmington, Del.: Michael Glazier, 1984), p. 116.

32. Wayne G. Broehl, Jr., *The Molly Maguires* (Cambridge, Mass.: Harvard University Press, 1964), pp. 365–70; Andrew Roy, *A History of the Coal Miners of the United States* (1905 [?]; reprinted Westport, Conn.: Greenwood Press, 1970), pp. 95–110.

33. Nicholas B. Wainwright, *One Hundred and Fifty Years of Collecting by the Historical Society of Pennsylvania, 1824–1974* (Philadelphia: Historical Society of Pennsylvania, 1974), pp. 97–98.

34. "Hill and West Testimonials . . . Total Amt. paid," and the Tiffany and Company bill are in the George A. Brackett Papers, Minnesota Historical Society, St. Paul, Minnesota.

35. *Minneapolis Tribune*, 11 September 1884, quoted from a typescript in the Hill Tray-accessions files, Minneapolis Institute of Arts.

36. Bills from A. H. Beal, the Pioneer Art Gallery, Minneapolis, 31 May 1884, Brackett Papers.

37. Francis J. Puig, "The Hill Tray," Minneapolis Institute of Arts *Bulletin*, vol. 64 (1978–80), pp. 42–53. I am grateful to Francis J. Puig, Curator at the Minneapolis Institute of Arts, for sharing the results of his recent research with me.

38. Ruth Zalusky Thorstenson, "The West Hotel" (3 parts), *Hennepin County History*, vol. 37 (Fall 1978), pp. 3–9; (Winter 1978–79), pp. 13–21; vol. 38 (Spring 1979), pp. 3–11. See also *Minneapolis Tribune*, 20 November 1884.

39. Accessions records, Munson-Williams-Proctor Institute Museum of Art, Utica, New York.

40. *Nineteenth Century America: Furniture and Decorative Arts* (New York: Metropolitan Museum of Art, 1970), no. 281; *American Renaissance*, p. 136; Carpenter, *Tiffany Silver*, pp. 146–48.

41. *The Adams Gold Vase*, 2d ed. (New York: Tiffany & Co., 1900), pp. 6–22. This was a bilingual publication prepared for the 1900 Paris Exposition.

42. David F. Burg, *Chicago's White City of 1893* (Lexington: University of Kentucky Press, 1976), pp. 138–41; Stanley Appelbaum, *The Chicago World's Fair of 1893: A Photographic Record* (New York: Dover Publications, 1980), pp. 57–59; Robert Twombly, *Louis Sullivan: His Life and Work* (New York: Viking, 1986), pp. 264–69.

43. John J. Flinn, ed., *The Handbook of Chicago Biography* (Chicago: Chicago Standard Guide Company, 1893), p. 330; Albert Nelson Marquis, ed., *The Book of Chicagoans* (Chicago: A. N. Marquis, 1911), p. 630.

44. [Testimonial and Presentation of the Transportation Department Vase to Willard A. Smith, 1893], six-page printed fragment in the Archives, Department of American Decorative Arts, Metropolitan Museum of Art, New York. See also Carpenter, *Tiffany Silver*, p. 147.

45. *Interborough Rapid Transit: The New York Subway* (New York: privately printed, 1904), pp. 13–25; Brian J. Cudahy, *Under the Sidewalks of New York: The Story of the Greatest Subway System in the World* (Brattleboro, Vt.: Stephen Greene Press, 1979), p. 23.

46. *New York Times*, 23 and 28 October 1904. I am grateful to Deborah D. Waters of the Museum of the City of New York for sharing the results of her research with me.

47. On the tray, see *Nineteenth Century America*, no. 285; *American Renaissance*, p. 217; and Carpenter, *Tiffany Silver*, p. 149.

48. Lawrence Beesley, *The Loss of the S.S. Titanic: Its Story and Lessons*, 2d ed. (Riverside, Conn.: 7c's Press, 1973), pp. 213–14.

49. *New York Times*, 29 and 30 May 1912.

50. "The Curtiss Marine Flying Trophy: The Triumph of Wings Over the Dominating Elements" (a three-page contestant's entry form for the 1919 race). Accessions Files, National Air and Space Museum, Smithsonian Institution. Gorham records identify the figures as Neptune and Mercury. The trophy required 1,034.35 ounces of silver. See Special Order IHA, estimates files, 1915. Archives, Gorham, Providence, Rhode Island.

51. "The Curtiss Marine Flying Trophy Races, 1915–1930," pp. 2–4, typescript in the Accessions Files, National Air and Space Museum, Smithsonian Institution, Washington, D.C.

52. "Gorham Trophies & Bronzes," undated photograph album, Design Department Archives, Gorham, Providence, Rhode Island.

53. Accessions records, Department of Decorative Arts, Museum of the City of New York.

54. Parkerson, *History of the New York Yacht Club*, vol. 1, pp. 102, 117.

55. Carpenter, "Nineteenth Century Silver in the New York Yacht Club," pp. 499, 501.

56. Parkerson, *History of the New York Yacht Club*, vol. 1, pp. 105, 113–14; vol. 2, pp. 614–15.

57. Carpenter, "Nineteenth Century Silver in the New York Yacht Club," pp. 500, 502–3. I am grateful to Mr. Sohei Hohri, Librarian of the New York Yacht Club, for introducing me to the history of the word "yacht."

58. Parkerson, *History of the New York Yacht Club*, vol. 1, pp. 117, 123; vol. 2, pp. 614–15.

59. *Nineteenth Century America*, no. 234; Carpenter, "Nineteenth-Century Silver in the New York Yacht Club," pp. 501, 503–4.

60. Parkerson, *History of the New York Yacht Club*, vol. 1, pp. 138–39; vol. 2, pp. 614–15.

61. Carpenter, *Tiffany Silver*, pp. 45–46; *American Renaissance*, p. 216. I am grateful to Janet Zapata, archivist for Tiffany and Company, for identifying the stock and special-order castings for me.

62. Don G. Seitz, *The James Gordon Bennetts, Father and Son: Proprietors of the New York Herald* (Indianapolis: Bobbs-Merrill, 1928), pp. 251–70.

63. John Leather, *The Northseamen* (Lavenham, Suffolk: Terence Dalton, Ltd., 1971), pp. 148, 162; John Leather, *The Big Class Racing Yachts* (London: Stanford Maritime, 1982), pp. 61–62.

64. Tiffany and Company archives, courtesy of Janet Zapata, archivist. A. F. Aldridge, "Famous Trophies," *Munsey's Magazine*, vol. 24 (January 1901), p. 621.

65. Parkerson, *History of the New York Yacht Club*, vol. 1, pp. 159–66.

66. Carpenter, "Nineteenth-Century Silver in the New York Yacht Club," p. 504.

67. We are indebted to Janet Zapata, archivist at Tiffany and Company, for this data.

68. *New York Times*, 6 June 1926.

69. Carpenter, *Tiffany Silver*, pp. 176–77.

70. [Chickering], *Arthur J. Stone*, pp. 6–7, 9, 11, 13, 21; Chickering,

"Arthur J. Stone, Silversmith," p. 275; Elenita C. Chickering, "Arthur J. Stone's Presentation Silver," *The Decorative Arts Society Newsletter*, vol. 2 (March 1985), pp. 1–6.

71. Darling, *Chicago Metalsmiths*, pp. 28, 61; David A. Hanks, "Robert R. Jarvie, Chicago Silversmith," *The Magazine Antiques*, vol. 110 (September 1976), pp. 522–27.

72. Phoebe Albert Driscoll, president of The Weeders Garden Club, to Ann Wood, 6 December 1986.

73. *Olaf Skoogfors, 20th Century Goldsmith, 1930–1975*. (Philadelphia: Falcon Press, 1979), p. 54.

74. *Pro Patria: A Testimonial Through the New York "Recorder" From 26,382 American Patriots to Benjamin Harrison, President of the United States* (privately printed, 1892); *New York Recorder*, 28 January, and 1, 7, 13, and 14 February, and 13 March 1892.

75. Secretary Tracy's statuette survives and is in the collection of the United States Navy Memorial Museum, Washington, D.C.

76. Ronald Spector, *Admiral of the New Empire: The Life and Career of George Dewey* (Baton Rouge: Louisiana State University Press, 1974), pp. 67, 105–6.

77. *New York Journal*, 11 May 1899, 6 September, 1 October, 29 May 1899.

78. Ibid., 24 September 1899; "Silver Ware Special II," special-order ledger (1889–99), p. 96, Archives, Gorham, Providence, Rhode Island. Sharon S. Darling, "Admiral Dewey's Loving Cup," *Silver*, vol. 9 (January-February 1976) pp. 10–12; Carpenter, *Gorham Silver*, p. 173; *American Renaissance*, p. 142.

79. *New York Journal*, 10 January 1900.

80. Trussell and Mitchell, *Silver Service*; Carpenter, *Gorham Silver*, p. 178; "USS *Pennsylvania* Presentation Silver Service," report from L. W. Hanagan, Assistant Deputy Commander, Naval Supply Systems Command, Washington, D.C., to Katharine S. Howe, 7 November 1985; Katharine Morrison McClinton, *Collecting American 19th-Century Silver* (New York: Bonanza Books, 1968), pp. 171–85.

81. "Gorham Battleship Silver," undated photograph album, Design Department Archives, Gorham, Providence, Rhode Island; "Agreement between Millard F. Davis and the Delaware Battleship Committee," and "Delaware Battleship Silver Service," eight-page report by George H. Ryden, State Archivist of Delaware, Dover, Delaware, 6 January 1940, through the courtesy of Rebecca J. Hammell, Historical Society of Delaware, Wilmington; "Beautiful Silver Service to be Presented To-day to the United States Battleship 'Delaware,'" *Jewelers' Circular*, vol. 61 (5 October 1910), pp. 1–2. See also *Silver Service: U.S.S. Delaware. Furnished by Millard F. Davis, Wilmington, Del. Designed and Manufactured by The Gorham Company* (1910?), nine pages. A meshwork fits into the bowl of the centerpiece to secure floral bouquets.

82. Pierre C. Cartier to Grace Tully, 22 December 1944, manuscript collections, Franklin D. Roosevelt Library, Hyde Park, New York. Miss Tully was President Roosevelt's secretary.

83. Hans Nadelhoffer, *Cartier: Jewelers Extraordinary* (New York: Harry N. Abrams, 1984), appendix: Cartier Family Tree and Chronology.

84. Franklin D. Roosevelt to Pierre C. Cartier, 9 January 1945, manuscript collections, Franklin Delano Roosevelt Library, Hyde Park, New York.

85. Ralph Destino, president of Cartier New York, to Katherine S. Howe, 16 January 1987.

86. Cost-estimate cards for the USS *Long Beach*, 1959–60, special-order numbers JNA through JNJ, Archives, Gorham, Providence, Rhode Island.

87. Richard L. Huggins to Katherine S. Howe, 16 June 1986; Carpenter, *Gorham Silver*, pp. 267–68.

88. *To William Cullen Bryant, at Eighty Years, from his Friends and Countrymen* (New York: Scribner, Armstrong & Co., 1876), p. 40.

89. "The Bryant Testimonial Vase," *Art Journal*, vol. 1 (new series) (May 1875), pp. 145–49.

90. The biographical medallions show Bryant as a journalist, as a translator of Homer, as a student of nature, and as a student of Homer at his father's knee. These medallions and the portrait have been attributed to Augustus Saint-Gaudens on the basis of letters in the Saint-Gaudens Collection at Dartmouth College; see John H. Dryfhout, *The Works of Augustus Saint-Gaudens* (Hanover, N.H.: University Press of New England, 1982), p. 78.

91. Samuel Osgood, "The Bryant Vase," *Harper's New Monthly Magazine*, vol. 53 (July 1876), pp. 245–51.

92. *To William Cullen Bryant*, pp. 28, 23–24. See also *Nineteenth Century America*, no. 220; Carpenter, *Tiffany Silver*, pp. 32–36; Doreen Bolger Burke et al., *In Pursuit of Beauty: Americans and the Aesthetic Movement* (New York: Metropolitan Museum of Art, 1986), pp. 254, 472–73.

93. John W. Jordan, ed., *Colonial Families of Philadelphia* (New York: Lewis Publishing Company, 1911), vol. 1, part 1, pp. 183–85.

94. *Samuel Kirk & Son* (Chicago: Chicago Historical Society, 1966), p. 17.

95. *New York Times*, 24 and 26 February 1887; *Anton Seidl: A Memorial by his Friends* (New York: Charles Scribner's Sons, 1899); Carpenter, *Gorham Silver*, pp. 163–64, 167. Although the *Times* identified the third scene as one from *Die Walküre*, in an interview with Katherine S. Howe, 21 October 1986, Robert Tuggle, archivist of the Metropolitan Opera Association, identified it as the opening scene from act 3 of *Siegfried*, first performed by the Metropolitan Opera on 9 November 1887. I am grateful to Robert Tuggle and Deborah D. Waters, Decorative Arts Curator of the Museum of the City of New York, for sharing the results of their research with me.

96. "Gorham Silver Company" special-order ledger (1 October 1887), item 167, Archives, Gorham, Providence, Rhode Island.

97. M.E. [?] Romera Rubino to Alexander R. Shepherd, 24 May 1888, Alexander Robey Shepherd Papers (container 4), Library of Congress, Washington, D.C. See also Katherine S. Howe, "The Batopilas Flask: A Nineteenth-Century Tale of Money, Mines, and Silver Manufacture," *Winterthur Portfolio*, forthcoming, 1988.

98. Carpenter, *Tiffany Silver*, pp. 77–79, 81, 98–99.

99. *Nineteenth Century America*, no. 283; *American Renaissance*, p. 216.

100. "The Kirby-Stewart Nuptials: Houston, Texas. Nov. 14th 1906," *Supplement, Southern Industrial and Lumber Review*, 20 December 1906, pp. 1, 4–5, Bess Kirby Tooke Black Papers, Junior League Collection, Houston Metropolitan Archives.

101. *Nineteenth Century America*, no. 282.

102. "A Freshman's Prayer on Thursday Night," *Harkness Hoot*, May 1934, as quoted in George Wilson Pierson, *Yale: The University College, 1921–1937* (New Haven, Conn.: Yale University Press, 1955), p. 570.

103. Ibid., pp. 135–37. See also Brooks Mather Kelley, *Yale: A History* (New Haven, Conn.: Yale University Press, 1974), pp. 224–27.

104. Carpenter, *Tiffany Silver*, pp. 260–61; Barbara McLean Ward and Gerald W. R. Ward, eds., *Silver in American Life: Selections from the Mabel Brady Garvan and Other Collections at Yale University* (New York: American Federation of Arts, 1979), p. 184.

105. *New York Times*, 7 March 1897; *New York Recorder*, 7 February 1892.

106. Jennifer Faulds Goldsborough et al., *Silver in Maryland* (Baltimore: Maryland Historical Society, 1983), p. 158.

107. *Beauty of Holiness: Ritual Art for the Jewish Home* (Philadelphia: National Museum of American Jewish History), cover, no. 87.

BIBLIOGRAPHY

American and European Silver from the Gilson Collection (exhibition catalogue). Milwaukee, Wis.: Milwaukee Art Museum, 1982.

American Church Silver of the Seventeenth and Eighteenth Centuries with a Few Pieces of Domestic Plate (exhibition catalogue). Boston: Museum of Fine Arts, 1911.

American Decorative Arts: From the Pilgrims to the Revolution (exhibition catalogue). Detroit: Detroit Institute of Arts, 1967.

The American Renaissance 1876–1917 (exhibition catalogue). New York: Brooklyn Museum, 1979.

American Silver: The Work of Seventeenth and Eighteenth Century Silversmiths (exhibition catalogue). Boston: Museum of Fine Arts, 1906.

American Silver and Pressed Glass: A Collection in The R. W. Norton Art Gallery (exhibition catalogue). Shreveport, La.: R. W. Norton Art Foundation, 1967.

American Silver 1670–1830: The Cornelius C. Moore Collection at Providence College. Providence, R.I.: Providence College, 1980.

Avery, C. Louise. *American Silver of the XVII and XVIII Centuries: A Study Based on the Clearwater Collection*. New York: Metropolitan Museum of Art, 1920.
———. *Early American Silver*. New York: Century Co., 1930.
———. *An Exhibition of Early New York Silver*. New York: Metropolitan Museum of Art, 1931.

Ball, Berenice. "Whistles with Coral and Bells." *The Magazine Antiques*, vol. 80 (December 1961), pp. 552–55.

Bartlett, Louisa. "American Silver." *The Saint Louis Art Museum 1984 Winter Bulletin*. St. Louis, Mo., 1984.

Beckman, Elizabeth D. *An In-depth Study of the Cincinnati Silversmiths, Jewelers, Watch and Clockmakers, Through 1850*. Cincinnati, Ohio: B. B. & Co., 1975.

Belden, Bauman L. *Indian Peace Medals Issued in the United States*. 1927. Reprint. New Milford, Conn.: N. Flayderman, 1966.

Belden, Louise Conway. *Marks of American Silversmiths in the Ineson-Bissell Collection*. Winterthur, Del.: Henry Francis du Pont Winterthur Museum, 1980.

Belknap, Henry Wyckoff. *Artists and Craftsmen of Essex County, Massachusetts*. Salem, Mass.: Essex Institute, 1927.

Betts, Charles Wyllys. *American Colonial History Illustrated by Contemporary Medals*. 1894. Reprint. Glendale, New York: Benchmark Publishers, 1970.

Biddle, James. *American Art from American Collections*. New York: Metropolitan Museum of Art, 1963.

Bigelow, Francis Hill. *Historic Silver of the Colonies and Its Makers*. New York: Macmillan, 1917.

Binder, Deborah J. *St. Louis Silversmiths*. St. Louis, Mo.: Saint Louis Art Museum, 1980.

Birk, Eileen. "New York Tributes and Trophies." *The Magazine Antiques*, vol. 95 (April 1969), pp. 464, 468.

Bohan, Peter J. *American Gold 1700–1860* (exhibition catalogue). New Haven, Conn.: Yale University Art Gallery, 1963.

Bohan, Peter, and Philip Hammerslough. *Early Connecticut Silver 1700–1840*. Middletown, Conn.: Wesleyan University Press, 1970.

Boultinghouse, Marquis. *Silversmiths, Jewelers, Clock and Watch Makers of Kentucky 1785–1900*. Lexington, Ky.: Marquis Boultinghouse, 1980.

Boylan, Leona Davis. *Spanish Colonial Silver*. Santa Fe: Museum of New Mexico Press, 1974.

Brix, Maurice. *List of Philadelphia Silversmiths and Allied Artificers from 1682–1850*. Philadelphia: privately printed, 1920.

Brown, Joan Sayers. "Charles A. Burnett." In *The Twenty-fifth Annual Washington Antiques Show* (program), pp. 70–73. Washington, D.C.: privately printed, 1980.
———. "Silver and Gold Owned by Stephen Decatur, Jr." *The Magazine Antiques*, vol. 123 (February 1983), pp. 399–405.
———. "William Adams and the Mace of the United States House of Representatives." *The Magazine Antiques*, vol. 108 (July 1975), pp. 76–77.

Brown, Michael K. "Paul Revere and the Late Reverend M. Prince's 'Church Cupp': The Study of a Commission." *The American Art Journal*, vol. 15 (Winter 1983), pp. 83–90.

Buck, John H. *Old Plate, Ecclesiastical, Decorative, and Domestic: Its Makers and Marks*. New York: Gorham Company, 1888.

Buhler, Kathryn C. *American Silver: From the Colonial Period through the Early Republic in the Worcester Art Museum*. Worcester, Mass.: Worcester Art Museum, 1979.
———. *American Silver and Art Treasures*. London: English-Speaking Union, 1960.
———. *American Silver 1655–1825*. Cleveland: World Publishing Company, 1950.
———. *American Silver 1655–1825 in the Museum of Fine Arts Boston*. 2 vols. Boston: Museum of Fine Arts, 1972; distributed by New York Graphic Society, Greenwich, Conn.
———. *Colonial Silversmiths, Masters and Apprentices* (exhibition catalogue). Boston: Museum of Fine Arts, 1956.
———. *Massachusetts Silver in the Frank L. and Louise C. Harrington Collection*. Worcester, Mass.: Barre Publishers, 1965.
———. *Masterpieces of American Silver*. Richmond, Va.: Virginia Museum of Fine Arts, 1960.
———. *Mount Vernon Silver*. Mount Vernon, Va.: Mount Vernon Ladies' Association of the Union, 1957.
———. *Paul Revere, Goldsmith, 1735–1818*. Boston: Museum of Fine Arts, 1956.
———. "The Pickman Silver." In *The Ellis Memorial Antiques Show* (program), pp. 19–29. Boston: privately printed, 1961.
———. *Silver Supplement to the Guidebook to the Diplomatic Reception Rooms*. Washington, D.C.: Department of State, 1973.

Buhler, Kathryn C., and Graham Hood. *American Silver: Garvan and Other Collections in the Yale University Art Gallery.* 2 vols. New Haven, Conn.: Yale University Press, 1970.

Burton, E. Milby. "Charleston Silver." *The Magazine Antiques,* vol. 97 (June 1970), pp. 915–17.
———. *South Carolina Silversmiths 1690–1860.* Charleston, S.C.: Charleston Museum, 1942.

Carlisle, Lilian Baker. *Vermont Clock and Watchmakers, Silversmiths, and Jewelers.* Burlington, Vt.: privately printed, 1970.

Carpenter, Charles H., Jr. "Gorham's Battleship Silver." *The Magazine Silver,* vol. 15 (November–December 1982), pp. 27–31.
———. *Gorham Silver, 1831–1981.* New York: Dodd, Mead, 1982.
———. "Nineteenth-Century Silver in the New York Yacht Club." *The Magazine Antiques,* vol. 112 (September 1977), pp. 496–505.

Carpenter, Charles H., Jr., with Mary Grace Carpenter. *Tiffany Silver.* New York: Dodd, Mead, 1978.

Carpenter, Ralph E., Jr. *The Arts and Crafts of Newport, Rhode Island, 1640–1820.* Newport, R.I.: Preservation Society of Newport County, 1954.

Casey, Dorothy Needham. "Rhode Island Silversmiths." *Rhode Island History,* vol. 33 (July 1940), pp. 49–64.

Catalogue of an Exhibition of Silver Used in New York, New Jersey, and the South (exhibition catalogue). New York: Metropolitan Museum of Art, 1911.

[Chickering, Elenita C.]. *Arthur J. Stone: Handwrought Silver 1901– 1937* (exhibition catalogue). Boston: Boston Athenaeum, 1981.

Chickering, Elenita C. "Arthur J. Stone, Silversmith." *The Magazine Antiques,* vol. 129 (January 1986), pp. 274–83.
———. "Arthur J. Stone's Presentation Silver." *The Decorative Arts Society Newsletter,* vol. 2 (March 1985), pp. 1–6.

Church Silver of Colonial Virginia (exhibition catalogue). Richmond, Va.: Virginia Museum of Fine Arts, 1970.

Clark, Grahame. *Symbols of Excellence.* Cambridge: Cambridge University Press, 1986.

Clark, Robert Judson, ed. *The Arts and Crafts Movement in America 1876–1916* (exhibition catalogue). Princeton, N.J.: Art Museum, Princeton University, 1972; distributed by Princeton University Press.

Clarke, Hermann Frederick. *John Coney Silversmith, 1655–1722.* Boston: Houghton Mifflin, 1932.
———. *John Hull: A Builder of the Bay Colony.* Portland, Me.: Southworth-Anthoenson Press, 1940.

Clarke, Hermann Frederick, and Henry Wilder Foote. *Jeremiah Dummer, Colonial Craftsman and Merchant, 1645–1718.* Boston: Houghton Mifflin, 1935.

Clayton, Michael. *The Collector's Dictionary of the Silver and Gold of Great Britain and North America.* New York: World Publishing Company, 1971.

Codman, William. *An Illustrated History of Silverware Design.* Providence, R.I.: Gorham Company, 1930.

Comstock, Helen. "The John Marshall Phillips Collection of Silver." *Connoisseur Year Book.* London, 1957, pp. 28–33.

Contemporary Industrial and Handwrought Silver. New York: Brooklyn Museum, 1937.

Cooper, Wendy A. *In Praise of America: American Decorative Arts 1650–1830* (exhibition catalogue). New York: Alfred A. Knopf, 1980.

Craig, James H. *The Arts and Crafts in North Carolina, 1699–1840.* Winston-Salem, N.C.: Museum of Early Southern Decorative Arts, 1965.

Crawford, Rachael B. "The Forbes Family of Silversmiths." *The Magazine Antiques,* vol. 107 (April 1975), pp. 730–35.

Crescent City Silver: An Exhibition of Nineteenth-Century New Orleans Silver (exhibition catalogue). New Orleans: Historic New Orleans Collection, 1980.

Csikszentmihalyi, Mihaly, and Eugene Rochberg-Halton. *The Meaning of Things: Domestic Symbols and the Self.* London: Cambridge University Press, 1981.

Curtis, George Munson. *Early Silver of Connecticut and Its Makers.* Meriden, Conn.: International Silver Company, 1913.

Cutten, George Barton. *The Silversmiths of Georgia: Together with Watchmakers and Jewelers, 1733 to 1850.* Savannah, Ga.: Pigeon Hole Press, 1958.
———. *The Silversmiths of North Carolina 1696–1850.* Raleigh, N.C.: State Department of Archives and History, 1948.
———. *The Silversmiths of Virginia (Together with Watchmakers and Jewelers) from 1694 to 1850.* Richmond, Va.: Dietz Press, 1952.

Dallett, J. "The Thibaults, Philadelphia Silversmiths." *The Magazine Antiques,* vol. 95 (April 1969), pp. 547–49.

Darling, Sharon S. *Chicago Metalsmiths.* Chicago: Chicago Historical Society, 1977.

Davidson, Ruth. "Museum Accessions." *The Magazine Antiques,* vol. 103 (April 1973), p. 676.

De Matteo, William. *The Silversmith in Eighteenth-Century Williamsburg: An Account of His Life and Times, and of His Craft.* Williamsburg, Va.: Colonial Williamsburg, 1956.

"The Diaries of John Hull, Mint-Master and Treasurer of the Colony of Massachusetts Bay." In *Transactions and Collections of the American Antiquarian Society,* vol. 3, pp. 109–316. Boston: privately printed, 1857.

Dillard, Maud Esther. *An Album of New Netherland.* New York: Bramhall House, 1963.

Dix, Morgan, ed. *A History of the Parish of Trinity Church in the City of New York,* vol. 3. New York: G. P. Putnam's Sons, 1905.

Dow, George Francis. *The Arts and Crafts in New England, 1704– 1775.* 1927. Reprint. New York: De Capo Press, 1967.

Dresser, Louisa. "Worcester Silversmiths and the Examples of Their Work in the Collections of the Museum." In *Worcester Art Museum Annual,* vol. 1 (1935–36), pp. 49–57.

Dunlap, William. *History of the Rise and Progress of the Arts of Design in the United States.* 2 vols. New York: George P. Scott and Co., 1834.

Durbin, Louise. "Samuel Kirk, Nineteenth Century Silversmith." *The Magazine Antiques,* vol. 94 (December 1968), pp. 868– 73.

Early New York Silver (exhibition catalogue). New York: Metropolitan Museum of Art, 1974.

The Early Plate in Connecticut Churches Prior to 1850. Hartford, Conn.: Wadsworth Atheneum, 1919.

Early Silver in California Collections: Old English and Early American Silverwork (exhibition catalogue). Los Angeles County Museum of Art, 1962.

Eldredge, Michael S. "Silver Service for the Battleship Utah: A Naval Tradition under Governor Spry." *Utah Historical Quarterly*, vol. 46 (1978), pp. 302–18.

Elias Pelletreau, Long Island Silversmith and His Sources of Design (exhibition catalogue). New York: Brooklyn Museum, 1959.

Emlen, Robert P. "Wedding Silver for the Browns: A Rhode Island Family Patronizes a Boston Goldsmith." *The American Art Journal*, vol. 16 (Spring 1984), pp. 39–50.

Fairbanks, Jonathan, and Robert Trent. *New England Begins: The Seventeenth Century* (exhibition catalogue). 3 vols. Boston: Museum of Fine Arts, 1982.

Fairbanks, Jonathan, et al. *Paul Revere's Boston: 1735–1818.* Boston: Museum of Fine Arts, 1975; distributed by New York Graphic Society, Greenwich, Conn.

Fales, Martha Gandy. *American Silver in the Henry Francis du Pont Winterthur Museum.* Winterthur, Del.: Henry Francis du Pont Winterthur Museum, 1958.
———. "The Britannia Cup." *The Magazine Antiques*, vol. 123 (July 1982), pp. 156–58.
———. *Early American Silver.* New York: E. P. Dutton and Company, Inc., 1973.
———. "The Early American Way of Death." *Essex Institute Historical Collections*, vol. 100 (April 1964), pp. 75–84.
———. *Joseph Richardson and Family: Philadelphia Silversmiths.* Middletown, Conn.: Wesleyan University Press, 1974.
———. *Silver at the Essex Institute.* Salem, Mass.: Essex Institute, 1983.

Feigenbaum, Rita. "A Faneuil Family Silver Cruet Stand Rediscovered." *The Magazine Antiques*, vol. 112 (July 1977), pp. 120–21.

Fennimore, Donald L. *The Knopf Collectors' Guide to American Antiques: Silver and Pewter.* New York: Alfred A. Knopf, 1984.
———. "Religion in America: Metal Objects in Service of the Ritual." *The American Art Journal*, vol. 10 (November 1978), pp. 20–42.
———. "A Solid Gold Testimonial: An American Medal for Lafayette." *The Magazine Antiques*, vol. 117 (February 1980), pp. 426–30.
———. "Thomas Fletcher and Sidney Gardiner." *The Magazine Antiques*, vol. 102 (October 1972), pp. 642–49.

Floyd, William Barrow. "Kentucky Coin-Silver Pitchers." *The Magazine Antiques*, vol. 105 (March 1974), pp. 576–80.

Flynt, Henry N., and Martha Gandy Fales. *The Heritage Foundation Collection of Silver, with Biographical Sketches of New England Silversmiths 1625–1825.* Old Deerfield, Mass.: Heritage Foundation, 1968.

Forbes, Esther. *Paul Revere and the World He Lived In.* Boston: Houghton Mifflin, 1942.

Fox, Ross. *Presentation Pieces and Trophies from the Henry Birks Collection of Canadian Silver.* Ottawa: National Gallery of Canada, 1985.

Frederiks, Johan Willem. *Dutch Silver: Wrought Plate of the Central, Northern and Southern Provinces from the Renaissance until the End of the Eighteenth Century.* The Hague: Martinus Nijhoff, 1960.

Fredrickson, N. Saye. *The Covenant Chain.* Ottawa: National Museum of Man, National Museums of Canada, 1980.

French, Hollis. *Jacob Hurd and His Sons Nathaniel and Benjamin, Silversmiths, 1702–1781.* Cambridge, Mass.: Riverside Press for the Walpole Society, 1939.

From Colony to Nation (exhibition catalogue). Chicago: Art Institute of Chicago, 1949.

Gaines, Edith, ed. "Collectors' Notes: The Forbes Family, New York Silversmiths." *The Magazine Antiques*, vol. 103 (March 1973), pp. 561–63.
———. "Collectors' Notes: Silver Made and Sold in New Orleans." *The Magazine Antiques*, vol. 104 (July 1973), p. 88.

Garvan, Anthony N. B. "The New England Porringer: An Index of Custom." In *Annual Report of the Board of Regents of the Smithsonian Institution for the Year Ended June 30, 1958, Publication 4354.* Washington, D.C.: U.S. Government Printing Office, 1959.

Garvan, Anthony N. B., et al. "American Church Silver: A Statistical Study." In *Spanish, French, and English Traditions in the Colonial Silver of North America. 1968 Winterthur Conference Report.* Winterthur, Del.: Henry Francis du Pont Winterthur Museum, 1968.

Gerstell, Vivian S. *Silversmiths of Lancaster, Pennsylvania, 1730–1850.* Lancaster: Lancaster County Historical Society, 1972.

Gibb, George Sweet. *The Whitesmiths of Taunton: A History of Reed and Barton, 1824–1943.* Cambridge, Mass.: Harvard University Press, 1943.

Gillingham, Harrold E. "Cesar Ghiselin, Philadelphia's First Gold and Silversmith, 1693–1733." *The Pennsylvania Magazine of History and Biography*, vol. 57 (July 1933), p. 254.
———. "Early American Indian Medals." *The Magazine Antiques*, vol. 6 (December 1924), pp. 312–15.
———. "Indian and Military Medals From Colonial Times to Date." *The Pennsylvania Magazine of History and Biography*, vol. 51 (1927), pp. 97–125
———. *Indian Ornaments Made by Philadelphia Silversmiths.* New York: Museum of the American Indian–Heye Foundation, 1936.
———. "Indian Silver Ornaments." *The Pennsylvania Magazine of History and Biography*, vol. 58 (1934), pp. 97–126.
———. "Indian Trade Silver Ornaments Made by Joseph Richardson, Jr." *The Pennsylvania Magazine of History and Biography*, vol. 67 (1943), pp. 83–91.

Gold, Annalee. "Crafts in Industry: Five Jewelers Join Skills with Reed and Barton." *Craft Horizon*, vol. 37 (August 1977), pp. 10–15.

Gold and Silver: Treasurers of New York (exhibition catalogue). New York: Museum of the City of New York, 1978.

Goldsborough, Jennifer Faulds, *Eighteenth and Nineteenth Century Maryland Silver in the Collection of The Baltimore Museum of*

Art. Baltimore: Baltimore Museum of Art, 1975.

————. *An Exhibition of New London Silver, 1700–1835* (exhibition catalogue). New London, Conn.: Lyman Allyn Museum, 1969.

Goldsborough, Jennifer Faulds, et al. *Silver in Maryland* (exhibition catalogue). Baltimore: Maryland Historical Society, 1983.

Goss, Elbridge Henry. *The Life of Colonel Paul Revere*. 2 vols. Boston: Howard W. Spurr, 1891.

Gottesman, Rita Susswein. *The Arts and Crafts in New York: Advertisements and News Items from New York City Newspapers.* New York: New-York Historical Society, *1726–1776* (1938); *1777–1779* (1954); *1800–1804* (1965).

Gourley, Hugh J., III. *The New England Silversmith* (exhibition catalogue). Providence, R.I.: Museum of Art, Rhode Island School of Design, 1965.

Gruber, Alain. *Silverware*. New York: Rizzoli International Publications, Inc., 1982.

Gustafson, Eleanor H. "Museum Accessions." *The Magazine Antiques*, vol. 110 (September 1976), p. 490; vol. 111 (April 1977), p. 735; vol. 114 (July 1978), p. 69.

Hale, Richard Walden. *Catalogue of Silver Owned by Nicholas Sever, A.B. 1701, in 1728*. Boston: Tudor Press, 1931.

Hamilton, John. *The Ames Sword Company*. Providence, R.I.: Mobray, 1981.

Hammerslough, Philip H. *American Silver Collected by Philip H. Hammerslough*. Hartford, Conn.: privately printed, 1958 (vol. 1), 1960 (vols. 2 and 3).

Hammerslough, Philip H., and Rita F. Feigenbaum. *American Silver Collected by Philip H. Hammerslough*, vol. 4. Hartford, Conn.: privately printed, 1973.

Hammond, Charles A. "Gold and Silver Trophies Awarded by the Massachusetts Society for Promoting Agriculture 1792–1830." In *Ellis Memorial Antique Show* (program), pp. 69–76. Boston: privately printed, n.d.

Haney, Robert W. *The Historic Silver of the First and Second Church in Boston* (exhibition catalogue). Boston: Museum of Fine Arts, 1980.

Hanks, David A. "Robert R. Jarvie, Chicago Silversmith." *The Magazine Antiques*, vol. 110 (September 1976), pp. 522–27.

————. "Silver at the Art Institute of Chicago." *The Magazine Antiques*, vol. 98 (September 1970), pp. 392–93, 418–22.

Harned, Henry H. "Ante-Bellum Kentucky Silver." *The Magazine Antiques*, vol. 105 (April 1974), pp. 818–24.

Harrington, Jessie. *Silversmiths of Delaware 1700–1850 and Old Church Silver in Delaware*. Wilmington, Del.: National Society of Colonial Dames of America in the State of Delaware, 1939.

Hiatt, Noble W., and Lucy F. Hiatt. *The Silversmiths of Kentucky, Together with Some Watchmakers and Jewelers 1785–1850*. Louisville, Ky.: Standard Printing Company, 1954.

Hill, Harry W. *Maryland's Colonial Charm Portrayed in Silver*. N.p.: privately printed, 1938.

Hindes, Ruthanna. "Delaware Silversmiths, 1700–1850." *Delaware History*, vol. 12 (October 1967), pp. 247–308.

Hipkiss, Edwin J. *Eighteenth-Century American Arts: The M. and M. Karolik Collection*. Boston: Museum of Fine Arts, 1941.

————. *The Philip Leffingwell Spalding Collection of Early American Silver*. Cambridge, Mass.: Harvard University Press, 1943.

The Historic Church Silver in the Diocese of Southern Virginia. Norfolk, Va.: Norfolk Museum of Arts and Sciences, 1953.

Holloway, H. Maxson. "American Presentation Silver." *The New-York Historical Society Quarterly*, vol. 30 (October 1946), pp. 215–33.

Honour, Hugh. *Goldsmiths and Silversmiths*. New York: G. P. Putnam's Sons, 1971.

Hood, Graham. *American Silver: A History of Style, 1650–1900*. New York: Praeger Publishers, 1971.

Hoopes, Penrose R. *Shop Records of Daniel Burnap, Clockmaker*. Hartford, Conn.: Connecticut Historical Society, 1958.

Hughes, Graham. *Modern Silver Throughout the World 1880–1967*. New York: Crown Publishers, 1967.

Hyde, Bryden Bordley. *Bermuda's Antique Furniture and Silver*. Hamilton, Bermuda: Bermuda National Trust, 1971.

In Pursuit of Beauty: Americans and the Aesthetic Movement (exhibition catalogue). New York: Metropolitan Museum of Art, 1986.

Irish Silver from the Seventeenth to the Nineteenth Century (exhibition catalogue). Washington, D.C.: Smithsonian Institution, 1982.

Johnson, J. Stewart. "Silver in Newark: A Newark 300th Anniversary Study." *The Museum*, vol. 18 (Summer–Fall 1966), pp. 13, 46–47.

Jones, E. Alfred. *The Old Silver of American Churches*. Letchworth, England: privately printed for the National Society of Colonial Dames of America at the Arden Press, 1913.

————. *Old Silver of Europe and America, from Early Times to the Nineteenth Century*. Philadelphia: J. B. Lippincott, 1928.

Kauffman, Henry J. *The Colonial Silversmith, His Techniques and His Products*. New York: Galahad Books, 1969.

"Kentucky Silversmiths before 1850." *Filson Club History Quarterly*, vol. 16 (April 1942), pp. 111–26.

Kernan, John D. "Gold Funeral Rings." *The Magazine Antiques*, vol. 89 (April 1966), pp. 568–69.

Klapthor, Margaret Brown. *Presentation Pieces in the Museum of History and Technology*, Contributions from the Museum of History and Technology, Paper 47. Washington, D.C.: Smithsonian Institution, 1965.

Knittle, Rhea Mansfield. *Early Ohio Silversmiths and Pewterers 1787–1847*. Cleveland: Calvert-Hatch Company, 1943.

Lay, Charles Downing, and Theodore Bolton. *Works of Art, Silver and Furniture Belonging to The Century Association*. New York: Century Association, 1943.

Leighton, Margaretha Gebelein. *George Christian Gebelein, Boston Silversmith, 1878–1945*. Lunenburg, Vt.: Stinehour Press, 1976.

Lightbown, R. W. "Victorian's Taste in Silver." *Apollo*, vol. 95 (March 1972), pp. 201–5.

Lowndes, Arthur Edward. *An Inventory of the Church Plate and Altar Ornaments Belonging to the Parish of Trinity Church in the City of New York*. New York: Knickerbocker Press, 1905.

Ludwig Yehuda Wolpert: A Retrospective (exhibition catalogue). New York: Jewish Museum, 1976.

McClinton, Katharine Morrison. "American Presentation Silver of the Seventeenth and Eighteenth Centuries." *Connoisseur*, vol. 166 (December 1967), pp. 256–66; vol. 167 (January 1968), pp. 58–63.
———. *Collecting American 19th-Century-Silver*. New York: Charles Scribner's Sons, 1968.
———. "Nineteenth-Century American Presentation Silver." *Connoisseur*, vol. 167 (March 1968), pp. 192–98.
———. "Some Early Nineteenth-Century American Presentation Swords." *Connoisseur*, vol. 177 (August 1971), pp. 287–95.

Macomber, Henry P. "The Silversmiths of New England." *The American Magazine of Art*, vol. 25, pp. 210–18.

The Magazine Silver (Whittier, Calif.), vols. 5–19 (1972 to the present).

Mastai, M-L. D'Otrange. "The Connoisseur in America." *Connoisseur*, vol. 162 (August 1966), pp. 288–89.

Merritt, Edward Percival. "The King's Gift to Christ Church, Boston, 1733." In *Publications of The Colonial Society of Massachusetts*, vol. 19: *Transactions 1916–1917*, pp. 299–331. Boston: privately printed, 1918.

Miller, V. Isabelle. *Silver by New York Makers, Late 17th Century to 1900*. New York: Museum of the City of New York, 1937.

Miller, William Davis. *The Silversmiths of Little Rest*. Kingston, R.I.: privately printed, 1928.

Minter-Dowd, Christine. *Finders' Guide to Decorative Arts in the Smithsonian Institution*. Washington, D.C.: Smithsonian Institution Press, 1984.

Monkman, Betty C. "American Silver in the White House." In *The Twenty-fifth Annual Washington Antique Show* (program), pp. 74–79. Washington, D.C.: privately printed, 1980.

Montgomery, Charles F., and Catherine H. Maxwell. *Early American Silver: Collectors, Collections, Exhibitions, Writings*. Portland, Me.: Southworth-Anthoenson Press, 1969.

Montgomery, Charles F., and Patricia E. Kane, eds. *American Art: 1750–1800, Towards Independence* (exhibition catalogue). Boston: New York Graphic Society, 1976.

Moody, Margaret J. *American Decorative Arts at Dartmouth*. Hanover, N.H.: Dartmouth College Museum and Galleries, 1981.

Morse, Edgar W., ed. *Silver in the Golden State: Images and Essays Celebrating the History and Art of Silver in California* (exhibition catalogue). Oakland, Calif.: Oakland Museum History Department, 1986.

Morton, Richard L. *Colonial Virginia: The Tidewater Period 1607–1710*, vol. 1. Chapel Hill, N.C.: University of North Carolina Press, 1960.

Natchez-made Silver of the Nineteenth Century (exhibition catalogue). Baton Rouge: Anglo-American Art Museum, Louisiana State University, 1970.

Needham, A. C. "Random Notes on Funeral Rings." *Old Time New England*, vol. 39 (April 1949), pp. 93–97.

New York Silversmiths of the Seventeenth Century (exhibition catalogue). New York: Museum of the City of New York, 1963.

New York State Silversmiths. Eggertsville, N.Y.: Darling Foundation, 1964.

Nineteenth Century America: Furniture and Decorative Arts (exhibition catalogue). New York: Metropolitan Museum of Art, 1970.

Norman-Wilcox, Gregor. "American Silver at the Los Angeles County Museum (The Marble Collection)." *Connoisseur Year Book*. London, 1956, pp. 62–70.

Nygren, Edward J. "Edward Winslow's Sugar Boxes: Colonial Echoes of Courtly Love." *Yale University Art Gallery Bulletin*, vol. 33 (Autumn 1971), pp. 38–52.

Olaf Skoogfors, 20th Century Goldsmith 1930–1975 (exhibition catalogue). Philadelphia: Falcon Press, 1979.

Patterson, Jerry E. *Antiques of Sport*. New York: Crown Publishers, 1975.

Pearce, John N. "Further Comments on the Lobate Bowl Form." *The Magazine Antiques*, vol. 90 (October 1966), pp. 524–25.
———. "New York's Two-handled Paneled Silver Bowls." *The Magazine Antiques*, vol. 80 (October 1961), pp. 341–45.
———. "Roman Catholic Church Plate in the Maryland Area, 1634–1800." *Connoisseur*, vol. 173 (April 1970), pp. 287–91; vol. 174 (May 1970), pp. 62–69.

Peterson, Harold Leslie. *The American Sword 1775–1945*. Philadelphia: Ray Riling Arms Books Company, 1977.

Philadelphia: Three Centuries of American Art (exhibition catalogue). Philadelphia: Philadelphia Museum of Art, 1976.

Philadelphia Silver. Philadelphia: Philadelphia Museum of Art, 1956.

Phillips, John Marshall. *American Silver*. New York: Chanticleer Press, 1949.
———. *Early Connecticut Silver 1700–1830* (exhibition catalogue). New Haven, Conn.: Yale University Art Gallery, 1935.
———. "Mr. Tyng's Bishop." *Bulletin of the Associates in Fine Arts at Yale University*, vol. 4, no. 3 (1932), pp. 148–49.

Pleasants, J. Hall, and Howard Sill. *Maryland Silversmiths 1715–1830*. Baltimore: Lord Baltimore Press, 1930.

Porcher, Jennie Rose, and Anna Wells Rutledge. *The Silver of St. Philip's Church, Charles Town, Charleston 1670–1970*. Charleston, S.C.: privately printed, 1970.

Precious Metals: The American Tradition in Gold and Silver (exhibition catalogue). Coral Gables, Fla.: Lowe Art Museum, University of Miami, 1975.

Prime, Alfred Coxe, ed. *The Arts and Crafts in Philadelphia, Maryland and South Carolina, 1721–1785: Gleaning from Newspapers*. 1929. Reprint. New York: Da Capo Press, 1969.

Prime, Mrs. Alfred Coxe. *Three Centuries of Historic Silver*. Philadelphia: Philadelphia Society of the Colonial Dames of America, 1938.

Prip, John. "John Prip and Reed and Barton." *Craft Horizon*, vol. 24 (March 1964), pp. 51–52.

Prucha, Francis Paul. *Indian Peace Medals in American History*. Madison, Wis.: State Historical Society of Wisconsin, 1971.
———. *Peace and Friendship: Indian Peace Medals in the United States* (exhibition catalogue). Washington, D.C.: National Portrait Gallery, Smithsonian Institution, 1985.

Publications of The Colonial Society of Massachusetts, vol. 24: *Transactions 1920–1922*. Boston: privately printed, 1923.

Rainwater, Dorothy T. *Encyclopedia of American Silver Manufacturers*. 2d ed. New York: Crown Publishers, 1975.

Reed, Helen Scott Townsend. "Church Silver in Colonial Virginia." *The Magazine Antiques*, vol. 97 (February 1970), pp. 243–47.

A Retrospective Exhibit of Silver Presentation and Commemorative Pieces, Presentation Swords, Yachting, Racing, Rowing, Shooting, and Rifle Cups, Made by Tiffany and Co. During the Past 25 Years. New York: privately printed, 1876.

Rice, Norman S. *Albany Silver, 1652–1825* (exhibition catalogue). Albany, N.Y.: Albany Institute of History and Art, 1964.

Riggs, Timothy A. *The Second Fifty Years: American Arts 1826–1876*. Worcester, Mass.: Worcester Art Museum, 1976.

Roach, Ruth Hunter. *St. Louis Silversmiths*. N. p.: privately printed, 1967.

Rosenbaum, Jeanette W. *Myer Myers, Goldsmith, 1723–1795*. Philadelphia: Jewish Publication Society of America, 1954.

Safford, Frances Gruber. "Colonial Silver in the American Wing." *The Metropolitan Museum of Art Bulletin*, vol. 41 (Summer 1983), pp. 1–56.

Schoenberger, Guido. "The Ritual Silver Made by Myer Myers." *Publication of the American Jewish Historical Society*, vol. 43 (September 1953), pp. 1–9.

Scoon, Carolyn. "Cornelia Duyckinck's Birthday Spoon Inscribed and Dated: August 25, 1696." *The New-York Historical Society Quarterly*, vol. 34 (October 1950), pp. 315–17.

Sewall, Samuel. *The Diary of Samuel Sewall, 1674–1729*. Ed. M. Halsey Thomas. 2 vols. New York: Farrar, Straus & Giroux, 1973.

Sharp, Lewis I. *John Quincy Adams Ward, Dean of American Sculpture*. Newark, Del.: University of Delaware Press, 1985.

Sherrill, Sarah B. "Current and Coming." *The Magazine Antiques*, vol. 119 (January 1981), p. 70.

"Silver and Silver Plate." *Harper's New Monthly Magazine*, vol. 37 (September 1868), pp. 433–48.

Skerry, Janine E. *Made by Design: American Silver from the 17th to the 20th Century*. Fitchburg, Mass.: Fitchburg Art Museum, 1983.

Smith, Dido. "Sterling in the '70s." *Craft Horizons*, vol. 31 (October 1971), pp. 12–17.

Sommer, Frank H., III. "The Functions of American Church Silver." In *Spanish, French, and English Traditions in the Colonial Silver of North America. 1968 Winterthur Conference Report*. Winterthur, Del.: Henry Francis du Pont Winterthur Museum, 1968.

Springer, Lynn E. "A Silver Tureen Made for Commodore John Rodgers." *Saint Louis Art Museum Bulletin*, vol. 10 (November–December 1974), pp. 93–94.

Sprunt, Douglas. "Silver Chalice and Paten: St. John's Church, Lafayette Square." In *The Twenty-fifth Annual Washington Antiques Show* (program), p. 102. Washington, D.C.: privately printed, 1980.

The Story of the House of Kirk, the Oldest Silversmiths in the United States Founded 1815. Baltimore: privately printed, 1914.

Taylor, Emerson. *Paul Revere*. New York: Dodd, Mead, 1930.

"A Tradition of Connoisseurship." *Apollo*, vol. 97 (March 1983), pp. 158–61.

Trophies. Philadelphia: Bailey, Banks, and Biddle, 1908.

Trupin, Bennett W. *Elias Pelletreau 1726–1810, Goldsmith of Southampton*. Southampton, N.Y.: Exposition Press, 1985.

Trussell, John B.B., and James R. Mitchell. *The Silver Service of the U.S.S. Pennsylvania*. Harrisburg, Pa.: William Penn Memorial Museum, 1981.

"Upon This Occasion": A Loan Exhibition of Important Presentation Silver from Colonial Times to Today. Newburyport, Mass.: Towle Silversmiths, 1955.

Van Hoesen, Walter Hamilton. *Crafts and Craftsmen of New Jersey*. Madison, N.J.: Fairleigh Dickinson University Press, 1973.

Wainwright, Nicholas B. "Major Thomas Biddles's Silver Vases." *The Magazine Antiques*, vol. 95 (January 1979), pp. 180–83.
———. *One Hundred and Fifty Years of Collecting by the Historical Society of Pennsylvania 1824–1974*. Philadelphia: Historical Society of Pennsylvania, 1974.

Ward, Barbara McLean. "The Craftsman in a Changing Society: Boston Goldsmiths, 1690–1730." Ph.D. dissertation, Boston University, 1983.

Ward, Barbara McLean, and Gerald W. R. Ward, eds. *Silver in American Life: Selections from the Mabel Brady Garvan and Other Collections at Yale University* (exhibition catalogue). New York: American Federation of Arts, 1979.

Ward, Gerald W. R. "Silver and Society in Salem, Massachusetts, 1630–1820: A Case Study of the Consumer and the Craft." Ph.D. dissertation, Boston University, 1984.

Warren, David B. "Bancroft Woodcock: Silversmith, Friend and Landholder." In *The Delaware Antiques Show Catalogue*, pp. 89–97. Wilmington, Del.: privately printed, 1967.
———. *Bayou Bend: American Furniture, Paintings, and Silver from the Bayou Bend Collection*. Houston, Tex.: Museum of Fine Arts, Houston, 1975.
———. "Southern Silver." *The Magazine Antiques*, vol. 99 (March 1971), pp. 374–79.
———. *Southern Silver: An Exhibition of Silver Made in the South Prior to 1860* (exhibition catalogue). Houston, Tex.: Museum of Fine Arts, Houston, 1968.

Wasserman, Abby. "Silver in the Golden State." *The Museum of California*, vol. 10 (September–October 1986), pp. 4–9.

Waters, Deborah Dependahl. "American Neoclassical Silver." *Decorative Arts at Amherst College: Mead Museum Monographs*, vol. 3 (Winter 1981–82), pp. 15–19.

Webster, Donald Blake, et al. *Georgian Canada: Conflict and Culture 1745–1820*. Toronto: Royal Ontario Museum, 1984.

White, Margaret E. *The Decorative Arts of Early New Jersey*. The New Jersey Historical Series, vol. 25. Princeton, N.J.: D. Van Nostrand Co., 1964.

Whitehill, Walter Muir. "Tutor Flynt's Silver Chamber-pot." In *Publications of The Colonial Society of Massachusetts*, vol. 38: *Transactions 1947–1951*. Boston: privately printed, 1951, pp. 360–63.

Williams, Carl M. *Silversmiths of New Jersey, 1700–1825: With Some Notice of Clockmakers Who Were Also Silversmiths*. Philadelphia: George S. MacManus, 1949.

Winterthur Point-to-Point Races: 1983 Program. Winterthur, Del.: Henry Francis du Pont Winterthur Museum, 1983.

Wolf, Edwin, II, and Maxwell Whiteman. *The History of the Jews of Philadelphia from Colonial Times to the Age of Jackson*. Philadelphia: Jewish Publication Society of America, 1957.

Wood, Elizabeth Ingerman. "Thomas Fletcher: A Philadelphia Entrepreneur of Presentation Silver." In *Winterthur Portfolio III*. Ed. Milo M. Naeve. Winterthur, Del.: Henry Francis du Pont Winterthur Museum, 1967, pp. 136–71.

Woodward, Arthur. "Highlights on Indian Trade Silver." *The Magazine Antiques*, vol. 47 (June 1945), pp. 328–31.

Wyler, Seymour B. *The Book of Old Silver*. New York: Crown Publisners, 1937.

INDEX

Page numbers in *italic* type indicate illustrations

PHOTOGRAPH CREDITS

Silver is an unusually difficult medium to photograph, The authors are grateful to the many photographers who contributed their work to this book. Arthur Vitols of Helga Photo Studio and Lynn Diane De Marco deserve special recognition. Mr. Vitols photographed silver for us throughout the entire New York metropolitan area. Ms. De Marco generously gave her time and counsel, traveling to thirty different locations in fourteen states on our behalf. All photographs were taken by Ms. De Marco expressly for this publication, with the exception of the following: Albright-Knox Art Gallery, Buffalo, N.Y.: 125. American Antiquarian Society, Worcester, Mass.: 55. The American Numismatic Society, New York City: 183, 184. Archdiocese of Santa Fe Collection in the Museum of International Folk Art, Museum of New Mexico: 8. Amy Blakemore, Houston: 82. Buffalo and Erie County Historical Society, Buffalo, N.Y.: 123, 124. Chicago Historical Society (C.D. Arnold): 180. Denver Public Library, Western History Department: 185. Gorham Textron, Providence, R.I.: 108, 221, 222. Helga Photo Studio (Arthur Vitols, Upper Montclair, N.J.): 3, 4, 5, 18, 19, 27, 28, 45, 46, 48, 51, 52, 53, 70, 71, 88, 96, 97, 98, 99, 103, 104, 115, 117, 120, 142, 143, 152, 157, 172, 178, 182, 187, 188, 189, 190, 191, 193, 197, 198, 214, 216, 217, 220, 225, 227. The Henry Francis du Pont Winterthur Museum, Inc., Winterthur, Del.: 144, 146. High Museum of Art, Atlanta: 155. Indiana Motor Speedway Corporation: 165. Edward Kelly, Hamilton, Bermuda: 25, 26. John Leather Collection, Fingringhoe, Essex, England: 196. Los Angeles County Museum of Art (Peter Brenner): 110. Melville McLean, Indianapolis: 203. Mead Art Museum, Amherst College, Amherst, Mass.: 128.

Memorial Art Gallery of the University of Rochester, Rochester, N.Y.: 77. The Metropolitan Museum of Art, New York City: 73. The Minneapolis Institute of Arts (Gary Mortensen): 175. Gary Mortensen, Minneapolis: 176. Munson-Williams-Proctor Institute Museum of Art, Utica, N.Y.: 177. Museum of Fine Arts, Boston: 1, 6, 15, 16, 17, 38, 64, 65, 66, 67, 74, 75, 76, 84, 91, 114, 127, 145. The Museum of Fine Arts, Houston: 57 (Paul Hestor), 107 (A. Mewbourn), 135 (A. Mewbourn), 136 (A. Mewbourn), 181 (A. Mewbourn), 223 (Paul Hestor). Museum of the City of New York: 106, 156, 194, 224 (Helga Photo Studio). National Museum of Natural History, Smithsonian Institution, Washington, D.C.: 129. National Portrait Gallery, Smithsonian Institution, Washington, D.C.: 10. The New-York Historical Society, New York City: 12, 61, 164, 192. North Carolina Museum of Art, Raleigh (Glenn Tucker): 134. Peabody Museum of Salem, Salem, Mass. (Mark Sexton): 89, 90, 95. Portland Museum of Art, Portland, Me., Pepperrell Silver Collection: 14. President and Fellows of Harvard College, Cambridge, Mass.: 11, 40, Society of Antiquaries of London: 7. State Historical Society of Wisconsin, Madison: 204. G. M. Tucker, Raleigh, N.C.: 21, 133. United States Navy, Naval Supply Systems Command: 167. Virginia Museum of Art, Richmond: 9 (Ronald Jennings). Wadsworth Atheneum, Hartford, Conn.: 93 (Joseph Szaszfai), 100 (Joseph Szaszfai), 122. Katherine Wetzel, Richmond, Va.: 13. The White House Collection: 168. Yale University Art Gallery, New Haven, Conn.: 31, 44 (Joseph Szaszfai), 56, 59, 60, 68 (Joseph Szaszfai), 69 (Joseph Szaszfai), 72, 79, 121, 148, 150 (Joseph Szaszfai), 151 (Joseph Szaszfai), 151, 154, 226.